AGRICULTURE, THE ENVIRONMENT AND TRADE -

Conflict or Cooperation?

Editor

CAROLINE T. WILLI

Published by the
International Policy Council on Agriculture and Trade

Published by the:

International Policy Council on Agriculture & Trade
1616 P Street, NW
Suite 403
Washington, DC 20036 USA

ISBN: 0-9636143-0-4

Library of Congress Catalog Card Number: 93-77535

recycled paper

Cover Design by: *Debra Naylor; Naylor Design, Inc.; Bryantown, MD*

About the International Policy Council

The *International Policy Council on Agriculture and Trade* was established in 1987 to develop consensus on feasible policy alternatives that could alleviate the problems facing global agriculture. The Council is comprised of 31 policy leaders in government, business, farming, and academia from 19 countries. Its members have expertise in all segments of the agricultural economy, from implementing policy to making investments.

The prominence of Council members affords them access to national and international leaders. The independence of the Council allows it to offer recommendations to governments, both publicly and privately.

Members of the board:

Lord Plumb of Coleshill (Chairman) - Member and former President, European Parliament. (United Kingdom)

Albert Simantov (Vice Chairman) - Former President, Governing Board, International Center for Advanced Mediterranean Agronomic Studies. (Greece)

William Miner - Senior Research Associate, Centre for Trade Policy and Law. (Canada)

David Swanson - President and Chief Executive Officer, Central Soya Company, Inc. (USA)

Robert E. Wise (ex officio) - Executive Director, International Policy Council on Agriculture and Trade. (United Kingdom)

Yutaka Yoshioka - Chairman, Japan Int'l Agricultural Council. (Japan)

Jorge Zorreguieta - President, Argentine Sugar Producers Council; Former Minister of Agriculture. (Argentina)

iii

Liberty Mhlanga - General Manager and Director, Agricultural and Rural Development Authority. (Zimbabwe)

Michael Shanahan - Director, Pivot Fertilizers; former Deputy Chairman, Australian Wheat Board. (Australia)

Ammar Siamwalla - President, Thailand Development Research Institute Foundation. (Thailand)

Stefan Tangermann - Professor and Director, Institute for Agroeconomy, University of Göttingen. (Germany)

Ajva Taulananda - Dep. Minister of Agr. and Cooperatives. (Thailand)

Robert L. Thompson - Dean of Agriculture, Purdue University. (USA)

Bruce Vaughan - Chairman, Dalgety Farmers Limited. (Australia)

Claude Villain - President, Interministerial Mission for Central and Eastern Europe. Former Inspector General of Finance. (France)

S.M. Wahi - Vice-President, National Institute of Agriculture. (India)

Aart de Zeeuw - Former Chairman, Agricultural Negotiations Committee, GATT. (The Netherlands)

Permanent Observers:

Alexandre Ivashchenko - Professor, Academy of Foreign Trade of Russia. (Russia)

Tianxi Wu - Research Fellow, Institute of Agricultural Economy, Academy of Agricultural Science; Advisor, Department of Policies and Laws, Ministry of Agriculture. (China)

Acknowledgements

The conference, "Agriculture, the Environment and Trade - Conflict or Cooperation?" was the result of the interest, cooperation, and efforts of numerous individuals and organizations. Similarly, the production and assembly of these conference proceedings required substantial guidance and support. As the conference director and proceedings editor, we gratefully acknowledge all of those who helped to bring the conference and these proceedings to fruition.

First and foremost, we wish to extend a heartfelt thanks to Piet Bukman, Minister of Agriculture, Nature Management, and Fisheries of the Netherlands. Dr. Bukman possessed considerable vision and foresight in proposing that a conference on these issues be held following the Rio Summit and we are proud that he asked the International Policy Council on Agriculture and Trade (IPC) to organize it. Furthermore, Dr. Bukman committed his Ministry's substantive and financial resources, in particular those of the Department for the Environment, Quality, and Nutrition, to assist the IPC. Moreover, throughout the duration of the conference, he remained personally committed to its success. Finally, in addition to hosting the Conference's Opening Reception at the Floriade International Horticultural Exhibit and the conference itself, Dr. Bukman opened the conference with a conceptualizing address. This event indeed would not have occurred without the dedicated support of the Minister and his staff.

Of special significance was the role of Aart de Zeeuw, Adviser to Minister Bukman and an IPC member. Mr. de Zeeuw initiated discussions on agriculture, the environment, and trade during his work on the April 1991 IPC Plenary meeting in The Netherlands, where Dr. Bukman was a guest speaker. It was at a later meeting between Dr. Bukman and Mr. de Zeeuw that the idea to have the IPC organize a conference on these issues was born. Additionally, Mr. de Zeeuw acted as the IPC's main contact at the Ministry, contributed substantively to agenda development, lent his personal advice on local arrangements and activities, secured conference participants, and singlehandedly raised the majority of funds to support the conference and its follow-up. His personal attention to this event and zealous activities on behalf of the Ministry and the IPC ensured the conference's success.

Also at the Dutch Ministry of Agriculture, Nature Management, and Fisheries, the IPC would like to recognize Piet Ritsema and Hans van der Kooi. Their wise counsel, advice, and support were essential for substantive and logistical coordination between Washington and the Hague. We also extend our appreciation to J.D. Gabor for providing the luncheon address on Tuesday, September 8th and to R. Dirkzwager, A.M.W. Kleinmuelman, and W.E. Geluk for their assistance. Furthermore, we note our sincere gratitude to Antoinette Mortensen-van der Veen for her capable assistance with protocol, with the Minister's cabinet, and with Codex Alimentarius. Finally, we thank Greta van Bemmelen and Wilma de Haan for their efforts to enhance coordination between Washington and the Hague and their general assistance throughout the project.

Secondly, we owe a debt of gratitude to the conference Advisory Committee, which bore the primary responsibilities of developing the agenda and recommending speakers. Advisory Committee members were: Pierre Crosson, C.J. de Bont, Aart de Zeeuw, Chet Dickerson, Joe Jensen, John Miranowski, Denise Owen, Jules Pretty, Kitty Reichelderfer, Norm Rosenberg, David Runnalls, Steiner Seljegard, Ann Tutwiler, and Hans van der Kooi.

Third, to all of the speakers, reactors, and their respective institutions, a heartfelt thanks for their thoughtful contributions to the conference and their timely replies to publishing deadlines. (See "About the Authors" on pages xix-xxvi for speakers' biographies.)

Fourth, an event like this is rarely possible without the financial and in-kind support of corporations, foundations, government agencies, and academic institutions. For this event, we are especially pleased to have had such a distinguished list of international contributors. We applaud their generosity and environmental progressiveness. (Financial and in-kind contributors are listed on page xi.)

Fifth, we would like to thank IPC members for their assistance with fundraising, securing conference delegates, and for their conference participation. In particular, we are grateful to the IPC's Chairman, Lord Plumb, and Executive Director, Robert Wise, for their committed assistance with fundraising and public relations and for their contributions to this volume. Finally, we note our sincere appreciation to Ann Tutwiler for her steady guidance, encouragement, and leadership and to Denise Owen for her loyal aid and cheerful follow-up throughout this project.

Finally, for their capable and dependable handling of organizational and administrative details before, during, and after the conference, we thank the IPC's Executive Assistant, Sandra Garner; IPC interns, Marcelle O'Connell, Richard Rivera, and Rachel Zylstra; and last, but certainly not least, the Leids Congres Bureau in Leiden, Holland. It was a pleasure to work with such a dedicated, hard-working group of individuals.

Washington, DC
February 1993

Tamara A. White
Assistant Executive Director

Caroline T. Williamson
Program Assistant

International Policy Council on Agriculture and Trade

Conference Contributors

Ministry of Agriculture, Nature Mgmt., and Fisheries (The Netherlands)
Royal Gist-Brocades nv (The Netherlands)
Rabobank Nederland (The Netherlands)
BP Nutrition (The Netherlands)
Sandoz Agro/Seeds (Switzerland)
Archer Daniels Midland (United States)
Monsanto Agricultural Company (United States)
Kraft General Foods International (United States)
Central Soya/Provimi Holding B.V. (The Netherlands)
Tradigrain, SA (Switzerland)
Organization for Economic Cooperation and Development

In-Kind Support

Agricultural Mortgage Corporation (United Kingdom)
American Farm Bureau Federation (United States)
Archer Daniels Midland (United States)
Booker Countryside (United Kingdom)
Business Council for Sustainable Development (Switzerland)
Central Soya Company, Inc. (United States)
Centre for Law and Social Policy (Canada)
CP Group of Companies (Thailand)
Economic Research Service, USDA (United States)
International Federation of Agricultural Producers (France)
International Food Policy Research Institute (United States)
Japan International Agricultural Council (Japan)
Ministry of Agriculture, Fisheries, and Food (United Kingdom)
Ministry of Agriculture, Forestry, and Fisheries (Japan)
Ministry of Agriculture, Nature Mgmt., and Fisheries (The Netherlands)
Ministry for Food, Agriculture, and Forestry (Germany)
Mitsui Corporation (Japan)
Monsanto Agricultural Company (United States)
National American Wholesale Grocers Association (United States)
Pioneer Hi-Bred International, Inc. (United States)
Resources for the Future (United States)
Sparks Companies, Inc. (United States)
University of Minnesota (United States)

1992
IPC General Funders

Sponsors

Anonymous (United Kingdom)
Archer Daniels Midland (United States)
Central Soya Co. Inc. (United States)
Kraft General Foods International (United States)
Mitsubishi Corporation (Japan)
Monsanto Agricultural Company (United States)
Unilever PLC (United Kingdom)
United Biscuits (Holdings)PLC (United Kingdom)

Contributors

Goodman Fielder Wattie Ltd. (Australia)
Groupe Saint Louis/Générale Sucriere (France)
Louis Dreyfus Corporation (United States)
Pioneer Hi-Bred (United States)
Unigrains (France)

Associates

Dalgety Farmers Ltd. (Australia)
Kellogg Company Ltd. (United Kingdom)
Mitsui & Co. (Japan)
Sam Yang Co. (Korea)

Table of Contents

xiv

xv

About the Authors

John Block

Mr. Block is currently President of the National-American Wholesale Grocers' Association and a member of the Board of Directors of Deere and Company, of the Farm Foundation, and of the Illinois Agricultural Leadership Foundation. He is also a member of the International Policy Council on Agriculture and Trade. From 1981-86, he was the Secretary of Agriculture of the United States.

Piet Bukman

Dr. Bukman is the Minister of Agriculture, Nature Management, and Fisheries of the Netherlands. His past positions include State Secretary for Economic Affairs, Minister for Development Cooperation, and President of the Dutch FAO Committee. He was also President of the European People's Party, General Secretary of the Christian Farmers and Market Gardeners' Association, and President of the Public Relations Bureau for Agriculture and Horticulture.

Brian Chamberlin

Mr. Chamberlin is on a one-year contract as Counsellor (Agriculture) at the New Zealand High Commission in London. He spent two years from mid-1990 as Special Agricultural Trade Envoy for New Zealand. Before that, he was President of the New Zealand farmers organization, Federated Farmers. He has spoken in many countries on New Zealand's experience of eliminating farm subsidies from a farmer's perspective, as well as on the merits of agricultural trade liberalization.

Kenneth A. Cook

Mr. Cook is Vice President for Policy at the Center for Resource Economics in Washington, DC. He was a principal designer of the conservation and environmental provisions in the 1985 and 1990 federal farm bills. Mr. Cook was formerly Director of Congressional Affairs and Director of Press Relations for the World Wildlife Fund and Conservation

Foundation. He served for several years as a policy analyst and writer on agricultural and environmental issues for environmental organizations and governmental agencies in Washington, DC.

Alex Dubgaard

Mr. Dubgaard is a Senior Lecturer in the Department of Economics and Natural Resources at the Royal Veterinary and Agricultural University in Denmark. He is presently coordinating a Nordic project investigating the economic aspects of less intensive agricultural practices. In the past, he has undertaken economic research for the FAO, the EC Commission, the "Commissariat General du Plan," the German and the Danish Agency for Environmental Protection, and the Danish Ministry of Agriculture.

Aart de Zeeuw

Mr. de Zeeuw is a member of the International Policy Council on Agriculture and Trade and was, until recently, Adviser to the Minister of Agriculture, Nature Management and Fisheries of the Netherlands. Formerly, he was Chairman of the GATT Agricultural Negotiations Committee, the Director General of International Agricultural Affairs for the Ministry of Agriculture (1987-89), and Director General of Agriculture and Food for the Ministry of Agriculture of the Netherlands (1973-86).

Richard Eglin

Mr. Eglin joined the Trade and Environment Division at the GATT Secretariat in 1991 and was made Acting Director of the Division in March 1992. Since December 1985, he has held various positions in the Research, Trade, and Finance Divisions, where he was responsible for the Uruguay Round negotiations on Trade, Related Investment Measures, and Functioning of the GATT System. From 1977 until 1985, he worked as an economist at the International Monetary Fund.

Tom Garvey

Mr. Garvey is the Deputy Director General in DG XI (Environment, Nuclear Safety, and Civil Protection) at the European Commission. His duties have included being Director of the Internal Market and Industrial Affairs Directorate General, preparing and implementing the

Commission's white paper of June 1985, and being Director in charge of PHARE Operational Service (External Relations). Before joining the Commission in 1984, Mr. Garvey was Chief Executive of An Post (a commercial state company), the first delegate of the Commission of the European Communities in the Federal Republic of Nigeria, and Chief Executive of the Irish Export Board.

John Gummer

Mr. Gummer is the Minister of Agriculture of the United Kingdom. Formerly, he served as Paymaster General (1984-85), Minister of State for Employment, and Under Secretary of State for Employment (1983-84).

Michael Franklin

Sir Michael serves as a non-executive director of Barclays Bank, as Chairman of the West European Program of the Royal Institute of International Affairs, and as a member of the International Policy Council on Agriculture and Trade. He has held prominent positions within the British Civil Service, including Head of the European Secretariat in the Cabinet Office and Permanent Secretary of the Ministry of Agriculture, Fisheries, and Food.

Tahar Hadj-Sadok

Mr. Hadj-Sadok is the Principal Adviser on economic issues in the UNCED Secretariat. Prior to being assigned to UNCED, he held a number of positions in the United Nations in the office of the Director-General for Development and Economic Cooperation then in the Department for International Economic and Social Affairs. Mr. Hadj-Sadok also held a number of research and management positions in private and parastatal organizations in Europe and served as a senior adviser in the Algerian national oil company, Sonatrach.

Dale Hathaway

Dr. Hathaway is the Executive Director of the National Center for Food and Agricultural Policy in Washington, DC and the Treasurer of the International Policy Council on Agriculture and Trade. His prior positions include: Vice President, Consultants International Group; Under-secretary for International Affairs and Commodity Programs, USDA; Director, International Food Policy Research Institute (IFPRI); Program Adviser, the Ford Foundation; and Chairman, Department of Agricultural Economics, Michigan State University.

C. Peter Johnson

Mr. Johnson is Chief Executive of Booker Countryside, the land management division of Booker Plc, in the United Kingdom. He has been affiliated with this company since 1978 when he developed a UK farming business for Booker Plc. Prior to joining Booker, Mr. Johnson was engaged in the management of a variety of agricultural enterprises in eastern England representing a wide spectrum of ownership.

Charles S. Johnson

Mr. Johnson is the Senior Vice President of Pioneer Hi-Bred International, Inc. Before being named to this position in 1988, he held various posts within Pioneer including Treasurer and Vice President of Finance. Mr. Johnson serves as Director of the Board of the National Association of Manufacturers and on the New American Realities Committee of the National Planning Association.

Kumbirai Kangai

Mr. Kangai is the Minister of Lands, Agriculture, and Water Development and a Member of Parliament in Zimbabwe. From 1980 until 1992, he held various government positions, including Minister of Industry and Commerce; Deputy Secretary of Economics; Minister of Energy, Water Resources, and Development; Minister of State for Industry and Technology; and Minister of Labor and Social Welfare. Mr. Kangai played an instrumental role in creating and in gaining international support for Zimbabwe.

Walter Kittel

Mr. Kittel is the State Secretary of the Ministry of Food, Agriculture and Forestry in Germany. He has served the government in several capacities, including posts in the Ministry of Economics and in the Permanent Mission of the Federal Republic of Germany to the EC in Brussels. Before being named State Secretary, Mr. Kittel was responsible for the Common Agricultural Policy of the EC and the International Agricultural Policy in his position as Permanent Deputy of the Ministry of Food, Agriculture, and Forestry.

H.O.A. Kjeldsen

Mr. Kjeldsen is the President of the International Federation of Agricultural Producers (IFAP) and Chairman of the Board of the Agricultural Council of Denmark. His former positions include Chairman of COPA (1987-88) and Member of the Board of The East Asiatic Company (1980).

Jim MacNeill

Mr. MacNeill is currently President of MacNeill Associates and a Senior Fellow at the Institute for Research on Public Policy in Ottawa. Formerly, he was the Secretary General of the World Commission on Environment and Development (the Brundtland Commission) and a principal architect of the Commission's 1986 report, Our Common Future. Before joining the WCED, he was Director of Environment for the Organization for Economic Cooperation and Development, the Permanent Secretary (Deputy Minister) of the Canadian Ministry of State for Urban Affairs, and a Special Adviser on the constitution and the environment in Prime Minister Pierre E. Trudeau's office.

Liberty Mhlanga

Mr. Mhlanga is the General Manager and Director of the Agricultural and Rural Development Authority in Zimbabwe and a member of the International Policy Council on Agriculture and Trade. His past positions include: former Assistant Director, Environment Training Program (ENDA)(1974-81); Fellow, Adlai Stevenson Institute, Chicago (1972-74); and Science adviser and researcher, United Nations Conference on the Human Environment, Secretariat Headquarters in Geneva, Switzerland (1971-72).

John A. Miranowski

Dr. Miranowski has been Director of the Resources and Technology Division of the Economic Research Service at the U.S. Department of Agriculture since 1984. In addition to his duties at ERS, he was on detail to the Office of the Secretary of Agriculture (1990-91), serving as Executive Coordinator of the Secretary's Policy Coordination Council and Special Assistant to the Deputy Secretary of Agriculture. Before joining USDA, Dr. Miranowski was Associate Professor of Economics at Iowa State University.

Henry Plumb

Lord Plumb is the Chairman of the International Policy Council on Agriculture and Trade and a Member of the European Parliament. Formerly, he was the President of the European Parliament (1987-89), of the National Farmers Union of England and Wales (1970-79), of the Royal Agricultural Society of England (1977), and of the International Federation of Agricultural Producers (1979-82). In addition, he was the Chairman of the British Agricultural Council (1975-79) and a non-executive Director of United Biscuits. Lord Plumb currently sits on the board of a number of international agribusiness corporations.

Jeffrey Rae

Mr. Rae is Head of the Agricultural Policies Division at OECD.

Jiro Shiwaku

Mr. Shiwaku is the Vice Minister for International Affairs at the Ministry of Agriculture, Forestry, and Fisheries in Japan. Since 1959, he has held various positions at MAFF, including: Director, Trade and Tariff Division, International Affairs Department (1975-6); Director, Fisheries Marketing (1976-8); Director, Agricultural Administration Department, Gunma Prefecture (1978-81); Director, Structure Improvement Project Division, Agricultural Structure Improvement Bureau (1981-85); Director-General, International Affairs Department, Economic Affairs Bureau (1985-88); and Director-General, Economic Affairs Bureau (1988-90).

Michael Smith

Since 1988, Mr. Smith has been President of SJS Advanced Strategies, an international trade and investment consulting firm in Washington, D.C. His former positions include Senior Deputy U.S. Trade Representative (1983-88), U.S. Ambassador to the GATT and Deputy U.S. Trade

Representative (1979-83), chief U.S. Textile Negotiator for USTR (1975-79), chief of Fibers and Textiles Division, Economic Bureau, U.S. Department of State (1973-74), and career Foreign Service Officer, U.S. Department of State (1959-88). Mr. Smith was a founding member of the Pacific Economic Cooperation Council.

Jan Sonneveld

Since 1989, Mr. Sonneveld has been a Member of the European Parliament from the Netherlands and has served on the Agriculture, the Fisheries, and the External Economic Relations committees. For 25 years prior to his appointment to the European Parliament, Mr. Sonneveld held a number of positions, partly at foreign posts, at the Dutch Ministry of Agriculture, Nature Management, and Fisheries.

W. Rob Storey

Mr. Storey is Minister of Transport, of Statistics, of Lands, of Survey and Land Information, and in Charge of the Valuation Department in New Zealand. Formerly, he was a member of the Parliamentary Service Commission, Chairman of the Publicity and Information Committee of the National Party, Director of Auckland Farmers' Freezing Company, Director of Combined Rural Traders Limited, and Chairman of Directors of the Point Blank Press Company. In addition, Mr. Storey was President of the Federated Farmers and Chairman of the New Zealand Committee of the Pacific Basin Economic Council.

P. J. Strijkert

Since 1985, Dr. Strijkert has been a Member of the Board of Management at Royal Gist-brocades nv. He is also a member of the Dutch Forum for Technology and Science, Chiron Corporation, International Bio-Synthetics BV, the Association of the Dutch Chemical Industry, the Bureau Eg-Liaison, and the Senior Advisory Group Biotechnology. Formerly, Dr. Strijkert was a researcher at the Council for Scientific and Industrial Research (1976-79) and a Professor of Biology at Eindhoven College (1973-75).

Robert L. Thompson

Dr. Thompson is Dean of Agriculture at Purdue University, a Board Member of the Farm Foundation, and a member of the International Policy Council on Agriculture and Trade. Formerly, he was Chairman of the National Center for Food and Agriculture Policy Advisory Council, the Assistant Secretary for Economics at USDA, the Agricultural Staff Adviser for the Council of Economic Advisers, and a Professor of Agricultural Economics at Purdue University.

Jan Diek van Mansvelt

Dr. van Mansvelt is President and a Member of the Board of the International Federation of Organic Agricultural Movements (IFOAM). In addition, he is an adviser to the Dutch National Institute of Public Health and Environmental Protection, a Board Member of the Dutch Platform of Biological Agriculture, and a Lecturer/Researcher at the Wageningen Agricultural University Department of Alternative/Ecological Agriculture.

A.I. van Niekerk

Mr. van Niekerk is Minister of Agriculture of the Republic of South Africa.

Caroline T. Williamson

Miss Williamson is Program Assistant at the International Policy Council on Agriculture and Trade. A 1992 graduate of Davidson College, she is presently a candidate for a Masters in International Management at the American Graduate School for International Management in Glendale, Arizona.

Robert E. Wise

Mr. Wise is Executive Director of the International Policy Council on Agriculture and Trade and Advisor to the Director General of the United Kingdom Agricultural Supply Trade Association (UKASTA). Formerly, he was Legislative Assistant to United States Senator Thomas A. Daschle and an Agricultural Economist with the Economic Research Service at the U.S. Department of Agriculture.

Foreword

Lord Plumb of Coleshill

For most of this century, the discussion of and debate over agricultural policy has been very much the exclusive preserve of the agricultural community itself, especially in developed countries. While stemming from issues of concern to a wider audience, such as food security in the 1930s, most agricultural policy discussion in the past focused largely on farm income goals: achieve a decent level of farm income and any other goals (such as food security) will be taken care of automatically. That being the commonly held view, there was never a compelling reason for others to get involved in the policy process.

Nothing stays the same forever, and today, in addition to farmers, it seems that taxpayers, consumers, ramblers, technologists, aid workers, and environmentalists alike have or believe they have a legitimate interest in and role to play in forming agricultural policy. Not only is the notion that governments will intervene in agriculture to protect farm income and provide affordable food under question, but many observers also believe that these policies may directly effect other aspects of socio-economic activity, both positively and negatively.

Nowhere is this relatively recent, broader interest in "traditional" agricultural policy more evident than in the scrutiny of the interactions of agriculture and agricultural policy with the environment and environmental policy. Similarly, many people, both in and outside of agriculture, are concerned about the interactions of agriculture and agricultural policy with trade and trade policy. The triangle can be completed by considering the relationship between trade and the environment.

Over the past ten to fifteen years, reform of agricultural policies in both developed and developing countries has begun to reflect these new concerns. While the process has been gradual, it would be wrong to assume that it has been completely smooth. For the first time, players with varying perspectives and interests have been involved in the policy process. Some of these players have come to view their counterparts as adversaries.

This conflict should not and need not be the case. As a farmer, with both owned and tenanted land, I see myself as a transient custodian of the land. Therefore, *prima facie*, I should be able to see eye-to-eye with anyone calling themselves an environmentalist. This conference was primarily about getting people together from different backgrounds to explore the issues at stake. In so doing, we hoped to develop a common and amicable ground for policy prescription.

The need for such a dialogue is patently obvious when one surveys the institutional mechanisms that are currently attempting to deal with agriculture, the environment, and trade. At a national level, most governments have departments or ministries individually devoted to each of these three areas. The civil servants within these agencies have their own particular constituencies to serve. Sometimes objectives between these departments have coincided; sometimes they have competed.

At the international level, the GATT was created in 1947 to deal with international trade issues. In the past, our agricultural policymakers, who for so long considered agriculture their own preserve, have managed to keep agriculture very much out of the GATT rules. That exclusion may finally be changing; the current Uruguay Round of negotiations, if successfully concluded, will impose GATT disciplines on agriculture as never before.

On the environmental side, we are at an even earlier stage of developing the necessary institutions for dealing with these issues globally. The work of the UN, most notably through the Brundtland Commission and the Rio Earth Summit, has both raised public awareness of environmental issues and created a stronger political imperative for policy action on these issues.

However, our analytical methods for investigating the impacts of economic and social activities on the environment are still developing. As yet, no clear consensus has emerged on the institutional arrangements that should be pursued in multilateral problem solving.   Thus, this conference came at an important juncture in world history: the stage has been set and the time to act is now.

The Netherlands is one of the countries at the forefront of these issues.   With incredible agricultural productivity from a relatively small land base, the Dutch have much to be proud of in terms of their agriculture.   However, this success has created its own environmental problems, such as the disposal of animal waste. Consequently, the Dutch are leaders in developing practices and policies to balance agricultural and environmental imperatives.

It should therefore come as no surprise that the International Policy Council on Agriculture and Trade (IPC) was invited by the government of the Netherlands to develop this conference. We are grateful to Minister Piet Bukman of the Ministry of Agriculture, Nature Management, and Fisheries for having the vision to develop a forum on these issue at a time when policymaking ground rules themselves are only just being laid down.

I believe that during the conference and in assembling this proceedings volume, we brought together some of the brightest minds currently working on these issues around the world. These proceedings will provide a much needed reference to the issues and will hopefully point to some of the directions policymakers should be taking.

Introduction

In September 1992, the International Policy Council on Agriculture and Trade (IPC) convened a conference on agriculture, the environment, and trade in Noordwijk, The Netherlands. The conference was organized at the request of Piet Bukman, Dutch Minister of Agriculture, Nature Management, and Fisheries. In light of heightened public concern about global environmental issues and the potential for national and international conflict over environmental policymaking, the need for a rational exchange of views on agriculture, the environment, and trade was clearly apparent.

The IPC, an independent, multinational body, was urged to convene a conference following the Earth Summit in Rio and preceding the conclusion of the Uruguay Round of the GATT. The timing of this event was seen as critical in order to build upon the experience and knowledge gained at Rio and to enable the IPC to offer advice to negotiators in the final stages of the Uruguay Round negotiations.

The IPC believes that the exchange of views between government, corporate, and agricultural leaders from developed and developing countries is essential for the formulation of policies that encourage mutually beneficial results for agriculture, the environment, and international trade.

Therefore, a key aim of the IPC in planning this conference was to provide an open forum and discussion that would help participants design agricultural policies which would be both environmentally sound and conducive to international agricultural trade.

One hundred and fifty delegates from over thirty nations participated in the conference. Delegates included eight Ministers of Agriculture, a dozen international agribusiness executives, and leaders from farmers' groups, universities, research policy institutes, and environmental organizations.

1

Section 1 offers a general overview of the topics discussed throughout this volume. In his key note address, Dr. Bukman notes that because environmental problems are global, multilateral cooperation is an absolute necessity. Citing the Netherlands as an example, he recommends two strategies for solving conflicts between agriculture and the environment and proposes a Benefactor Benefits Base initiative. Mr. Gummer argues that because surpluses are not eternal, agriculture must prepare for increased demands for food production in the future. Like Dr. Bukman, Mr. Gummer suggests the use of direct payments to farmers for encouraging environmentally sound practices.

Mr. MacNeill states that the challenge is "to initiate a process in which agriculture, the environment, and trade are mutually supportive and in which sustainable forms of agriculture become the order of the day." He urges every round of the GATT to be a "green round." Dr. van Mansvelt outlines the features of organic agriculture and describes their future potential.

Section 2 is entitled "How do agricultural practices and policies affect the environment?" Dr. Miranowski notes the problems between agriculture and the environment in the United States but says that the conflicts are not as serious as is often suggested. He proposes trade reform, research and technology, and development of "green alternatives" as possible policy options for improving the environment.

Mr. Dubgaard notes the growing concern about agriculture's effects on the environment in the European Community and suggests that a policy remedy is one which "combines price support with input levies on fertilizers and pesticides." Citing evidence from OECD countries, Mr. Rae states that agriculture is the custodian of the natural and man-made environment despite some adverse problems.

Mr. Mhlanga makes particular references to Africa and to his native Zimbabwe and notes that population, natural sources, farmers, and technology all affect the environment. Mr. Sonneveld reacts to the above speakers, saying that market and price policies are environmentally blind.

Section 3 concerns "reforming agricultural policies to protect the environment." Mr. Kjeldsen stresses the importance of including farmers in the reform process and in multilateral negotiations. Mr. Kittel outlines new approaches in Germany for environmentally benign farming and for environmental policies, government, farmers, and agribusiness, while Mr. Shiwaku notes the sustainability of Japanese agriculture and the examples it can provide to the rest of the world. Mr. van Neikerk cites South Africa's history and outlines possible roles for government, agribusiness, and farmers in reforming national policies.

Section 4, "Agribusiness: Protector or Polluter?" discusses the positive and negative links between agribusiness and the environment and the role of regulation. Mr. Charles Johnson states that the nature of modern agricultural production practices pose major health risks for farmers and cites sustainable agriculture and biotechnology as possible ways both to ameliorate these risks and to achieve broader environmental stewardship goals.

Mr. Cook suggests that policies should involve a commitment to recognize and cope with agriculture's negative environmental effects. To do so, he recommends taking a farm level view and developing ways for agribusiness and farmers to maximize production and environmental objectives. Mr. Strijkert illustrates the ways in which agriculture is a polluter of the environment and indicates how biotechnology could be used to remedy these problems.

Mr. Peter Johnson asserts that while some regulation comes about for the wrong reasons, regulation generally benefits enterprise and environmental quality. He notes that in the United Kingdom, the activities of agribusiness were formerly unquestioned but now agribusiness is often seen as a major polluter. Mr. Kangai claims that agribusiness is not a polluter in Zimbabwe or in the rest of the developing world.

Section 5, entitled "How Will Environmental Concerns Affect Trade? Do We Need a Green Round?" completes the triangle of topics. Mr. Eglin states that causes of trade friction include claiming jurisdiction over another country's resources and internalizing environmental costs but says that it is too soon to know whether or not we need a "green round."

Mr. Smith asserts that because trade and the environment are in conflict, their problems are complicated to resolve. He argues,

3

however, that GATT must include the environment or it will be revolutionized. Mr. Garvey examines agriculture, the environment, and trade in the European Community, asserting the Community's commitment to enhancing the role of international environmental law. Mr. Hadj-Sadok discusses UNCED's earth conference in Rio in June 1992 and its impact on the future.

Citing New Zealand's environmental experiences, Mr. Storey recognizes the importance of increasing the focus of environmental issues within the GATT. Mr. Chamberlin further explains New Zealand's history of agriculture and the environment without subsidies and states that the Uruguay Round must be completed before a "Green Round" can be initiated.

Section 6 is a summary of the conference as seen through the eyes of the section moderators and of Lord Plumb of Coleshill, Chairman of the IPC. Robert Wise, Executive Director of the IPC, concludes the proceedings with an overall summary and conclusions.

Section I: Agriculture, the Environment, and Trade - Conflict or Cooperation?

An Outline of the Issues

Driven by mounting public concern, the critical link between agricultural trade and environmental issues has been thrust into policy dialogues at local, national, and international levels. While some perceive the protection of environmental and trade interests to be in conflict, others view the objectives of a cleaner environment and freer trade as compatible. Finding solutions that simultaneously promote the compatibility of agriculture and the environment and encourage international trade is a complex task of concern for both food exporting and importing nations.

Speakers and papers in this session addressed the key arguments in this debate, including:
- Are agricultural trade and environmental issues in cooperation or conflict?
- Do international trade agreements force standards to the lowest common denominator?
- Do trade agreements and open borders abrogate a nation's sovereignty over its environment?
- Will higher environmental standards raise food prices and render farmers uncompetitive?
- Are today's conditions eternal?
- Can environmental and agricultural demands be brought together without endangering the food supply?
- What is the role of the market?

- How can organic agricultural techniques be used to achieve sustainable agriculture?
- Should conflict be resolved multilaterally or unilaterally?

Chapter 1

Agriculture, the Environment, and Trade - A Dutch Perspective

Piet Bukman

Cooperation is a Must

Agriculture, the environment, and trade: conflict or cooperation? That is the question. To me the answer is obvious. Cooperation is a must. There is no viable alternative. However harsh the contrasts may be or seem to be, cooperation is an absolute necessity. This position is not only ideological (even though cooperation fits in well with my political ideology) but purely rational. On balance, cooperation is the only road that is open. If this cooperation fails to materialize, the development of both rich and poor countries will take a turn for the worse. This is sad for the former but a tragedy for the latter.

Environmental Problems are Global

The Present Situation in Rich and Poor Countries

Agricultural development causes environmental problems in both rich countries and poor countries. The problems and causes, however, are as different as night and day. In rich countries, environmental problems in agriculture are generally due to attempts at improving productivity and intensification. Contamination of soil, water, and air and deterioration of nature and landscape values are the dark side of the gold medal of growth and technological innovation and the by-products of prosperity and development.

Environmental problems in poor countries, however, are entirely different. There they are by-products of under-development, inadequate technologies, and population explosion. This combination causes an unrestrained exploitation of the environment. A poignant example: each year the Sahara expands by three times the surface area of the Netherlands (i.e. by about 100,000 km^2). Obviously, it is much more difficult to obviate the negative by-products of poverty and under-development than those of prosperity.

Solution Requires Different Approaches

Because the causes of agricultural and environmental problems in rich and poor countries are fundamentally different, they will have to be addressed in different manners. For the benefit of the environment, the governments of rich countries will have to make prerequisites for agricultural production. This action could lead to extensification or to cleaner production methods without affecting their intensiveness. Unlike the poor countries, the rich countries have the option of choosing and therefore can avoid some problems. The challenge for both rich and poor countries is the same though: however difficult, the tide must be turned even if only out of self interest.

In the poor countries there are three tracks that should be followed: 1) The population explosion should be brought to a halt until population rates are more in line with the environmental carrying capacity. The present explosion is the result of a quite strong reduction in the death rate without similar adjustments in the birth rate; 2) The rich world should transfer more appropriate technology and expertise to the poor countries. Fortunately, this notion is widely accepted today by policymakers. Practice, however, is still lagging behind; 3) The poor countries should gain easier access to the world market. Poverty can be fought effectively only if poor countries are able to integrate into the world economy. In the long run, isolation will solve nothing.

The Netherlands Provides an Example

Successful Agriculture and Its Environmental Burden

There are few rich countries in the West where the problems between agriculture and the environment stand out as clearly as in the Netherlands. Each and every day we are made to face the facts and so we are spurred to find solutions. In short, although it is modern, efficient, and successful, Dutch agriculture is a heavy burden on the environment. Therefore, the Netherlands provides an excellent example of what we are discussing at this conference.

Dutch agriculture has prospered since the war. It is a remarkable feat when a small industrialized country is the world's third largest exporter. Sixty percent of our agricultural production goes abroad -- a magnificent economic achievement, a gold medal.

There are drawbacks, alas, particularly in regard to the environment, of which we have become more and more aware during recent years. We use the largest amount of fertilizers and pesticides per hectare in the world and lose quite a bit into the environment. Intensive livestock production produces tons of manure, which are hard to discard and consequently become a risk to ground and surface water quality. In addition, ammonia released from the manure contributes significantly to acid rain, which affects our forests.

Dutch Policy for Agriculture, the Environment, and Nature

Therefore, the Netherlands has developed a coherent policy on agriculture, the environment, and nature. The policy focuses on the concept of "sustainable development" as introduced by the Brundtland Commission, which we wish to realize in the near future.

Because the implementation of our policies will have far-reaching consequences for our farmers, however, achieving this goal is easier said than done. For example, in the year 2000 the amount of manure applied to the land may not exceed the amount that can be taken up by the crops, resulting in an enormous manure surplus. So why not reduce the numbers? A reduction in herd numbers will affect the farmer's income and is bad for the national economy. Do you see the dilemma we are in?

The goal of our pesticide policy is to reduce use by 50 percent in the short run and by 70 percent in the long run. Here too the question arises of whether there are alternatives to maintain both quality and quantity of production. Of this the same answer is true: farmers and growers have to make a living and our economy is the better for it. Again the dilemma.

Strategies for the future

It is nice, of course, to put one's finger on these dilemmas, but far more relevant to determine the solution and strategies to achieve it. I offer two strategies.

Benefiting the Environment and Achieving Market Orientation

First, my policy is aimed at realizing adjustments for environmental benefit while maintaining our products' market positions. Obviously, a farm which does not pay is unable to take measures to protect the environment. Closing borders is not an option since there are developing countries who we want to give opportunities in our market. In practice, tighter environmental requirements are not facilitating competition with countries using less strict requirements.

Therefore, in our market orientation we aim to satisfy the wishes and preferences of modern, critical consumers with purchasing power. Experience shows that consumers all over the world are paying more attention to the quality of products and production methods and less attention to prices. If a producer is able to demonstrate that his product was produced in an environmentally friendly manner, he should, in principle, be able to obtain a better price. This is why I am working on a system of environmental labelling. We have the advantage that consumers in the rich countries are spending an increasingly smaller share of their income on food and drink (in the Netherlands it amounts to only 18 percent).

Transforming Land-Use Systems

My second strategy is to transform the present land-using systems into ones which are more sustainable and less detrimental to the environment. Much research and extension are required to develop and improve these systems and to introduce them into practice. They compromise new systems of production, new resistances, and new housing systems, which are all geared to reducing the emission of harmful substances to the environment. At the same time, more stringent legal requirements are necessary. Farmers are responsible for adjusting their farms to the requirements made for environmental protection. There is no systematic protection against the importation of products which do not meet these same prerequisites.

The Netherlands: A Leader in Agro-Environmental Reform

Some in our country are afraid that this approach will affect the competitive position of Dutch agriculture. Although I can understand their fears, I do not share them in all respects. Measures to protect the environment can be compared with other factors (such as climate, soil type, infrastructure, working conditions, geographic location relative to markets, etc.) that determine whether a certain type of agriculture will be successful in country A or B and hence the type of economic activity. An alleged competitive disadvantage may be turned into a competitive advantage. And this is what will happen here when agricultural producers succeed in selling their environmental efforts on a market that is becoming more susceptible to environmentally friendly methods of production. I already see possibilities.

It is true that it is generally better to lead the way than to bring up the rear. The EC member states do not have the possibility of keeping out imports if these imports satisfy Community quality requirements. In some fields, the Netherlands uses stricter quality requirements than the EC. Nevertheless, it is my impression that the Dutch agricultural sector so far has not suffered greatly for the stricter national position. On the contrary, our agricultural exports have strongly increased. I intentionally use the words "so far" to avoid the impression that there is no need to further harmonize the agro-environmental policy of the EC. For the need is great, but this does not preclude that it is possible to take advantage of a difficult situation.

Reforming the Common Agricultural Policy

Regarding the Common Agricultural Policy (CAP), in May an agreement was reached on the partial replacement of price support by direct income support, particularly for cereals. I doubt whether the entire package of reforms will suffice to solve problems of surpluses and to curb spending. I am no advocate of *laissez faire* or *laissez aller* as the answer to world problems. The questions are whether government intervention in the agricultural sector has not overshot the mark and whether a farmer's doings are still sufficiently influenced by the market. Stating the question like this is more or less implying the answer. I think there is a fair chance that within a few years we will once again enter into discussions on reforming the CAP. We will then have to decide which way we want to go. Budgetary restrictions, trade politics, and environmental problems will require further adjustments in the future.

The EC is currently breaking new ground on an income support system. This is a positive development for farmers, who otherwise would immediately be faced with the consequences of declining prices. In our society though, the support measures serve a social purpose and give farmers time to adjust to new price relationships which conform more to the market. This conformity is not achieved through permanent income support.

Also important is the question of whether such income support without *quid pro quo* is politically tenable in the long run. I have grave doubts about it. I do not believe in it. Indeed, I am convinced that a next discussion on the CAP will center on what to ask for in exchange for the right to permanent income support.

Linking Agriculture and the Environment

The Benefactor Benefits Base

This brings me back to the discussion on agriculture and the environment. Permanent forms of direct income support might be linked up to a clearly defined fair return in the context of nature and landscape maintenance. I feel sure that it will become an item for discussion. Analogous with the Polluter Pays Principle, this might be labelled the Benefactor Benefits Base. It will not be easy to realize such a policy. It may turn out to be an inexpensive way to keep the farmer's income at a reasonable level, to avoid rural depopulation, and to maintain nature and landscape values.

Cross Compliance

Another possibility is a form of cross compliance by linking up with environmental objectives (e.g. hectare support if production satisfies certain environmental requirements). It may be possible to bridge the gap between agriculture on the one hand and nature, landscape and environment on the other. I am convinced that permanently guaranteed income from public funds is not tenable without a socially relevant fair return.

The Agriculture, Environment, and Trade Triangle

Free world trade and the environment are not always reconcilable, which may have been one of the reasons why the item "environment" was not very high on the Uruguay Round agenda.

The recent tuna fish panel is an example of the tension that may be created if one country takes restrictive measures based on its national environmental policy because another country does not satisfy the first country's environmental standards. Under its national environmental legislation, the United States has banned the import of several tuna fish species because the catch methods used are detrimental to dolphin stocks. A GATT panel considers this import ban a contravention of the GATT treaty not because the panel deems the protection of dolphins unnecessary but because it sees the <u>unilateral</u> character of the United States' measure.

At the same time, this case pointed out the possibility of realizing the desired end by <u>multilateral</u> cooperation. The Netherlands strongly advocates multilateral approaches. The effect of such approaches is by definition more profound than that of unilateral trade measures. It is important that agreement is reached in the GATT context on the circumstances and criteria for deviating from the general GATT principles for environmental reasons.

In this respect, the Uruguay Round developments in the area of veterinary and phytosanitary measures are very interesting. The GATT is studying a draft decision containing further arrangements on the prerequisites for measures to be taken under Article XX that may affect free trade. A similar procedure could perhaps be followed with regard to environmental protection by creating a kind of environmental code for all parties. Amending the GATT Article is another possibility but, in view of the problems this will cause, it might be less effective.

I, therefore, propose that the GATT should be transformed into a world trade organization whose primary objective would be fair trade. It should be fair with regards to environmental and consumer requirements, to the position of the poor countries, and to food safety and food security.

Chapter 2

Agriculture, the Environment, and Trade - A British Perspective

John Gummer

(Transcribed from conference tapes.)

Agriculture, the environment or trade - conflict or cooperation? No previous generation would have had this question on their agenda, which proves that it is nonsense. The failure to study history is the root cause of the unbelievable arrogance of the 1990s.

Three Green Heresies

Exclusion of Mankind from the Environment

It is a reflection of three fundamental green heresies that we come to discuss this issue in this form. First, there are those whose view of the environment is that it would be very much better if mankind had nothing to do with it. The speeches round the EC and beyond of these doom-laden environmentalists remind one of Archimedes, who said that if only someone would give him a platform outside the world, he would use levers to move the world. The greens of this kind want a platform outside the world in order to look at it proceeding down its uninterrupted environmental way.

That is not the world of which we were intended to be stewards. That is not the world in which we were placed and have our place. The concept that the fundamental activities of mankind should be in contradiction with the environment is itself utterly wrong. For the environment which we seek to preserve is the creation of agriculture and trade and is not in some way a besmirched and damaged original creation which needs to revert to some nobler, more savage condition.

The Fascist Perspective

The second heresy is that unless some exterior action is taken, there will be a fight between the noble ideals of the environment and the sordid activities of man growing, feeding, and trading the results of what he grows. That is the incipient fascism of those who wish to impose upon the whole of mankind rules and regulations which they will lay down and which will not be able to be gainsaid by national interests, agricultural concerns, or trading needs because of the one single justification that it is environmentally good. That attitude towards the environment is one which has grown and which is seen so clearly in those who suggest that there is no way in which freely and in cooperation we can find a solution on these occasions in which conflict exists.

I hear all the time from groups, largely unelected and self-important, that people should behave in particular ways. They are, of course, the very groups who would object to that if I imposed rules for some religious or political reason. Because they can claim that it is for an environmental reason though, all is justified. That has been the case for fascism down the ages. Fascism is believing that it is alright for you to tell other people what to do as long as they do not try to tell you what to do, because your reasons are good and theirs are bad.

The Marxist Claim

The third heresy lurks more deeply and more carefully covered because it is less fashionable. It is the Marxist belief that inherently freedom, free trade, free expression, free discussion, and free choice are opposed to environmental good. It is the last resting place of the Marxist interpretation of history. It is the final hope of those who have seen their beliefs prove false in practice.

16

They constantly suggest that in small things or in medium size things freedom is okay. However, in these great global matters, we have to have ways of restricting people, lest ultimate destruction befalls us all.

Heresies Should Not Distort Assessment of Problems

These three mechanisms of the extremists should not distort our rational and sensible assessment of the problems of agriculture, trade, and the environment, which are not in conflict anymore than any other series of activities need to be in conflict. A wise commentator once said that civilized men never follow their arguments to their ultimate conclusions. That is a very true statement because what it seeks to emphasize is that you only get into that position of conflict if your concentration upon one side of the issue or one aspect of the matter is such that none other can play its proper part or restore the proper balance.

I start in the sharp manner I have because I doubt if the farming position or the trading position will be overstated. The danger at the moment is that the environmental position will be extolled beyond its proper place in today's world. In the past, the danger was that the agriculture position was going to be extolled beyond its proper place and perfectly rightly there has been a reaction among those who are particularly concerned to correct the balance. What we must make sure in a conference like this is that the balance does not give way to a new distortion which destroys the proper equilibrium in a different way.

Today's Surpluses Are Not Eternal

If that is the case, where do we find that balance? I hope we start by believing that today's conditions are not inevitably eternal.

The Old Beliefs

If I dare step upon dangerous ground, when the Brundtland report was produced, it was the last flurry of an attitude which was born of a generation that believed that food shortages were inevitable and eternal. I was born of that generation. We believed -- well, everyone in the world told us -- that increasingly the battle in the world would be between North and South about food, because population would do that to us, and that all the old arguments would be displaced by this one, overwhelming, essential, and ineluctable kind of debate.

Indeed, it was sometimes put, as the club of Rome did, in even more extreme language that we would have to batten down the hatches in the West if we were to conserve any of our food for ourselves because the pressures from the rest of the world would be so great and our moral duty so obvious that we would find it difficult to feed ourselves at all. Therefore, all the demands were to produce more and more and more. We gave a moral justification to what had been a direct economic, post war need.

The New World Situation

Then, suddenly the world situation changed. Those who could afford to pay for food could pay for food in abundance so much so that they had piles of it everywhere. Even the poorest began to see that the real issue was not the supply of food but the distribution of it both in economic and in social terms.

Instead of learning the lesson that any generation ought to learn -- that what is true today may well not be true tomorrow --, we learned the lesson that because we were no longer in shortage and were now in surplus, we would always be in surplus. I notice that speeches prepared for me still tend to have that feeling that I have to talk about the dangers of overproduction and I have to emphasize how much we have. I am prepared to say that is true today and I think it will be true tomorrow and it may well be true the next day but it will not be true forever.

Therefore, any way you look at the agricultural environment, you must accept that there is an environmental and an agricultural imperative to ensure that we can produce food in abundance and that we do not use what is the temporary fact of surplus of temperate foods to excuse any failure on our part to ensure an adequate level of future food production.

Why Surpluses Are Not Eternal

There are a series of reasons why the moment will come when we shall seek again from our farmers higher not lower production. I can give all kinds of logical, sensible arguments for that, including the most powerful argument of all: that it has always been so. Every time we have had surplus, people have said that it will never be the same again. They said it in the 1880s. They said it in the 1930s. They always said it will never be the same again but it always was because life is like that. Population pressures, climatic change, and peoples' desires to have variety and choice in their diets lead one to believe that the capacity to produce temperate food will again be outgrown by the demand.

Therefore, for our part of the world the one thing we must not do is to assume that surplus is eternal. We must prepare the future on the basis that agriculture will need to be able to use the current land area to produce as much food as is needed and that what it will need to produce may well be considerably more than is now satisfactory.

Agricultural Policy Cannot Destroy Farmers' Ability to Produce

Therefore, you cannot evolve an agricultural policy which is going to destroy the ability of farmers to produce food. In other words, you cannot either go to what is called in some of the sillier circles "traditional farming methods," as if you could ever get anyone to hoe beet by hand today. Nor can you suggest that we say about agriculture what we would say about no other industry: that technology stops today; we are not going to develop; we are not having any new systems; we are not investing; we are not thinking of better and more efficient means of production. It would be impossible to do that if we are to protect ourselves from the increased demands which will be made on us sooner or later.

No Excuses Will Be Allowed

Let's be clear about it -- there will be no excuses. Any group of governments, whether through intellectually respectable organizations like GATT or the European Community or nationally, which have made it impossible to feed their people effectively will not be forgiven in the future. Anybody who is in politics ought to recognize that they are not getting away with the statement which says, "I'm sorry we haven't got enough wheat. We thought it was better for the environment." We have to recognize that the environment does not stand comparison with hunger. We must prepare ourselves for a world in which you must be able to bring together the demands of the environment and of agriculture while not endangering our food supply.

Trade Must Play a Role

Of course, trade must play its part. Trade is the vehicle by which man has discovered the ability to progress. Exciting and innovative, trade is the one of the things which has most changed mankind. I was brought up in Kent and my earliest memories are of wandering about what were then the very busy Docklands in London, there at the mouth of the river, down where the sea pilots and the river pilots changed. I have always had that very British and, if I may say so, Dutch romantic view about trade. It is not a dirty, unpleasant thing. It is an exciting way in which human beings exchange their goods, find markets, and learn about each other. Do not allow anybody to remove that great romance.

Indeed, the three subjects we are discussing are the three great romantic activities of mankind: tilling the land, selling our products, and passing onto the next generation something better

20

than we received ourselves. Therefore, they cannot be allowed to be seen in conflict. They must be brought together so that they enhance rather than detract from each other.

Rebuilding the Rural Economy

If we believe that to be so, what should we be doing? The fundamental changes which are taking place in order to restore that balance must be allowed to take place against the background that every acre of land now in production ought to be capable of producing as long as possible. I think it was nonsense for the European Commissioner to suggest in a speech once that every farmer who now farms in Europe should be able to farm in ten years time. That statement is neither true nor sensible. There will not be anything like as many farmers in Europe in ten years time or we will have betrayed our principle of needing to be able to produce efficiently. I think one of the dangerous things in Europe is this belief that somehow or other it is sensible to produce inefficiently because it means a lot of people have a job. Those countries that are still maintaining that view are doing great disservice to agriculture.

There are other ways of rebuilding the rural economy. I can now work at home in the country because of the fax, the telephone, and other speedy means of communication. More people will find their home and their work in the rural areas because of those changes in life. It will not be necessary for farming to provide the jobs it once provided. The countryside can come to the rescue of that utterly artificial concept: the town. We will be able to bring people back to a more healthy way of life because they will run their life from the countryside and provide the jobs there. Those who seek to make the farm an outpost of Victorian industry will gravely damage agriculture. So, of course, we must accept that there will be a continuing decline in the number of people involved in agriculture.

Direct Payments Must Be In Return for Environmental Practices

We are in the business of helping farmers directly but those direct payments must be in return for environmentally acceptable agriculture and cannot be merely paid for being farmers. There is no justification in the argument that a farmer must be paid because he is a farmer.

I always remember speaking in Bavaria, if Mr. Kittel will not mind me quoting this, where I was welcomed by the farmers who were not going to have a go at me. The man they were having a go at was the representative of the German Ministry of Agriculture. It was summed up by a leader of the Bavarian farmers who said to him (in English, for my benefit) "Look, you pay the postman. You pay the train driver. Why do you not pay the farmer? We are all civil servants." Indeed, it is very much that attitude -- the view that the farmer has a right to be paid -- which has so undermined a sensible way of looking at agriculture.

There is a great danger in believing that numbers are the sign of support for agriculture. Maintaining larger numbers and doing things inefficiently does two terrible things: first, it distorts the market and increasingly annoys the tax payers who ultimately will cut off the funds; and secondly, it suggests that our rural land should be a museum and not part of the life of the community.

Reforming the CAP

What we have to do is to have an environmental protection policy integrated into our system so that the wildlife and the countryside benefit from it. All EC Ministers reaffirmed their commitment to this approach earlier this year when we completed the historic reform of the CAP. I shall certainly take this forward in our Presidency.

Furthermore, all member states must be required to take measures to safeguard the environment on farms that are benefiting from direct subsidies. I do not think we can go on paying subsidies to people who do things which are wholly contrary to the demands of the environment. If I am going to pay them money, they must perform in a way which is recognizably of advantage to the taxpayer who provides that money.

Farmers Need Adequate Incomes

Farmers cannot do this, of course, without proper incomes. Those who suggest that we can allow the market as a whole to pay do not understand what the market is. Agriculture does not merely produce food. It looks after the land. Eighty percent of Britain, for example, is farmed. You cannot look after eighty percent of the land in a way which is acceptable to the public and expect the cost to be returned in prices in a world where you are competing with people who do not care about the environmental results. I cannot produce pigs as cheaply as they can in Thailand because Thailand does not have the same rules about how you get rid of the pig muck. I can deal with competition in other ways but what I cannot do is to demand that my farmers spend vast sums of money ensuring that they do not destroy the environment in their own back yard and then compete equally with those who do not.

It will no longer be possible to accept that somehow or other the environment in agriculture is a matter of subsidiarity whereas everything else is not. I do believe we are going to be in trouble with this word subsidiarity if we are not careful about what the word means. What it means is meeting the same overall needs in your own national way. It does not mean avoiding the overall needs and leaving others to pay for the problems. What we need to do is to ensure that in each of the countries of Europe, we do not meet the same specifications. That we do not constantly demand that we do things in exactly the same way but that we always accept that there are overriding standards of environmental requirements which should be placed upon all our farmers and without which they do not get their money. There cannot be a future for the direct payments for the environment without cross compliance. Agriculture is a business and has got to pay its way. We have to pay for it and we do so in partnership with farmers.

Let us not suggest that we could look after the countryside without farmers. They must be able to work these things in their own manner and as much freedom as possible must be given. In the end, there must be a return to the taxpayer in terms of environmental benefit. We need to discourage the actions which will do damage to the environment.

The Future Is At Stake

Like the whole of the British government, I am very determined that we should proceed on the basis of Maastricht. The reason I think that is because my children do not see their heritage as Britain. They see their heritage as Britain in Europe. We have a very real interest in the protection of our historic countryside in Britain and in the protection of the historic countryside of the Netherlands. When Minister Bukman spoke of this beautiful part of his country, he was speaking for all Europeans about a beautiful part of our country. In that sense, we cannot accept policies which would not enable our children to benefit and enjoy an environment in Europe as a whole. Therefore, I believe that they will not forgive us if the European Community does not ensure that all governments of Europe protect their heritage. The next generation will expect to enjoy an inheritance that reaches from Sicily to Scotland, from the Atlantic right across to Europe's eastern borders.

The principles of environmentally friendly farming must be part and parcel of the CAP. No member state can opt out of the duty to conserve Europe's landscape for future generations. That is because we are all stewards in a deeply, fundamentally, theologically, and philosophically important way. This is not our land to do what we wish with. In a memorable phrase of the former Prime Minister, "We are not freeholders. We are leaseholders with a full, repairing lease." We have received this countryside of ours from those who have gone before and we must pass it on so that our children can enjoy their rightful inheritance.

If that is true in Europe, it is also true in the wider world. The approaches will be very different but it is still crucial to encourage and to enable a multilateral approach not with uniform standards and practices but with a range of options which however wide will be seen in this overall framework of multilateralism.

Customers Will Demand The Terms of Trade

It will be increasingly true that customers will demand standards from imported products which will have to be met by producers. There has been a tendency in the United States to believe that the customer is right as long as he does not disagree with the views of the administration and that it is perfectly reasonable for other people to have their standards as long as those standards are the same as the United States. I went to an international conference in London in which a spokesman for the administration explained about the standards of meat inspection in the United States in which it was made clear that they were the highest in the world, that we should all come into line with it, and that it was quite improper for a customer to say that they wanted different standards. I said you try telling that to a supermarket in Britain. The farmer who says "my standards are higher than yours and you will accept my standards" does not get the business.

There is a danger in GATT that we shall suggest that the customer's standards do not count. We have to be very careful about protecting in free trade the customer's right to decide the standard at which he wishes his product to be produced. There is an area of very considerable concern. If I want my meat killed according to EC standards and people want to sell it to me in the United States, I can say they should not have hormones. I can say this with great freedom because I voted against making the use of natural hormones illegal. Britain has never held that view. But if that is what the Community wants, then that is what it must be able to demand of its suppliers. That is the nature of capitalism. I am not going to be told by anybody that I am not allowed to say that because there is a greater good before which I have to bow. It is for us, the customer, to decide the terms of the trade. Just as others abroad tell us how we shall meet their requirements. That is how business works.

Conclusion

Therefore, I repeat what an indictment it is that we should have to question the compatibility of agriculture, the environment, and trade. These three core concerns of the human race must be held in balance. Together they can produce a world which offers greater choice to more people, greater opportunity to the poorest as well as the richest, and greater access to the best of what the world has to give to developing and developed nations alike. We can achieve this by multilateral action, setting the highest standards within the most flexible framework. We must beware of believing that what is true today will be true forever. We must never lose sight of agriculture's primary role: to produce the food on which we rely. Yet, in all our efforts we must never forget that we are stewards in this world, not proprietors. Our responsibility to the Creator and the generations to come demands that we hand on what we have received, improved, and enhanced so that the balance between agriculture, trade, and the environment can continue to be preserved.

Chapter 3

Agriculture, The Environment, and Trade - A Complex Relationship

Jim MacNeill

This conference addresses what is clearly one of the most compelling issues confronting the world today. The sub-theme of the conference, "conflict or cooperation," captures in two words the essential character of the global struggle for hope. If we can find the wit and the imagination to discover formulas for successful cooperation, we will be able to avoid destructive conflict. Conversely, if we don't, we won't. In my view, that is the single most important lesson to emerge from the last twenty years of environmental politics.

Geopolitical and Attitudinal Earthquakes

In preparing these notes, I felt like I was standing on ground that has been moving and shifting week by week for the past five years, as in a slow-motion earthquake. Under these conditions, there is simply no point in trying to be consistent and defend the past. If I can mix my metaphors, this is a perfect time to reexamine sacred cows that no longer produce milk, even under supply management.

I cannot think of a better metaphor to describe the past five years than "earthquake." The end of the Cold War, the revolution in Eastern Europe, and the collapse of the Soviet Union have caused a break with our geopolitical past that is without precedent. The ongoing realignment of Europe, the regional trading blocs forming here and in North America and elsewhere, and, we hope, the successful conclusion of the Uruguay Round, followed perhaps by a "Green Round," ensures years of aftershocks for the world's trading system.

There are even more tremors built into the massive and ongoing shift in public values, a shift that forced environmental issues to the top of the political agendas prior to the current recession and will almost certainly bring them back to the top after the recovery. Who in 1987 when the Brundtland Commission presented its report to the General Assembly would have predicted that, within a few years, government leader after leader and the CEO's of perhaps twenty percent of the companies listed in the Fortune 500 would undergo a public baptism as born-again environmentalists? Or that sustainable development would become a regular feature of the debates of the UN system, the OECD, and the annual summits of the G7? Or that an Earth Summit, the largest ever held with 103 heads of government, would be convened this year to address the critical issues of environment and economic development, including environment's place in the international trading system?

Relationships between the Environment and the Economy

These geopolitical and attitudinal quakes have been accompanied by another, more intellectual in nature but nonetheless significant. I am referring to the abrupt change that has occurred in our understanding of the relationships between the environment and the economy.

Not long ago, most of us believed that the whole world's economic and the earth's ecological systems were two separate systems. We now know that is not true. We now know that the incredible growth of the past 40 years has thrown the world's economy and the earth's ecology literally into each other's arms. They have become one system, totally intermeshed and interlocked, one with the other "till death do them part."

28

We used to believe that the impact of one system on the other was marginal at worst. We now know that the impact is enormous. It is growing rapidly and it could soon be decisive for the economy as well as the environment. In some areas it already has. For example, take the ozone hole or global warming. What are they? Well, they are both essentially a form of feedback from the world's ecological system to its interdependent economic system. Or take water, something closer to home in an agricultural conference. The Brundtland Commission found that water is a serious constraint on agricultural development in eighty countries today, with over forty percent of the world's population. If the oil wars have begun, the water wars may not be far behind.

Do Trade Agreements and Open Borders Reduce Environmental Sovereignty?

A global economy totally and irreversibly interlocked with the earth's ecology in one system is the new reality of the late 20th century. And it relates directly to the first question put to this session by the Conference organizers. "Do trade agreements," they asked, "and open borders reduce or abrogate a nation's sovereignty over its environment?" The answer, clearly, is "yes," at least to the same degree that open borders have long-since reduced or abrogated a nation's sovereignty over its economy.

Nations have been trying to adapt their notions of sovereignty and governance to the realities of economic interdependence ever since World War II. It hasn't been easy but the Bretton Woods institutions, OECD and now the G7 are evidence of serious intent and some success. Nations must now struggle to adapt their notions of sovereignty and governance to the new reality of a single world system, including the trading system, embracing both the economy and the environment.

The Earth Summit in Rio confirmed that we are entering an era when a nation's environmental, economic, and trade policies will be increasingly determined by actions beyond its borders. The Convention on International Trade in Endangered Species (CITES) and the Montreal Protocol to the Vienna Ozone Convention pioneered the use of trade measures to deal with global environmental problems. Nothing is more controversial. The acid test will come, I believe, when the climate convention signed in Rio is strengthened to include targets and timetables for reducing greenhouse gases.

The Role of the Environment in Trade Negotiations

If trade is now a part of environmental negotiations, environment is becoming a part of trade negotiations, at least at the regional level. Witness recent events in North America. Environment was ignored in the negotiations between Canada and the United States on the 1988 Free Trade Agreement. It could not be ignored in the recently concluded negotiations on the North American Free Trade Agreement (NAFTA). The new politics of environment, especially in the United States, would not permit it. Four years is a long time in this earthquake-prone field.

North American Free Trade Agreement

NAFTA may be the first trade agreement to commit the participating countries to undertake joint and separate measures to reconcile trade with the goals of environmental protection and sustainable development. The negotiations have just concluded. I have not seen the text (I do not think it exists yet) but according to my sources the agreement will enable Canada and the United States not only to maintain but also to strengthen their higher standards for health, safety, and the environment. It will discourage all three countries from lowering standards to attract investment, although it appears that, contrary to the demands of the environmental movement, they will not suffer any sanctions if they do.

NAFTA will also establish rules to prohibit standards and regulations that are unnecessary obstacles to trade. It is the first trade agreement to be subjected to an "environmental assessment."

And it will establish a Tri-National Standards Committee to monitor implementation and resolve disputes.

Lessons from NAFTA

We will not know what it all means, of course, until we see the fine print later this year. Whatever the fine print, the NAFTA experience has established a new direction for trade policy and trade negotiations. Countries must now begin to ensure that environment is fully considered in all aspects of national trade policy, in regional negotiations like the NAFTA, and in future multilateral trade negotiations in GATT. Every round must be a "Green Round."

And environmentalists should note that the reverse is also true. Countries must now begin to consider trade in all aspects of environmental policy. In an interlocked system of environment and economy, assessment must work both ways: the impact of environmental policies on trade and the impact of trade policies on the environment.

The Impact of Environmental Policies on Trade

Until recently, talk about the environment-trade connection implied concern about one thing and one thing only: the potentially negative impact of environmental policies on trade. And this concern centered on one thing and one thing only: the steady proliferation of national health, food, safety, and environmental standards and the fact that there were often differences between them that could act as a cover for non-tariff barriers.

Differences in Standards

Differences in standards may be quite legitimate. They can reflect the fact that nations have different environmental endowments, or that their electors have different levels of income

31

and awareness and demand different levels of environmental quality.

The differences may also be totally contrived. Governments may want different standards in order to use them as a convenient cover for non-tariff barriers. That is a reality and we should not pussyfoot around it. I directed one of the largest international harmonization programs, the OECD Chemicals Program, for seven years and I have looked into the cold, smiling eyes of too many ministers protesting their innocence to have any doubts.

Should We Harmonize Standards Upwards or Downwards?

Because of this, the debate often generates more heat than light. Formal declarations usually call for international harmonization, and studiously avoid the real question, which is whether we should direct our international bodies to harmonize upwards to higher standards, or downwards to lower standards. That's not a technical or even a scientific question-- although formal declarations sometimes pretend it is. It's a political question, and it requires a political answer.

The answer is complicated especially by some of the other questions put to this session. "Are lowering environmental standards a product subsidy and, vice versa, are higher standards a burden on competitiveness? More specifically, will higher standards raise food prices and render farmers uncompetitive?" And the old standby: "Will they encourage production and food processing to move to countries with lower standards?"

It would appear that the leaders of many governments and industries would still answer each of these questions in the affirmative, an unequivocal "yes." But would they be right in doing so? Not according to the OECD. In 1984, following several years of study, OECD's International Conference on Environment and Economy found that high environmental standards could have a strongly positive effect on innovation and productivity.

Michael Porter of Harvard, who is well known for his work on the competitiveness of nations, puts it very clearly. "The conflict between environmental protection and economic competitiveness," he says, "is a false dichotomy. It stems from a narrow view of the sources of prosperity and a static view of competition. Strict environmental standards . . . trigger innovation and upgrading. . . . Nations with the most rigorous requirements often lead in exports of affected products." In this area it is better to lead the way than bring up the rear.

Examples of Harmonization

There are many illustrations of harmonization. It is no international secret that Canada's forest industry is in deep trouble. It is no longer competitive. A major reason is that, unlike the Scandinavian forest industry, it was never challenged to innovate by high environmental standards. Its capital plant was allowed to die a natural death and now entire communities are dying with it.

During the 1970s and early 1980s, Japanese and some European industries were pressed by both high world oil prices and tight environmental standards. In response, they invented most of the industrial technologies of the 1980s and 1990s. Those technologies were not only energy and resource efficient but environmentally efficient and internationally competitive. They stole market share in almost every sector from automobiles to pulp and paper, food processing, the service industries, and communications. They are still gaining market share.

The modern agricultural industry provides a classic story of rising productivity stemming from better machinery, better management, and better seeds. Some of this innovation has been driven by high production costs; in the future, more of it will be driven by changing environmental conditions.

Parts of Europe and Japan appear to have learned these lessons more easily than Canada and the United States. If they continue to pursue competitiveness goals in this way, their industries, including their agricultural industry, will be forced to invent the technologies of the first decade of the new millennium. And, in the process, their economies will become cleaner and healthier.

Unfortunately, this is not where the environment-trade debate stands. I am afraid that with some outstanding exceptions, much of it remains stuck in the intellectual mud of the 1970s.

Problems of Harmonization

If we attempt to harmonize upwards, we run up against the old fear in OECD countries that higher standards are necessarily the enemy of competitiveness. We also encounter resistance in developing countries on the grounds that higher standards will result in barriers against the products they export.

If we attempt to harmonize downwards, we run into other problems. The voters, the media, and even some leading industries in OECD countries will simply refuse to support them. And those industries that understand the technology-forcing and market-leading impact of high standards will simply go it alone.

In a global, competitive economy, higher standards are not luxury goods. We cannot impose them on newly industrializing countries like Mexico and, conversely, they cannot impose lower standards on us.

Requiring advanced nations to lower their standards in the name of harmonization may well be politically out of reach. Moreover, with global communications, international advertising, and rising awareness, the growing middle class of developing countries like Mexico and India will slowly demand higher standards of their own governments. The Indian middle class is already greater than the population of France. It won't be easy, but trends and power relationships are such that it is only a matter of time.

The European Communities' proposal to GATT puts it very well. It states: "Countries which have achieved a high health status will find it difficult to systematically relinquish their national standards in favor of lower, albeit "international" standards. It will therefore be necessary to provide for countries to continue to apply more stringent standards, where appropriate."

Outlook for the 1990s

The good news in all of this, I believe, is that conflicts over internationally inconsistent standards have been held to a minimum, in spite of a few high-profile cases. The bad news is that they are bound to grow. The 1990s will probably see a greater increase in both the number and variety of national standards than occurred in the whole of the past five decades. The political climate is favorable and will likely become even more favorable.

Green consumerism is now entrenched in parts of Europe, it is sweeping Canada, it has a toe hold in Japan and the United States, and it is emerging in some newly industrializing countries. It is hitting industry after industry, especially resource-based industries. In many countries, it is aided by government-sponsored labeling programs covering every sector, including food and agriculture. As these programs gain momentum and spread throughout the world, they will affect markets and trading patterns. That is the whole point, of course, and there is nothing illegal about it. The GATT Secretariat makes that very clear in its recent annual report. "In general," it says, "a country can do anything to imports or exports that it does to its own products."

While countries can do whatever they wish to protect the environment against damage from either domestic or imported products, there is growing concern that some large governments will use their trading clout in a unilateral manner to force other countries to change certain environmental practices. Minister Bukman referred to the most recent example last night, the tuna/dolphin case involving the United States and Mexico. The GATT panel, as he mentioned, ruled against the United States in this case. That is very interesting but what is even more interesting is that during the last Congress there were over 30 draft bills in play that would have placed trade restrictions on imports from another country if those countries did not change certain environmental practices. In most cases, the legislation sought changes in processes of production and resource-extraction rather than in products themselves.

These process issues have become very contentious in forestry, fishing, agriculture and other sectors. They could become even more contentious. Everyone favors multilateral approaches over bilateral or unilateral measures. But multilateral approaches are too often ineffective. Governments that want to move ahead on an issue often find themselves paralyzed in multilateral fora by governments that do not. If this continues, and Rio is the latest example, I fear that unofficial consumer boycotts could become the most prominent form of unilateralism in the future.

You are familiar with what this has done to the Canadian seal hunt and the world's fur trade. The forest industry today faces a growing demand for wood products that come from sustainably managed forests. Companies in Canada and several tropical countries have been threatened with boycotts if they will not measure up. The agricultural industry is also confronting a rapidly changing demand pattern rooted in new values with emphasis on "organically grown" produce.

The Impact of Trade Policies on the Environment

What about the reverse? According to OECD, "trade policies can contribute to environmentally adverse patterns of production, unsustainable exploitation of natural resources, and commerce in polluting or hazardous products." In fact, the impact of trade and trade-related policies on the environment is significant and it is growing rapidly.

Reasons Trade Policies Impact the Environment

1. **Tariff and non-tariff barriers often distort global patterns of production in ways that accelerate the degradation of a nation's environment and the depletion of its ecological capital (e.g. its forests, fisheries, soils, waters, etc.).** OECD countries are responsible for the biggest distortions, by any measure, and they impact most heavily on developing countries. There are many examples. We are all aware of the tariffs against cane sugar imports and other products in which developing countries enjoy a strong ecological comparative advantage. We are also aware of tariff walls that increase with the level of processing, such as Japanese tariffs that favor the importation of raw logs from Southeast Asia.

2. National trade policies do not and cannot take international externalities into account. Trade policies are blind to the different environment and resource endowments of nations and, in the absence of a global environmental regime, they will remain blind. We need an international Polluter Pays Principle.

3. Most importantly, government interventions in the market are simultaneously economically perverse, ecologically destructive, and trade-distorting. We have them in agriculture, as you all know. Subsidies which cost OECD taxpayers and consumers over $300 billion a year encourage overproduction, market gluts, and trade wars. They also underwrite a fast drawdown of our most basic farm capital, our souls, wood, and water, not only here in the North, but also in the South where we dump our surpluses and undermine their agriculture.

We have them in energy: over $40 billion a year for conventional fuels in the US alone; perhaps $4 billion in Canada for fossil fuels; billions more in the countries of the former East Block, China, India, and Europe. These subsidies tilt the playing field in favor of fossil fuels. They result in more acid rain and global warming, and they penalize efficiency and renewables.

We have them in forestry. Most governments offer various tax concessions and sweetheart leases that encourage overcutting and species loss. We have them in water development, regional development and other sectors.

The Brundtland Commission recognized that the market could be one of the primary forces for sustainable development. We were well aware of market failures, especially in the environmental field. But, quite frankly, when I total up the costs of these perverse interventions, I sometimes think that we have more to fear from the visible hand of government than from the invisible hand of the market.

Free market liberals, fiscal conservatives, budget-balancers, and environmentalists all agree that these perverse incentives should be eliminated. But, instead, they simply keep on growing in accordance with some political Parkinson's law.

What Should We Do?

As in the current Uruguay Round, we can continue to try to persuade governments to reduce if not eliminate clearly perverse incentives in agriculture, energy, and other sectors. I know that this course is favored by many and I would have no real objection to it if I thought it would work. But I do not. I have met very few industrial leaders who are prepared to swear off subsidies, tax abatements, and other forms of assistance and even fewer politicians who are prepared to swear off promising them. It is not only a proven path to power; it is often the only instrument they have to maintain social peace.

Rather than forego their right to intervene in the market in ways that win votes, I think it might be more realistic to try to get governments to agree that, when they intervene, they will do so in ways that encourage sustainable forms of development and trade.

Minister Bukman hinted at a couple of policy directions which I would personally favor. Europe has started to decouple farm subsidies from production. I would like to see all governments begin to recouple subsidies to land classification, conservation, and the promotion of sustainable agricultural practices. I am sure that we can design agricultural incentive systems that are political winners and do not encourage ecologically destructive or trade-distorting practices. We can support farm income (a prerequisite for sustainable agriculture) in ways that encourage farmers to adopt practices that enhance rather than degrade their basic farm capital: soil, wood, and water.

Trade Liberalization

Benefits

Phasing out tariff and non-tariff barriers and export and production subsidies of all kinds through trade liberalization would not only make good economic sense, it could make good environmental sense -- leading to more sustainable patterns of energy, agricultural, forestry, and industrial production. It may free resources that could be used to augment our natural as well as man-made capital assets.

Trade liberalization can broaden export opportunities for developed countries. If OECD governments are serious, it can broaden export opportunities for developing countries in areas in which they have an ecological as well as an economic comparative advantage. It could also broaden opportunities for the new democracies in Eastern Europe at a time when they need it desperately.

Caution Required

But, again, we have to be careful. We have to ensure that trade liberalization does not accelerate the net drawdown of our forests and soils and other basic capital assets. It could easily do so. We also have to ensure that trade liberalization agreements do not limit goals. It has been suggested that certain policies to internalize the external costs of production could be considered trade distortions under GATT (e.g. taxes to ensure full cost pricing of chemicals, energy and other products that impact on the environment). If this is true, then GATT's rules should be reexamined against the overriding global imperative to promote more sustainable forms of development. A recent OECD paper puts it very well. "Unlike sustainable development, free-trade is not an end in itself."

Conflict or Cooperation?

Everyone knows that environment and economic development, including agricultural development, can be mutually destructive. History is full of examples of civilizations that collapsed because they failed to manage or they overconsumed the ecological capital on which their agriculture depended. That is not in question. What is in question, and given the population and other trends, it is a survival question, is how to initiate a process in which environment and agriculture and trade become mutually supportive and in which sustainable forms of agriculture and trade become the order of the day. That is the real challenge before society and before this conference.

Chapter 4

Organic Agricultural Production: Evaluation and Accreditation

Jan Diek van Mansvelt

Looking for a road to sustainable agriculture, many experts see themselves caught in a deadlock between environmentally sound but socially unacceptable extensification and high external input strategies, which feed the world but exhaust the environment. This deadlock concept complies with a basic notion that humans have to compete with nature in order to survive. Within an economically and highly competitively society, this choice between the environment, nature, and people leads to a fight.

In the Brundtland Report and again in UNCED's Agenda 21, another basic notion is proposed -- Our Common Future. "We need a new form of 'collective engagement' . . . to establish a new North-South relationship, based on mutual enlightened self-interest," said the Brundtland Report. Section 1, Chapter 2 of UNCED's Agenda 21 states: "Environment and trade policies should be mutually supportive." This notion argues that human cooperation is the key for human survival and, moreover, that human life is dependent on the same environmental conditions as those required for the survival of nature. Thereby, the stabilization of the environmental conditions requires optimal efficacy of natural processes (i.e. that humanity, nature, and the environment are mutually dependent on each other for survival).

Against this background, the challenge for all efforts in favor of a sustainable development is to identify roads that merge the benefits of the environmentally-sound extensification approach with those of a productive, high external input strategy. At stake here is the optimization of the synergy between quality and quantity and between food and the environment.

A preliminary statement on this issue might be that this challenge demands a conceptual competition to get away from increasing food and resource competition -- more of an "as well as" approach than of an "either or." This strategy needs to and can be facilitated by stressing the multi-purpose efficiency of natural systems and subsystems. It allows for and inspires autonomous cultivation of agro-ecosystems so as to optimize the benefits of their diversity. Being fully aware of ongoing improvements and adaptations needed to make it feasible to all farmers everywhere, the options of organic types of agriculture are increasingly recognized as interesting for further research and, most importantly, implementation.

Basic Concepts of Organic Types of Agriculture

Autonomous Ecosystem Management

Like all types of agriculture, organic types of agriculture are implementations of any basic concept, model, or mental map. In organic types of agriculture, the common denominator can be defined as "Autonomous Ecosystem Management." This includes such notions as optimizing the primary production efficiency of agro-ecosystems in compliance with the local soil/climate conditions (carrying capacity) and the social needs of the region. In view of the management requirements, these types of agriculture demand an attitude in favor of an 'eco-intelligence for non-renewable inputs' swap. Agriculture, in this concept, is more a policy for land-use, including agro-, sylvi-, and aqua-culture in mixed or integrated agro-ecosystems. Pest prevention, well-balanced mineral flows, and sustainable resource management result in low external inputs (chemical fertilizers and non-renewable energy).

Cultivating Multi-Purpose Efficiency

To optimize the production of agro-ecosystems in the framework of autonomous ecosystem management, it is important to cultivate the multi-purpose characteristics of the relevant kingdoms of nature. Over-stressing any single production aspect of any subsystem might easily deteriorate the balanced efficiency of the whole system. Orchestrating the benefits of diversity or optimizing the synergy of soil-crop-animal interactions are therefore the foremost challenges of organic agriculture. This strategy includes using animals to upgrade the non-foods produced with food, and manuring the soils for food and feed production.

Within this framework, the multi-purpose efficiency per eco-subsystem can be listed as follows:
- soils (mineral-clay-humus complexes, sandy, loamy, peaty)
- source and store/buffer of nutrients for crops
- biotype for general waste-feeders
- basis of agricultural production
- crops (mainly floriferous plants)
- human food and fiber producers
- animal feed producers
- soil producers
- water harvesters
- husbandry (mainly vertebrates but also fowl, fish, bees)
- human food and fiber producers
- roughage feeders
- manure production
- intelligent traction
- pollinators
- climate (sunshine, rain, temperature, wind)
- temporization and regulation
- source of external energy input for primary plant production.

Aspects of Soil Management

Compliant to farmers' traditions in many regions, organic types of agriculture regard soil improvement, by means of well-balanced

43

stewardship, as a key issue of its professional ethics. Conservation of the soil's fertility is the basic requirement; regeneration of degraded soil is a challenge for farms in conversion; and leaving a better soil for successors is proof of craftsmanship and the ultimate goal. Appropriate liming and rock-dust applications are accepted as medication of soils in need of special care (nutrient deficiencies). Thereby, considerations on non-renewable energy and other resource depletions are critical and stress the need for minimal input strategies. On-site nutrient mining by deep rooting crops, improving nutrient availability with mycorhiza's and optimal nutrient recycling are part of the multi-purpose approach. Within the agro-ecosystem, specific crop-rotation and manuring strategies for different soil types, structures, and exposures are part of the craftsmanship.

Aspects of Crop Rotation

Within the framework of the multi-purpose efficiency of crop production, crop rotation is instrumental in orchestrating the complementary characteristics of various crops in their mutual and plant-soil relationships. Inter-cropping, after-cropping, alley-cropping, and mixed-cropping are examples of spatial and temporary alternations, chosen according to the specific crop and soil cycles, needs, and gifts. Sophisticated crop rotations are also instrumental in biological pest prevention (fungi, insects, weeds).

Additional multi-purpose aspects of crops are: legumes as nitrogen fixers and protein food/feed producers; leguminous ley-grasslands as nitrogen-fixers, feed producers, and weed suppressors; corns as producers of staple food and feed, animal housing, and manure catch material; vegetables as vitamin and mineral sources; roots as staple food, feed, and silage; fruits; herbs; flowers; seeds for propagation, elevation, oils; and hedges and woodlands for feed, shelter, housing, burning, landscaping, soil stabilization, and humidity regulation.

Aspects of Mixed Husbandry

Within the framework of multi-purpose efficiency of animal husbandry, cultivation of the animal-specific characteristics is instrumental. As with crop rotation, implementation always depends on the actual farm situation, soil-climate conditions, and inter-species interactions of local or adapted breeds. The multi-purpose approach of animals focuses on manure, roughage, and waste production to the food conversion capacity of the animal. This is an important key to avoid competition on human food in a world of limited resources.

Cultivation Cycles and Development Phases

In order to optimize or "orchestrate" the mentioned eco-subsystems in their multi-purpose potential, the whole scale of different qualities of developmental phases, seasons, and other cycles must be taken into account. For example,
- specific properties of the seedling, growing, flowering, ripening, decaying and dormant phases in crops (selective cropping for food, feed, fuel, and timber in forestry; crops for green manuring harvested before flowering; special after-sowing of crops for nitrate catching; seed production on-farm and local)
- specific properties of the young, adult, and mature phases in animals (meat versus reproduction, dairy and traction, health and longevity breeding)
- the alternating consumption of plant-food in the growing season and animal-food in the "hunger season"
- anticipating on bio-meteorological cycles, like sun-spots and locust plagues, moon cycles, and cassava planting.

Organic Agro-Ecosystem Management and Its Standards

The Ideal. The cultivation of the fore-mentioned properties in compatible quantities, appropriate qualities, and sound timing is a craft demanding a good deal of eco-intelligence together with a well-developed feeling for the organism. Thus, organic agriculture or autonomous ecosystem management could also be defined as managing bio-diversity. From this description, it is clear that the autonomous system is not a physically closed system as the chemo-technically sophisticated hydroponics. Organic agriculture is more eco-conceptually consistent than physically closed.

A leading motto of this eco-organic strategy can be summarized by saying that the well-being of the whole agricultural system (farm-organism and agro-ecosystem) depends on the well-being of all its subsystems (farm-organs or agro-biotopes). The objective of each of the subsystems is to support the whole agro-ecosystem as an organism.

The Basic Standards. Although each item in the highly qualitative system mentioned above could be illustrated with figures from literature, they would not be easily translated into clear norms for organic agriculture or organic production standards. This is because each soil-climate-infrastructure situation has special conditions, with different farmers or groups of farmers having their own set of priorities. To achieve internationally acceptable norms defining what is regarded as organic and what is not, a profound process of interprofessional expert discussions was set up by International Federation of Organic Agricultural Movements (IFOAM) in the late 1970s. The single but still quite demanding pretention was to define the lowest common denominators of all participating movements. Thus, the IFOAM Standards are explicitly basic or minimum standards. They leave ample room for extra requirements, which exceed the basic standards and can by no means be used as a guideline for organic agriculture. That is why the preface of the standards explains the basic principles of organic agriculture.

Performances of Organic Types of Agriculture

On Pesticide Inputs and Nitrogen Losses

As chemical pesticides are excluded from use in organic types of agriculture, it is no wonder that the main pesticide problems are those of ubiquitous stress, in-soil remnants of pre-conversion times, and drifting sprays from neighbors.

As far as nitrogen leaching is concerned, more mineral balance accounting than comparative monitoring has been done. Here we present the data available from Dutch research. One set is from a research farm on clay while the other compares organic mixed and conventional, practical farms on sandy soils. On the clay, the nitrogen level in the water matched the EC level; on sand they were close and well below the Dutch drinking water level. Considering additional denitrification on the way to water intake points, these data allow for a good perspective on drinking-water production on organic farms even on sand. Total nitrogen losses per year show how much lower they were in organic than conventional agriculture, in sand as well as in clay. Thereby, it should be realized that the averages on farmed lands are higher than the mean of the range that covers all clay and sandy soils.

Species, Habitat, and Landscape Diversity

An increasing number of agro-policy makers realize that agriculture not only produces foods and fibers but also environment and landscape. Parameters have been chosen to discuss the quality of nature production and the diversity of plant and animal species. Lately, species diversity has been extended to biotope or habitat diversity, as a meta-parameter over species diversity. Here, even less data from monitoring are available than for environmental performance. Considering the basic concepts of organic types of agriculture as described above, it seems rather obvious to suppose that a multi-purpose or bio-diversity management approach leads to more species per plot and more plots per farming system.

In view of the recent discussions on extensification and sustainability in agriculture, increasingly the question is raised of whether besides food, the cluster of environment-nature-landscape should or should not be regarded as a valuable product of agriculture. The stances in this discussion can be summarized as the segregationist (separation of functions) and the integrationist (merging of functions). The description and definition of values of

47

nature over and above those of species and sometimes habitats is still in a preliminary phase.

Recently, two landscape students made a pilot study into the question of how to identify and describe the contribution of agriculture to those landscape values. They selected four biodynamic farms in Sweden, Germany, and the Netherlands and compared them to their neighbors that implemented conventional types of agriculture.

In their study, "Differences in Appearances," they found that the biodynamic farms they visited as compared to their neighbors showed: more compliancy of land-use and natural subsoil; a more clearly interwoven structure of land-use; a larger number of land-uses; a larger number of human participants in the production; a greater labor diversity, including in farm processing; a greater diversity in biotopes (arable crops, vegetables, fruits, and brambles); a greater diversity in husbandry; a larger surface area planted with a larger number of shrub and tree species better integrated in the farm management structure; a greater diversity in "wild" flora; and a greater overall offer of sensorial perceptions.

They conclude that, in principle, biodynamic/organic types of sustainable agriculture bear a remarkable potential for landscape enrichment. Obviously, this pilot study completes the interesting evidence of the previously mentioned findings on biodiversity. This potential, which is also important for the implementation of the MacSharry CAP proposal on positive extensification, seems appropriate for a thorough large-scale monitoring of its general validity.

Yields

As the whole set of agro-chemical inputs developed over the last decades was intended to boost yields, it no wonder that yields in organic types of agriculture tend to be lower than in conventional agriculture. However, for a scientifically sound comparison, each level of observation brings its own demands. Comparisons at scientific plot-level are different from those in practice, and experimental and practical levels differ considerably per country and region. Here we show a few data to indicate the magnitude of the differences found between high external input conventional (100 percent) and organic agriculture (56 percent for potatoes to 96 percent for beet roots). It goes without saying that the lower the external inputs in the region's conventional agriculture, the closer organic agriculture comes to the 100 percent or higher. In studies on national or regional scales, the differences between farms and farmers within each group often approach the differences between the groups, complicating the conclusions somewhat. In any case, looking for multi-purpose performance (yields, energy and resource efficiency, and environmental impact), it will be clear that organic types of agriculture are quite an interesting option.

Farm Level and Food Sufficiency

Regarding the economic feasibility of organic agriculture, it should be realized that prices are largely a product of policy on local, national, and international levels. It is only within that framework that farmers and their partners in the whole food chain can adapt to the balance between input and output of goods and money. Each of these levels includes a certain amount of free choice, subject to priority decisions by those responsible: farmers, traders, consumers, and authorities. It is only within this framework of considerations that comparisons on farm or national economy are possible, because hard as any set of data on economy might be, they are but a reflection of a soft system, a set of interlinked validations made by society or its representatives. The most obvious debate on prices in conventional agriculture regards their lack of environmental accounting, resulting in lower prices than those from organic production. This makes quite a difference, because environmental agriculture exteriorized the environmental impacts to the national budget, whereas organic agriculture interiorized it into its own farm budget. Thus, the competition between conventional and organic produce on the market is regarded as unfair from this point of view.

For this paper, we selected data on the economic performance at the farm level, focusing on farm and labor income per person. As with yields, we found that on a national or regional scale, differences between farms and farmers within each group often approach the differences between the groups, thus complicating the conclusions. Furthermore, the differences between years can be considerable, influencing different farms in different ways. Thus, in studies over longer periods, the differences between the systems diminish. Generally, conventional farm income is slightly higher than or equal to organic agriculture, whereas labor income per person tends to be lower in organic agriculture. It could be argued that the premium prices plus the reduced input costs can largely balance the lower yields and the higher labor input. It is mainly the increased farm and crop diversity that is not yet covered by the premium price. Here the MacSharry farm income support might be added to an equitable environmental accounting system, to support fair competition in a truly sustainable agriculture at large.

As the last type of economic data, we selected several papers on food sufficiency. One of the most frequent and fair questions raised in discussions on the feasibility of organic types of agriculture regards its feeding capacity in view of the increasing world population. Until now and as far as we know, the data on organic agriculture have not been included in global modelling of agriculture. This situation will change in the near future but results are not yet available. However, in several European countries, national exercises on this question have been carried out. Their common message is that when consumption complies with recent concepts of healthy nutrition, these countries could very well produce enough for their own people. Avoiding wide-spread over-consumption, especially eating less meat and sugar, is thereby a key issue for healthy nutrition and agriculture.

This data shows that organic agriculture, applying the principles of autonomous ecosystem management as the basis for a diversified production system, have a remarkable potential for an efficient and sustainable land use.

The Role of Food Trade

Market Potential

Organically grown products which satisfy organic standards (e.g. the Register of Organic Food Standards in the United Kingdom) traditionally find their way to consumers in specialized retail trade (health food) stores. However, in recent years, supermarket chains have also started to serve their clients with organically grown products.

This illustrates favorable prospects for conventional industry to participate by reallocating capital to sustainable agriculture. Reasons mentioned by food companies and supermarkets include: taking a position in this rising market segment, improving their public image, contributing to solving environmental problems, and increasing profits. Estimates of the potential penetration of organic produce in the retail food market in the 1990s for vegetable sales are five to ten percent. A recent study by the Agriculture Economic Institute in the Netherlands on the prospects of organic products is moderately positive, specifically for the export market.

In order to achieve this potential, the area of organically grown products should increase concomitantly. In the Netherlands, the total area of organic agriculture has increased from 40 hectare in 1970 to 1,600 hectare in 1980 and to 7,500 hectare in 1990. In West Germany, a comparable growth occurred; 5,000, 15,000, and 54,000 hectare, respectively. In the United Kingdom, the surface of organically treated soils increased from around 3,600 in 1980 to about 20,000 in 1990. The rapid growth of consumer demand for organically grown products might impose problems for the production sector as it takes several years to convert from a conventional farming system to an organic one. If the demand for organically grown products continues to increase, the number of farmers who are willing to convert to organic will likely also increase. The extensification subventions (CAP of the EC; the MacSharry plan) have objectives that are quite in line with the performances of organic types of agriculture and are already used to support the above-mentioned conversion in several countries.

Redirecting Markets Towards Sustainable Agriculture

When mentioned in global colleges, arguments in support of reallocating investments into environmentally sound technology tend to elicit the question of why the poor should pay and resign from well-being in order to diminish the pollution created by the rich. When focused on agriculture, the usual reaction is to state that without the usual high external inputs, starvation will continue to extend with increasing population.

Well-being, wealth, economic growth, high external inputs, and related high turn-over rates are, in the minds of many decision-makers, very closely linked. Although that system is undeniably consistent with high wastes, pollution, and environmental degradation, this way of understanding economy makes decisions in favor of sustainable solutions highly unpopular.

This notion supports the remarks of personalities, like India's Kemla Choudhury at the FAO-SARD conference in 1991 when he argued that all efforts to change the actual policy towards a more socially and environmentally sustainable one of global citizenship are doomed. Unless compatible, considerable revisions of attitudes and ethics are achieved both individually and publicly, no one and nothing can change the current course of events.

These considerations show how agriculture and all other technology can be recognized as expressions of social structures and cultural paradigms.

Conceptual Constraints of a Sustainable Economy

The basic opposition between economy and ecology, which is a part of today's orthodox economic theory and political practice of decision-making, is essentially an ideological, conceptual opposition. It roots partly in the self-understanding of modern society in its defensive, suppressive, competitive relation toward nature, which regards nature as being nothing but commodity, completely at the mercy of human high-handedness. Only the instrumental value of nature is being considered, denying its intrinsic value.

As far as the economic growth mania is concerned, it roots in identification of human socio-cultural development with the material, ego-oriented youth-phase development of nature, fructification and ripening phases: the phases that offer an extensive amount of short-time and sheer idea of moderating physical commodity consumption is widely sensed as limiting individual realization.

Hierarchies of interdependent networks of vital relationships between eco-partners, including humans, on the global scale of our home planet, require substantial human responsibility for our common future. Thus, a concept of fraternal economy must be developed, based on cultural efforts to share commodities world-wide, as well as to adapt the humane physiological needs to match the natural limitations of global resources. This fraternal economy contrasts with the classical "competitive" economy, originating from a social-darwinistic view on human relations.

To facilitate these urgent developments, extensive reflections on current concepts and compliant reconsiderations of ethics are at stake. Technical implementations can only contribute to globally sustainable resource management when they are conceived from appropriate images and used within appropriate attitudes.

Trade in the Food Chain

Within the fore-mentioned context, trade has a sensitive and key position. With its function basically and historically being to link producers and consumers, it inevitably occupies the central position in the chain and the place where most information available in that particular chain comes together. As knowledge represents a main basis for power, it is again inevitable that trade is continuously tempted to use its knowledge-power for its own benefit, according to the "divide and rule" principle (*Divide et Impera*). Kampfraath recently pointed out that for this decade, it is crucial to develop models for an acceptable sharing of the profits made in the product-chain over all participants in that product chain. In the case of the food chain, this is aiming to revise the fore-mentioned principle toward its sustainable version -- "link and serve" (*Liga et Serve*).

Although there is obviously an historic reason for some "mercantophobia" in the field of organic agriculture, this fear, as a result of critical evaluations, needs creative positive action to contribute to a common solution. However, critical evaluation of development programs points to the importance of trade in the empowerment of developing communities. Buying the products from such communities supports sustainable developments much more than "just" pouring in well meant but foreign money or commodities. These "supports" act as "alien" external inputs, remarkably much like the physical external inputs in agriculture. But, to facilitate trade's instrumentality in favor of sustainable developments, clear standards and compliant accreditation procedures for trade must complement those for sustainable (organic) production and processing.

On a conceptual basis, this means that besides the principle of fraternity (or sisternity as some prefer to phrase it) mentioned as leading in the ecological realm of global, sustainable sharing of common goods, the principle of equity must be appropriately developed to meet the demands of fair competition and reliable consumer warranty in the realm of legal provision. Both should comply with and support the need for a highly diversified agriculture world-wide, freely adapting to and cultivating the local geo-climatological and socio-economical difference, fully challenging the mental capacities of those involved.

For a full copy of this paper, including all tables and references, please contact the author at the following addresses:

Drs. J.D. van Mansvelt
President
IFOAM
General Secretariat
clo Okozentrum Imsbach
D-6695 Tholey-Theley
Germany

or

Department of Ecological
  Agriculture
Wageningen Agricultural University
Haarweg 333
6709 RZ Wageningen
The Netherlands

Section II: How Do Agricultural Practices and Policies Affect the Environment?

An Outline of the Issues

Because agriculture differs both within and among countries, it is extremely difficult to generalize the relationship between production practices followed and the alleged environmental negatives associated with them. Speakers in this session concentrated primarily on the United States and Europe and on the impact of agricultural policies rather than of production practices on the environment. They emphasized that the empirical evidence of causality between practices and the environment is not always clear cut.

The questions addressed by the speakers include:
- What are the linkages between farm programs and environmental quality?
- How can reforms enhance agriculture's contribution to the environment?
- How can agricultural and environmental policies be integrated to achieve the goals of sustainable agriculture?
- What are some of the factors that impact agricultural production and environmental degradation?
- How do agricultural policies encourage environmental damage? What evidence is there of such linkages?
- How do environmental policies affect agriculture?
- What are the anticipated or witnessed effect of recent policy changes (e.g. in the United States, in the Common Agricultural Policy, and in the OECD) on the environment?

55

How Do Agricultural Policies and Practices Affect the Environment in the United States?

John A. Miranowski

Introduction

This presentation will address four questions that are critical to the agriculture-environment interface in the United States. First, how do agricultural activities affect the environment in the United States? Second, what policy initiatives were implemented in the 1985 Food Security Act and the 1990 Food, Agriculture, Conservation, and Trade Act to improve consistency between agricultural and environmental goals in the United States? Third, how would agricultural commodity policy and trade reform further affect the environmental outcome? Finally, following trade reform, what alternatives are we left with to further improve agricultural-environmental conditions and sustainability? Most of my remarks are limited to the United States case but may apply to most developed countries and to some developing countries as well.

The Current State of the Agri-Environment

In the United States, environmental problems associated with agriculture have been recognized for many years. Many of our current soil conservation programs had their origins in the 1930s. The 1970s and 1980s were decades of growing awareness and response to potential problems associated with agricultural chemicals, water quality, and food safety.

Since the 1970s, the United States has witnessed an increasing demand for environmental quality. Personal incomes have increased; knowledge of the impact of our production and consumption activities on the environment has improved; and the public has become more aware of the possible linkages between agricultural activities and environmental quality. Concerns have been expressed over sediment, fertilizers, and pesticides polluting ground and surface waters; pesticide residues contaminating the food supply; wildlife habitat and wetlands being converted to cropland; and fragile ecosystems being disrupted or destroyed by agricultural chemicals and intensive cultivation practices, limiting biological diversity.

Actual damage from agriculture is not as serious as often suggested. Some of the areas where the detrimental effects of agriculture on the environment can be measured are 1) the loss of soil productivity, 2) ground water pollution, 3) surface water pollution, and 4) loss of species diversity.

Loss of Soil Productivity

If current erosion levels continue for 100 years, crop yields will fall less than four percent, even assuming constant technology. These results do not necessarily imply that soil erosion is not a significant problem nor that serious local losses of soil productivity will not occur. Rather, it implies that overall soil productivity in the United States is not threatened.

Groundwater Pollution

Groundwater is a source of public drinking water for nearly 75 million people in the United States. Most commonly reported contamination comes from industrial and municipal sources. However, pesticide residues from agricultural use have been detected in the groundwater of a number of states. The Environmental Protection Agency's (EPA) National Survey of Pesticides in Drinking Water Wells found that about half of the wells contained detectable amounts of nitrate, but only one percent of community water systems and two percent of private domestic wells contained nitrates at levels above those recommended as safe by EPA. About ten percent of the community wells and four percent of the private domestic wells contained detectable levels of one or more pesticides, but less than one percent contained pesticide concentrations that could pose a risk to human health.

Surface Water Pollution

The runoff of nitrogen and phosphorus fertilizers plays a role in increasing nutrient levels in estuaries. A study of 78 major estuaries in the United States found that on average agricultural runoff contributed 24 percent of all nutrient loadings and 40 percent of total sediment loadings.

Damages from waterborne sediments may exceed $10 billion per year. About one-third of these damages are due to cropland erosion. Sedimentation reduces the flood-control benefits of reservoirs and the navigation of waterways, increases the operating costs of water-treatment facilities, and reduces the recreational and commercial value of water bodies.

Wildlife Habitat Diversity

Agricultural activities, especially changes in the use of land area and soil ecosystems, can reduce the diversity of plant and animal species in the ecosystem. Land changes that may be crucial include the drainage of wetlands, the removal of fence rows and ditches, and reduction in crop rotations. In addition, sensitivity to pesticides may threaten certain species of plants and animals.

How Agricultural Policies Affect Environmental Quality

What is it about agricultural programs that causes them to impact the environment? Commodity programs in particular impact the economics of crop production decisions. Such programs can affect what is produced; where it is produced; how it is produced; with what inputs it is produced; and how much is produced. Particular crops may be associated with more erosive production practices and more intensive chemical and capital input use, may be more damaging in environmentally-sensitive areas, and may be more price responsive in chemical use.

Thus, commodity programs can alter the scale, location, mix, and technology of crop production. Frequently, these alterations lead to more crop production, more environmentally-damaging crops being produced, production occurring in more environmentally-sensitive areas, and more intensive technology (higher purchased input levels) being used. Alternatively, commodity programs cause a series of price and production distortions that can have significant environmental consequences. Related agricultural programs such as input subsidies, export enhancement, and insurance and credit programs introduce additional relative price distortions and add to the environmental impacts of agricultural production activities.

Trade and agricultural policy reform increases reliance on world markets to determine the prices that drive agricultural production decisions regarding how much, where, what, and with what. Both national and international studies indicate that global as well as most country environmental loadings from agricultural activities will be reduced.

Dimensions of Current Farm Programs

Farm policies prior to World War II were designed to support farm incomes and to stabilize agricultural prices. In the 1950s, programs began to include provisions for promoting United States' exports to expand world demand for United States' produce. In the 1970s, support prices were more closely tied to market prices and voluntary acreage reduction was implemented to control growing supplies. By the 1980s, concern about the environmental effects of agricultural policies were incorporated into farm legislation, resulting in the Conservation Compliance, Swampbuster, and Sodbuster provisions of the 1985 Food Security Act, along with the Conservation Reserve Program. Current farm programs include provisions or instruments to stabilize agricultural prices, support farm income, reduce supply, insure quality for consumers, promote exports, and protect against environmental degradation.

Linkages Between Farm Programs and Environmental Quality

Crops supported under government programs (e.g. cotton, corn, wheat, grain sorghum, barley, rice, and oats) tend to be higher-value crops. This may be due in part to government price supports. Raising the value of marginal product for these crops can result in an increase in derived demand for inputs to produce the higher-value crops. Program crops tend to be the more input-intensive crops.

Crops that have lower-value (e.g. grassland, hayland) tend to have lower-input intensity. These alternative uses of cropland have not typically been supported by government programs, except as they are indirectly impacted through other commodity policies, such as the dairy program.

It is important to remember that farm programs are voluntary. Farmers participate in programs when world prices are low relative to target prices. If world supplies fall, resulting in higher world prices, farmers are under no obligation to stay in the program. Environmental provisions attached to farm programs only apply to farmers actively participating in government programs.

Maintaining crop prices above the world prices increases output through additional production area and input intensification. Increasing cultivated area can encourage cultivation of highly erodible land, wetlands, and other environmentally sensitive acreage. Increasing input intensity can heighten the potential for agricultural externality problems.

Researchers have pointed to a correlation between government price supports that raise the value of output and increases in input use that raise yields per acre. Part of the increased use of fertilizers and chemicals in the United States may have been in response to government support prices. The 1985 Food Security Act included provisions for lowering target prices and loan rates and freezing base acreages and yields.

Acreage Reduction Programs (ARPs) are designed to reduce supply. ARPs may result in higher input use per acre (input intensification) by raising the relative price of farmland. Research has shown that there is not a one-to-one decline in chemical use relative to acreage reduction, indicating that producers intensify chemical use on acres remaining in production. Base acreage requirements (total acreage planted to the program crop and eligible for deficiency payments) can reduced the number of crops in the rotation. Decreased crop rotations may raise pest populations. This can result in increased use of pesticides to control pest damage. Flex acres (portion of base acreage not covered by deficiency payments) allow farmers to choose other crops to plant on program crop base acres. In 1991, less than six million flex acres were planted to non-program crops from a potential 20 million flex acres. In 1992, six million flex acres were planted to non-program crops from a pool of 25 million flex acres.

Removal of base acreage requirements may improve environmental quality by freeing farmers to plant non-program crops on more acreage. By allowing farmers more planting diversity, pesticide use could be reduced by increased cropping diversity and shifting to less input-intensive crops.

Environmental Provisions in Farm Programs

Three compliance mechanisms were introduced in the 1985 Food Security Act. The Swampbuster provision precludes farmers who cultivate wetlands from collecting government farm program payments, including deficiency payments, disaster relief payments, and CCC loans. The 1990 Food, Agriculture, Conservation, and Trade Act introduced graduated penalties for particular violations. Over 300 producers have been denied benefits and the rate of wetland conversion from all sources and the economic incentives to convert have decreased.

The Sodbuster provision withdraws government program benefits from farmers who bring highly erodible land under cultivation. Almost 800 producers have had to forego program benefits. At the same time, current incentives to cultivate highly erodible land are limited. If market prices increase substantially and commodity program participation becomes less attractive, then the environmental leverage provided by compliance will decrease.

The Conservation Compliance provision requires conservation plans for farms with highly erodible land by 1990 and full implementation by 1995. If farmers do not farm according to the provisions of the plan, they will forfeit farm program benefits. Estimates indicate that when fully implemented, Conservation Compliance could reduce erosion by 50 percent on highly erodible land. Once again, the effectiveness depends on the attractiveness of farm program participation.

The Conservation Reserve program is a ten-year environmental land retirement program introduced in the 1985 Food Security Act. In return for an annual rental payment, farmers agree to take highly erodible land out of crop production for ten years. The land must be planted in a cover crop, such as grass or trees, and cost-sharing payments are available for cover establishment. To date, over 36 million acres have been enrolled in twelve sign-ups. Significant soil erosion reductions, water quality improvements, wildlife habitat benefits, and supply control have occurred. The Conservation Reserve Program is estimated to have cost less in government outlays than the value of off-site water quality related benefits by reducing soil runoff.

The Environmental Conservation Reserve Program (ECARP) is the latest version of the Conservation Reserve Program (CRP). The ECARP provision of the 1990 Food, Agriculture, Conservation, and Trade Act redirected the CRP bid screening process to include environmentally sensitive land. Another ECARP provision is the Wetlands Reserve Program, a voluntary program to reimburse farmers for restoring wetland acreage that is currently being farmed. The program involves longer term easements with a lump sum or ten annual payments, 75 percent cost-sharing for restoration, and ten states in a pilot program.

How Environmental Policies Affect Agriculture

Through programs based on education and technical and financial assistance, current policies attempt to correct for externalities and for the problems resulting from the lack of information. Environmental programs (administered by the EPA) that have the potential to affect agriculture include the Clean Water Act, the Safe Drinking Water Act, the Toxic Substances Control Act, the Coastal Zone Management Act, and the Federal Insecticide, Fungicide, and Rodenticide Act.

Responsibility for non-point source pollution control has largely been left to the states. About half the states have cost sharing programs (incentives) that attempt to induce farmers to engage in best management practices (BMP). Seventeen states have enforceable water pollution control laws (regulatory instruments) that deal with non-point source problems.

All pesticides are required to be registered with EPA's Office of Pesticide Programs which reviews attendant health, safety, and environmental effects and is charged with restricting the use of those that are judged to present unreasonable, adverse effects on the environment or public health.

Agricultural Trade Policies and Environmental Quality

The United States and its major trading partners are in the final months of the Uruguay Round negotiations for the General Agreement on Tariffs and Trade (GATT). Efforts are underway to reduce support through agricultural programs that are linked to production (i.e. price stabilization, income supports, and some investment and input subsidies). These programs can adversely affect ground and surface water quality, soil erosion, and wildlife habitat.

Phasing down price and income supports in response to GATT results in two opposing environmental effects in the short term. With revised programs, the incentive price, which is the price farmers use for planting decisions, will likely fall (incentive prices are typically greater than market prices or loan rates), signaling farmers to reduce input use. Studies in the United States indicate that there are reductions in fertilizer and pesticide use and that only minor adjustments will occur in the mix and location of crop production.

Over time, farmers may adjust to changes in prices and the increase in available land by substituting land for chemicals and machinery, which could have an effect on soil erosion and surface water quality. Substituting land for other inputs could be expected to increase soil erosion due to increased cultivated acres, especially in the short run. The accompanying shift from more intensive to more extensive cropping practices, especially in the intermediate to longer run, should offset most of the increase in overall soil erosion.

The United States' case is not necessarily indicative of the potential environmental gains from trade reform. Already the 1985 Food Security Act and the 1990 Food, Agriculture, Conservation, and Trade Act have linked commodity programs and environmental objectives so that the potential gains are more limited. Also, the increased role of market-based price signals in production decisions has already induced a reduction in purchased input use.

The Critical Story of Prices and Technology

Based on the concept of induced technological change, technological change takes place in the direction of enhancing the scarce factors of production. For example, if labor is one of the scarcest factors of production, as is typically reflected in a high relative cost or price, new technologies will frequently be designed to augment or save this scarce input (e.g. machines, chemical weed control). If land and labor are scarce and costly, technologies conducive to high-intensity, such as confined livestock systems, are likely to evolve or be induced.

Government commodity programs and trade policies can aggravate the situation when they interfere with the relative price structure facing producers. In land scarce countries, cheap feed grain prices may encourage concentrated livestock production near ports and accompanying waste disposal problems. Artificial land scarcity induced by land set-aside and retirement programs for supply control increases the relative price of land and the incentive to develop and use higher-yielding cultivars. Additionally, if the price of land is high relative to agricultural chemicals, incentives exist to increase chemical use and develop new chemicals to further augment or increase the productivity of the scarce land resource.

Pesticides provide an illustrative case of the potential importance of relative prices, induced technology, and input use. Between 1950 and 1990, pesticide costs in the United States decreased relative to the costs of all other major inputs. Pesticide costs relative to labor costs decreased over 80 percent, and pesticide costs relative to crop prices decreased over 40 percent. The costs of pesticides relative to machinery costs and fuel costs are only available beginning in 1965; but from 1965 to 1990, the cost of pesticides relative to machinery decreased over 60 percent and relative to fuel costs decreased 50 percent.

Agricultural pesticide use (pounds of active ingredients) increased 250 percent during the 1965-1990 period while labor, fuel, and machinery inputs all declined. Although this casual empiricism is not intended to be a test of the induced innovation hypothesis, it does demonstrate that less costly inputs are substituted for scarcer or more costly ones. The decline in the price of pesticides relative to the prices of other major agricultural inputs was likely due to technological advances in the chemical industry designed to enhance the relatively most scarce inputs (i.e. land and labor).

What Policy Options Remain for Environmental Improvement?

Trade reform will lead to environmental gains, especially in some regions such as the European Community. It is important to recognize that the potential environmental improvements will vary by country and depend on the sectoral consequences of trade reform.

The portfolio of environmental policy instruments needs to be reconsidered. Possibilities include incentives to producers for incorporating externality costs in production decisions, revenue generation mechanisms coupled with financial, educational, and technical assistance, and regulations combined with incentive schemes.

Our major emphasis has been on reducing the trade distortions caused by commodity programs. Further research and analysis needs to be devoted to assessing the "green alternatives" that will replace commodity programs. Present commodity programs are tied to income support, price stability, and landscape preservation. The distribution of environmental problems is frequently different than the distribution of agricultural concerns. Environmental solutions need to be targeted to environmentally-sensitive areas and adapted to local resource conditions.

Research and technology may offer the most palatable longer term solution for addressing environmental concerns related to agriculture. We lack market signals for externalities and the demand for environmental quality. Thus, we need to provide signals to direct or induce technologies that save scarce environmental resources. Agricultural sustainability cannot succeed without "getting prices right" in the system.

Finally, trade reform will cause markets to send more accurate price signals to farmers, especially if accompanied by sound environmental policy that is designed to incorporate external costs into market prices. Only with time and improved market signals can we get technology right.

Chapter 6

Agriculture and the Environment in the European Community

Alex Dubgaard

Introduction

The Common Agricultural Policy (CAP) of the European Community (EC) is confronted with two major problems: 1) considerable surplus production creating a serious strain on EC-finances and on EC-relations with its major trading partners; and 2) growing concern over the environmental effects of modern agricultural practices.

This combination of problems has developed as a result of the lack of integrated policies to facilitate an appropriate trade-off between competing agricultural and environmental objectives. In principle, environmental protection has now become an integral part of the overall policy strategy for agriculture. In practice, however, the farm income goal still dominates agricultural policy decision-making.

To reduce surplus problems, the EC has now introduced an obligatory land set-aside program in combination with guaranteed price reductions for crop products. With a large element of quantitative supply control, the present CAP reform points to an even less market-oriented policy mix than before. Environmentally, the reform seems quite inadequate. The obligatory, rotational set-aside program is one of the least attractive elements of the reform from an environmental, an economic, and an administrative point of view.

Alternatively, the CAP should be integrated with environmental policies in such a way that surpluses and environmental stress could be reduced simultaneously without obligatory set-aside. The main point is that as long as quantitative measures are needed to limit surpluses, it would be more rational to force fertilizer and pesticide levels down than to set aside non-marginal land.

How Endangered is the Environment?

Traditionally agriculture has not been associated with environmental damage. Rather, farmers were seen as the "guardians of the countryside". The notion that agricultural practices may have detrimental effects on the environment has developed gradually over the past couple of decades. The EC Commission's 1985 Green Paper on the CAP stated that: "In the last decades agriculture has undergone a technological revolution which has profoundly changed farming practices. There is growing concern about the effects of such changes on the environment."

Nitrate and Pesticide Contamination of Groundwater

Enlarged concentrations of nitrate in groundwater is an increasing problem in several regions in Europe with intensive crop production or animal husbandry (e.g. the Southeast of England, the Netherlands, Flanders, several parts of Germany, Brittany, the Northwest of Italy) (see Baldock and Bennett, 1991; Young, 1991). In (West) Germany nitrate concentrations in groundwater have increased at an average rate of 1-1.5 mg/l per year during the last ten years and in several aquifers a sudden nitrate breakthrough has been experienced due to an exhaustion of the denitrification capacity of the substratum (see Schwarzmann and Meyer, 1991). The Federal Health Authority regards nitrate contamination as the greatest long-term problem for drinking water in Germany (op. cit.).

In certain parts of Europe, pesticide residues in water is a growing problem. In (West) Germany, for example, it is estimated that ten percent of the groundwater extraction sites are polluted with pesticide residues above the European threshold (op. cit.).

Nutrient Pollution of Surface Waters

In 1990, a UN Advisory Panel reported rapid destruction of marine (coastal) habitats worldwide. It concluded that "if unchecked, these trends will lead to global deterioration in the quality and productivity of the marine environment" (GESAME, 1990). The Panel considers an overload of nutrients (mainly nitrogen (N) and phosphorus (P) from sewage, agricultural runoff, and erosion) as the most widespread and serious coastal pollution problem.

Excess nutrients overfertilize marine waters, causing algal blooms that deplete oxygen as they decay and possibly resulting in fish kills in severe cases. Nitrogen, originating mainly from agriculture, is considered the limiting factor on marine plant growth while phosphorus, originating mainly from urban waste water, limits freshwater plant growth (see Isermann, 1990). Increased algal blooms have been reported from coastal areas around the world. In Europe, eutrophication is a widespread problem (e.g. the Baltic Sea, the North Sea, the Kattegat and Skagerrak, the Dutch Wadden Sea, and costal waters around Brittany).

Agriculture's share of N and P emissions into surface water in Western Europe (FRG, the Netherlands, Italy, Denmark, Switzerland, Norway) ranges from 37 to 82 percent for N and 27 to 38 percent for P. Its share in the flush into the North Sea catchment basin is about 60 percent for N and 25 percent for P related only to the material carried by the rivers. Agriculture's share in atmospheric N emissions into the North and Baltic Seas can be estimated to about 65 percent and 55 percent, respectively (see Isermann, 1990).

Landscape and Habitat Degradation

In addition to being the basis for food production, agricultural land serves as a habitat for wildlife, a space for recreation and aesthetic values, and the embodiment of history and tradition. In many parts of Europe, modern farming has reduced the amenity and recreational value of the rural landscape through drainage and cultivation of wetlands, conversion of semi-natural grasslands to arable land, infilling of ponds, and removal of hedgerows.

There has also been a dramatic increase in the rate of species extinction in Europe. Many studies point to changes in agricultural practices and land use as the main causes of the loss of wildlife diversity and abundance (Baldock, 1990). The principle agricultural factors responsible for the reduction in wildlife density are a combination of habitat loss, specialization, and growing intensity of crop production leading to vegetational uniformity. Danish investigations indicate that the rapidly increasing pesticide intensity has contributed significantly to the decline in farmland bird species experienced during the last couple of decades (see DEPA, 1989).

Soil Erosion

In the EC, soil erosion is primarily a problem in the Mediterranean region because of a combination of steep slopes, fragile soils, and dry climate. In Spain, for example, official figures suggest that about 17 percent of the land is subject to very serious erosion and 28 percent to moderate erosion (from Baldock, 1990).

Price support has contributed to the erosion problems since high grain prices have created incentives to take marginal land, which is more suitable for extensive pasture and forestry, into intensive crop production (see Ferreira, 1991). Massive EC and national development programs have also contributed to the conversion of fragile soils to cropping or plantations dominated by fast-growing tree species (eucalyptus) with negative impacts on both soils and ecosystems (see Baldock, 1990).

How Do Agricultural Policies Encourage Environmental Damage?

In the EC, environmental problems created by agriculture cannot be ascribed to market failure alone. They can also be associated with policy failure. The CAP support schemes have created major distortions in agricultural price relations and contributed to increasing the intensity of inputs detrimental to the environment (e.g. nitrogen fertilizer and pesticides).

Still, there is a tendency, I believe, to overemphasize the environmental potentials of output price reductions. Generally, the use of fertilizer and pesticides is rather insensitive to changes in crop prices (see Dubgaard, 1990; and Dubgaard, 1987). Probably, the most environmentally damaging effects of price support have been the incentives to take marginal land and habitats into intensive cropping.

EC Policies Encouraging Environmental Protection

The "Single European Act" (1987) created a legal basis for integrating environmental considerations into the Community's other policies. For agriculture, it added a new aspect to the original objectives of the CAP: recognition of the farmer as a landscape warden.

Where environmentally detrimental effects are concerned, the EC Commission's 1985 "Green Paper" stated that the Polluter Pays Principle ". . . must of course apply to agricultural activity as it does elsewhere." Nevertheless, environmental aspects have not really been integrated in the CAP. Most EC (and Member State) initiatives in the environmental field are of a regulatory character, often confined to environmental protection areas. Economic incentives and disincentives play a minor role apart from subsidies to extensification and land diversion in designated areas.

The recent CAP reform addresses environmental aspects through a set of accompanying measures (mainly aid to environmentally benign practices in "environmentally-sensitive areas"). However, the scope of this scheme is far too limited. With some exceptions, EC Member States and regions have designated only a few percent of the agricultural area as Environmentally Sensitive and the aid given to environmentally benign activities is often rather symbolic.

Economic and Structural Consequences of Agro-Environmental Policies

In the EC, most pollution abatement programs for agriculture have been formulated and implemented at the Member State or regional level within a framework specified by the EC for some of these policies (e.g. the nitrate directive). The agro-environmental policies adopted by Member States differ to such an extent in scope and character that it would be difficult to give a general assessment of the economic effects for EC agriculture as a whole.

Taking Denmark as an example, a quite extensive but probably not sufficient agro-environmental program has been implemented during the past six to seven years. The most costly part of the program is an upgrading of storage facilities for animal manure to nine months' capacity. It has been estimated that the required investments will amount to about 350 million ECU (see Dubgaard, 1991A). (For a comparison, annual investments in farm buildings in Denmark average about 200 million ECU). Per farm, investments in manure storage facilities amount to an average of 15,000-20,000 ECU. Farmers are being offered a subsidy covering about 30 percent of the costs of upgrading the manure storage facilities to the required capacity. Among the other measures of potential economic and structural significance to Danish agriculture are limits on manure application levels which are in agreement with maximum nutrient limits specified in the EC nitrate directive. Until now, these programs have had no measurable effects on production levels or structural development in Danish agriculture (see Dubgaard, 1991A).

Still, the economic and structural impacts of environmental regulations could be severe in other parts of Europe. This will certainly be the case in areas where overstocking is a region-wide problem (e.g. the Netherlands) unless cost effective slurry dehydration methods are invented that will make long-distance transportation of animal waste economically feasible.

Environmental Effects of EC Agricultural Policy Reform

To reduce surplus problems, the EC has decided to introduce an obligatory land set-aside program in combination with reductions in guaranteed prices for crop products. The reform will to some extent replace price support by income transfers in the form of acreage payments. In contrast to price support, acreage payments are not linked to yield and therefore preferable from an environmental point of view since they create no incentives to increase intensities of inputs detrimental to the environment. On the other hand, the new acreage support scheme is not fully de-coupled since it requires that land must be cropped to be eligible for support. This means that many marginal and environmentally sensitive areas will remain in intensive cropping.

Similarly, the obligatory lands set-aside program requires rotational set-aside, which is unfortunate from an environmental point of view. In fact, there is a risk that nitrate leaching will increase due to inadequate plant cover of set-aside land. Where amenity is concerned, scattered uncultivated fields will scarcely contribute to the visual qualities of the landscape.

It is still too early to tell to what extent farmers will reduce intensities of fertilizers and pesticides in response to the price cuts of the CAP reform. However, as already mentioned, model simulations indicate that the use of fertilizer and pesticides is rather insensitive to changes in crop prices (see Dubgaard, 1991A; and Dubgaard, 1987).

In many regions of Europe, animal manure is the main source of nitrate pollution. Price cuts will not help solve this problem since a reduction in output prices creates no incentives to enhance the utilization rates for nutrients in animal manure. In contrast, nitrogen and phosphorus taxes on chemical fertilizers would increase the value (shadow price) of these plant nutrients in animal manure. This would create economic incentives for farmers to handle manure in such a way that most of the nutrients were taken up by crops rather than being lost to the environment (through ammonia evaporation, leaching, and runoff).

How Can Reforms Enhance Agriculture's Contribution to Environment?

A First-Best Solution?

EC agriculture is producing too much food with too high intensities. From an economic point of view, the solution to this "paradox" seems simple: abolish price support and let market forces establish an equilibrium between supply and demand at a lower production level. Environmental problems should be handled in accordance with the Polluter Pays Principle by imposing eco-taxes on environmentally detrimental activities in proportion to the (marginal) social costs of the damage.

Eco-taxes on fertilizers and pesticides would help solve the surplus problems by reducing the intensity of these yield increasing inputs. Nevertheless, according to economic theory, surplus problems do not justify the use of eco-taxes.

I am sceptical about the validity of this policy prescription. The claim that eco-taxes should not be used as a supply control instrument rests upon the assumption that a first-best solution is attainable (i.e. supply control can be achieved through output price adjustments).

However, the recent CAP reform demonstrates that there is still a political desire to secure a certain transfer of income to agriculture through producer prices (above world market levels) and to rely on quantitative restrictions for supply control. As already mentioned, this combination of price support and quantitative supply control is rather unattractive from an environmental point of view.

Best Second-Best Solution

As an alternative to the present CAP reform, I would suggest a policy which combines price support with input levies on fertilizers and pesticides. With such a policy mix, a certain level of support to the primary factors (land and labour) could be maintained through price support schemes without subsidizing the use of yield increasing and environmentally detrimental factors of production such as fertilizers and pesticides.

Admittedly, eco-taxes are not a first-best solution to the supply control problem. However, set-aside is not a first-best solution either. In contrast to rotational set-aside, an <u>overall</u> reduction in the intensity of chemical fertilizers and pesticides would have both positive environmental effects and output supply effects. Therefore, as long as the output price instrument is not applied to the extent needed to control supply, it seems rational to remove some of the chemical inputs from agricultural production rather than to set aside agricultural land which is not environmentally sensitive.

Tentatively estimated, crop production would fall by 10-15 percent if the use of nitrogen fertilizer was reduced by one- third and pesticide intensity was halved. For the EC, the grain surplus is 15-20 percent of total production. Thus, the outlined reduction in nitrogen and pesticide intensities would result in an appreciable alleviation of surplus problems.

Environmental Policies and International Trade Agreements

According to free trade economics, a removal of trade barriers would improve resource allocation in agriculture worldwide and thus improve total economic welfare. However, the environmental aspects of trade liberalization are usually not incorporated in these analyses. If external (environmental) costs are not internalized to producers worldwide, free trade will not generate prices reflecting the private and the external costs of production.

In this case, a removal of trade barriers might not improve global resource allocation (see Baumol and Oates, 1988); that would depend on whether external costs (environmental damage) would increase worldwide by a redistribution of production between countries and whether a possible increase in the external costs would off-set the reduction in internal costs associated with a reallocation of (market) resources.

For example, if barriers to agricultural imports were removed altogether, a significant part of the present crop production in the EC would be transferred to third countries, *inter alia* a number of developing countries. This would create more pressure on land resources in this part of the world implying more clearings of rain forests with global environmental repercussions. The production and use of fertilizer and pesticides and animal welfare are other (transboundary) aspects of agricultural production which ought to be considered in a trade policy context. Therefore, in the absence of a global environmental policy, some (agricultural) trade barriers may be necessary to ensure that global environmental damage is not increased through international trade.

If the EC adopted a common environmental policy for agriculture, which ensured that external costs were effectively internalized to its own agricultural producers, arguements for not unconditionally accepting agricultural imports at world market prices would be strengthened.

Conclusions

In the "Best of All Worlds," as found in economic theory, the price mechanism can be adjusted in such a way that both market and non-market resources are allocated as efficiently as possible. In the real world, equity considerations often lead to second-best policies such as price support supplemented by quantitative supply control measures as seen in the new CAP reform.

The obligatory, rotational set-aside program is one of the least attractive elements of the CAP reform from an economic and an environmental point of view. As long as quantitative measures are needed to limit surpluses, it seems more rational to force fertilizer and pesticide levels down. Therefore, a Common Agro-Environmental Policy would be a valuable adjunct to the CAP.

References

Baldock, D. Agriculture and Habitat Loss in Europe. AP
   Discussion Paper No. 3. London: WWF International, 1990.

Baldock, D. and G. Bennett. Agriculture and the Polluter-Pays-
   Principle. A study of Six EC Countries. London: Institute for
   European Environmental Policy, 1991.

Baumol, W. J. and W.E. Oates. The Theory of Environmental
   Policy. 2nd ed., USA: Cambridge University Press, 1988.

Danish Ministry of Agriculture (Landbrugsministeriet).
   Kvælstoftilførsel og kvælstofudvaskning i dansk
   planteproduktion, gennemsnitsopgørelse for perioden 1978-
   1982 (Nitrogen Application and Nitrate Leaching in Danish
   Crop Production). Copenhagen: Arealdatakontoret, 1984.

DEPA (Danish Environmental Protection Agency/
   Miljøstyrelsen). Fugle foretrækker usprøjtede marker (Birds
   Prefer Un-Sprayed Fields). No. 1-2. Copenhagen: Miljø
   Danmark (Danish Environment), 1989.

Dubgaard, A. Anvendelse af afgifter til regulering af pe
   sticidforbruget (Taxation as a Means to Control Pesticide
   Use), (English Summary). Report No. 35. Copenhagen:
   Statens Jordbrugsøkonomiske Institut (Institute of
   Agricultural Economics), 1987.

Dubgaard, A. The Danish Nitrate Policy in the 1980s. Report
   No. 59. Copenhagen: Statens Jordbrugsøkonomiske Institut
   (Institute of Agricultural Economics), 1991A.

Dubgaard, A. The Need for a Common Nitrogen Policy in the EC; in Nitrate-Agriculture-Eau. R. Calvet, Ed. Proceedings from an International Symposium organized by Institut National Agronomique, Paris, 1990.

Dubgaard, A. Pesticide Regulation in Denmark, in Farming and the Countryside: An Economic Analysis of External Costs and Benefits, N. Hanley, Ed., UK: C.A.B. International, 1991B.

Ferreira, A. G. "Impacts of Agricultural Policies on Soil Erosion in Two Regions of Portugal." in M.D. Young, Ed., Towards Sustainable Agricultural Development. London: OECD/Belhaven Press, 1991.

GESAME (Group of Experts on the Scientific Aspects of Marine Environment). The State of the Marine Environment. Nairobi: United Nations Environment Program, 1990.

Isermann, K. "Share of Agriculture in Nitrogen and Phosphorus Emissions into the Surface Waters of Western Europe against the Background of their Eutrophication." Fertilizer Research. 26: 253-269, 1990.

OECD. OECD Environmental Data Compendium 1991. Paris, 1991.

Rude, S. and A. Dubgaard. "Regulering af næringsstofbe lastningen fra landbruget med særligt henblik på kvælstof (Policy Instruments to Control the Use of Nitrogen)," in Midler til reduktion af næringsstofbelastningen fra landbruget, Arbejdsrapport fra Miljøstyrelsen. No. 19. Copenhagen: Miljøstyrelsen (Danish Environmental Protection Agency), 1989.

Schwarzmann, C. and H. von Meyer. "The Federal Republic of Germany." (Chapter 4) in D. Baldock and G. Bennett. Agriculture and the Polluter-Pays-Principle. A study of Six EC Countries. London: Institute for European Environmental Policy, 1991.

World Resources Institute. World Resources 1992-93. New York, 1992.

Young, M. D., Ed. Towards Sustainable Agricultural Development. London: OECD/Belhaven Press, 1991.

Chapter 7

Agriculture and the Environment in OECD[*]

Jeffrey Rae

Introduction

During recent decades, agriculture in OECD has been characterized by increasing conflicts between it and the environment (as well as growing economic costs and disruptions in world commodity markets). To a significant degree, these increasing environmental conflicts are a consequence of the recent evolution in agricultural production systems and the failure to recognize the full extent and importance of the interdependencies between agriculture and the environment when framing policy. While agriculture has impacted the environment negatively, agriculture has also significantly contributed to the environment and to the amenity of rural areas.

Agriculture and State of the Environment in OECD

Despite far-reaching changes in the nature and scale of economic activities in OECD over the past four decades, agriculture continues to be a major custodian of the natural and man-made environment. Indeed, in the case of some natural

---

[*]This paper represents the personal views of the author and does not engage the responsibility of the OECD or of its Member countries.

resources (e.g. land and water), agriculture is often the dominant user (see Tables 1 and 2).

Historically, this association between agriculture and the environment in OECD has been marked by many positive effects. The drainage of land for farming has helped to eliminate disease, control flooding, and improve water quality. In some countries, wildlife has adapted to agriculture to such an extent that certain plant and animal species are now wholly dependent on it. In most countries, agriculture is an important element in recreational, educational, and tourist facilities, as well as in the maintenance of rural populations and infrastructure.

While agriculture has had these beneficial associations, the 1970s and 1980s witnessed heightened concern about the environmentally damaging effects of agriculture. These include agriculture's impacts on natural resources, on plants and animals and their habitats, and on the general amenity value of rural areas.

The most recent OECD report in the series The State of the Environment reviewed progress over the past two decades in OECD countries towards environmental objectives (OECD, 1991f) and examined the policy agenda for the 1990s by comprehensively assessing environmental impacts and issues at both the global and the OECD level. The following is a brief resume of that assessment as it applies to OECD agriculture. (The report also assessed the impacts on agriculture of pollution from non-agricultural sources, but they will not be addressed here.)

Impact on Soil

Agricultural Practices effect soil in OECD countries in numerous ways.
- Inappropriate tillage leads to wind and water erosion. Cropping arrests natural soil formation and exposes the land to erosion. The maximum rate of soil erosion consistent with maintaining soil productivity is exceeded on a substantial part of the agricultural land in Australia and the United States.
- Poor agronomic practices and overgrazing can lead to desertification. The drier regions of OECD, including

Australia, Spain, Turkey and the United States, are affected by this phenomenon.
- Heavy farm machinery can compact soil.
- Irrigation can cause waterlogging and salination. In the mid-1980s, 5.2 million hectares (or 27 percent) of irrigated land in the United States were damaged by salination.
- Intensive fertilization can have many undesirable side effects, notably the accumulation of phosphates and heavy metals (e.g. copper or cadmium) in soils, which lowers soil fertility and results in undesirable residues in crops.
- Pesticide residues can accumulate in soils and in the livestock and crops raised on them. Since the early 1970s, Japan has had some 7,050 hectares of land contaminated by heavy metals.

Impact on Foodstuffs

The presence of pesticides and heavy metals in foodstuffs is of increasing concern in OECD countries. This concern has focused upon more accurate identification of such residues in foodstuffs and on research about their long term consequences for human health and for vulnerable groups such as children. In the meantime, there is growing pressure by consumers to reduce the use of agricultural chemicals, to develop disease-resistant animals and plants that utilize such inputs more effectively, and to encourage environmentally preferred methods of pest and disease control (such as biological pest control).

Impact of Pesticides

Pest management is an important part of modern agriculture. Pesticide usage is widespread in OECD, particularly where value-added per hectare is high. In 1980, nearly 80 percent of all agricultural chemicals by value used in OECD was applied to just seven crop categories (1).

Intensive pesticide use has witnessed growing resistance to certain pesticides by several of the targeted pests. A similar evolution has been noted with herbicides. Moreover, non-specific pesticides and herbicides can eliminate benign species and natural predators which will increase pest problems. These problems are aggravated by large scale, continuous cropping which provide ideal conditions for pest growth. In addition, continuous cropping can degrade soil fertility, necessitating increased use of fertilizers. Where output concentrates on a limited range of high yielding varieties, there is also the risk of eliminating lower yielding but more pest resistant strains from the gene pool.

Impact on Water Systems

Agricultural water use can have adverse impacts on water tables and on the capacity of arterial water systems to absorb wide variations in supply. In some countries, salination of water systems is also a major problem. In others, agricultural soil erosion can lead to blocked water courses and siltation of water supply and hydroelectric power reservoirs. Generally, however, these direct impacts are not of great significance for most OECD members.

By far the most significant problem in OECD comes from the leaching of agricultural chemicals into water systems. Agriculture is the major source of nitrate pollution of water systems due to the following developments:

- *Conversion of permanent grassland to cropping* was a major source of nitrate pollution in Europe in the 1950s and 1960s but has since ceased to be so with the subsequent stabilization of the arable area.
- *Use of nitrogenous fertilizers*, which can cause nitrates to leach into groundwater, mainly occurs when they are applied in excess of recommended application rates or when the recommended conditions for application are not observed.
- *Intensive livestock production* produces large concentrations of animal manure which can pollute water systems through leaching, flooding, or a breakdown of manure storage facilities.

Nitrate pollution of groundwater is of serious concern in Europe and elsewhere. Increasing nitrate levels in deep groundwater, which have been reported in parts of France, the Netherlands, and the United Kingdom, will take a very long time to be reduced to acceptable levels. Moreover, contamination can also lead to undesirable nitrate residues in crops grown with such water.

Finally, fertilizers can lead to eutrophication of surface waters. In some European rural areas, 70 to 85 percent of the nitrogen and more than 30 percent of the phosphorous in surface water comes from agriculture. Similar problems can arise with manure from intensive livestock production.

Impact on Flora and Fauna

Land reclamation and development can reduce natural and semi-natural wildlife habitats. Some OECD countries with long agricultural histories have plant and animal communities dependent on certain agricultural practices for their survival; a change in practices can lead to the loss of those flora and fauna. On the other hand, fertilizer use can rapidly reduce floral diversity in pasture land. In European countries, the conversion of permanent pasture to cropping and the removal of hedgerows and uncultivated field margins is particularly important. Finally, the area of wetlands declined in many OECD countries during the 1980s (see Table 3) and important European wetlands remain at risk as a result of agricultural irrigation.

Agricultural chemicals can also have negative impacts on flora and fauna. While certain highly persistent pesticides (e.g. DDT and dieldrin) have been banned or substantially restricted in OECD countries, past applications will continue to be felt for some time as they accumulate in food chains. Moreover, because some of the pesticides still in use are sufficiently toxic and/or environmentally mobile, their improper use or disposal can generate serious problems.

The overall threat to flora and fauna is illustrated in Table 4, which shows the proportion of known species in OECD countries which were threatened or vulnerable to destruction at the end of the 1980s. In most member countries, more than 20 percent of known species fell into this category. Even so, the data on land use devoted to forestry (Table 1) and on major protected areas (Table 3) reveal some encouraging developments over the 1980s so that

86

in virtually all OECD countries, the changes in these two categories have generally been positive for the environment.

Impact on the Amenity of Rural Areas

The effects of agriculture on rural amenity are quite diverse. Intensive livestock production may result in air pollution. Ammonia from stored manure may acidify the environment and adversely affect plant life. In addition, a loss of rural amenity can result from the erection of farm buildings, the adoption of agricultural monocultures, the elimination of hedgerows, the disappearance of permanent grasslands, or damage to historical or archeological sites. Such problems occur mainly in the European members of OECD.

Of more widespread concern in some countries are the changes in the distribution of rural populations induced by structural changes, particularly in agriculture which is often the dominant source of employment in rural areas. While the significance of this issue goes beyond traditional environmental concerns, it has an important environmental dimension and is a matter of public concern, particularly in Europe and Japan.

The Environment and Recent Structural Changes in OECD Agriculture

Whether the risks for the environment inherent in modern agricultural production systems will be heightened or lessened depends upon the general nature of structural change in agriculture. For instance, as agricultural production increases its intensity of environmentally risky inputs and farm practices, these risks will be enlarged. On the other hand, the extension of production into new areas will widen the set of environmental impacts associated with a given input mix and production technology.

The geographical scope and intensification of agricultural production systems can be measured by a number of indicators which give an overall view of the trends, despite variations in the agronomic, ecological and social circumstances of individual OECD countries. It is for these reasons that certain indicators of agricultural input usage have been included in the work by OECD on environmental indicators (OECD, 1991d and 1991e). This work on indicators has concentrated attention on the more environmentally risky farm inputs and practices, such as farm machinery, agricultural chemicals and irrigation.

The evolution of the key agricultural indicators over the period 1970-88 (Tables 5 and 6) reveals the following developments:

- While agricultural land area has declined in OECD, agricultural output has increased overall by 20 to 30 percent during the last decade (2). More recently, policy measures which encourage fallowing or setting-aside agricultural land have accentuated the decline.
- Irrigated land area as a proportion of the arable area reached a peak for OECD in the early 1980s but has since declined (see Table 6). Despite this overall decline, growth has continued in European member countries.
- Farm employment has declined in OECD by 30 percent since 1970 with the trends most pronounced in some European countries and Japan. A major factor behind these trends has been the substitution of machines for manual labour.
- Total energy consumption per agricultural land unit has increased by 39 percent during the period 1970-88, which reflects trends to substitute capital for labor.
- The fertilizer application rate is a further indicator of intensification and specialization in agriculture. It also shows the quantities of manufactured chemicals released into the environment. For OECD as a whole, total fertilizer application decreased in the 1980s, after steady growth through the 1970s. However, utilization has continued to rise in Europe and Japan during the more recent period.
- The rate of application of pesticides by arable land unit varies considerably but there is a tendency for heavy usage of all types of pesticide. While the data on trends are sparse, they suggest a fall in application rates in the OECD during the 1980s, with the exception of insecticides.

Agricultural Policies and the Environment

The structural changes outlined above have occurred against a range of agricultural policies in OECD countries which have exerted varying influences on both the pace and direction of these changes. For this reason, OECD agricultural policies have also been a substantial, if indirect, factor in many of the environmental consequences associated with structural changes in agricultural production systems. Indeed, in a number of instances, policy has also had an explicit environmental dimension.

Producer and Consumer Subsidy Equivalents

The synthesis report, National Policies and Agricultural Trade and an associated series of country reports (3) analyzed the consequences of national agricultural policies for trade and the functioning of world markets. To elaborate and analyze these consequences, the concepts of Producer and Consumer Subsidy Equivalents were adopted. The Producer Subsidy Equivalent (PSE) is the assistance to farm production; the Consumer Subsidy Equivalent (CSE) is the implicit tax this assistance imposes upon consumers of agricultural commodities (4).

In 1987, the OECD Ministerial Council concluded (OECD, 1987a) that National Policies and Agricultural Trade highlighted:

- the existence of serious structural imbalances in world markets for agricultural commodities;
- the considerable costs which agricultural policies impose on public sector budgets, consumers, and OECD countries' economies;
- the increasing distortion of competition in world commodity markets which flowed from these policies; and
- the damage which these policies did to many developing countries.

OECD Council Reforms Agricultural Policies

As a result, the Council agreed to reform OECD agricultural policies (OECD, 1987a). The long-term objective of this reform was to allow market signals to influence the orientation of farm production. This was to be achieved by a progressive and concerted reduction of agricultural assistance and by all other appropriate means. In pursuing this long term objective, Ministers also agreed that consideration could be given to social and other concerns, such as protecting the environment or maintaining rural populations. Furthermore, they agreed that farm income support should be provided by way of budgetary assistance, which would not be linked to agricultural output or input usage.

OECD Monitors the Reform

The Council also initiated a process to monitor the progress in implementing this reform. Consequently, since 1987, the OECD has published an annual report, Agricultural, Policies, Markets and Trade: Monitoring and Outlook, which assesses policy developments in each member country against the agreed reform (5). Each year these reports update and estimate the PSEs and CSEs for production of the major temperate agricultural commodities in each of the OECD countries (6). More recently, they have sought to sharpen the focus on the relationships between agricultural policies and the environment. This work has enabled the OECD to build up a good picture of the evolution of agricultural polices and assistance levels and their environmental consequences.

Tables 7 and 8 set out two of the key PSE indicators for OECD countries for the period 1979-91. From the Percentage PSEs in Table 7, one can see that agricultural assistance accounted for nearly 40 percent of the farm-gate value of production in the OECD in 1979 (7). The Producer Nominal Assistance Coefficients (NACs) in Table 8 express this another way; namely, that unit returns to farmers, including assistance, were equivalent, on average, to 1.5 times the prices at the border (8). Equally important, some 80 percent of this assistance was provided by assistance measures directly linked to agricultural output or inputs (9). Such measures encourage the expansion of productive capacity and the adoption of relatively more intensive production techniques than would otherwise be the case.

Since 1979, an already high rate of agricultural assistance in OECD has increased by 50 percent. By 1991 unit returns to farmers had risen to nearly 1.8 times the prices at the border (10). Moreover, the trend to increasing rates of assistance was even more pronounced in Finland, Norway and Switzerland, despite the fact that their rates of assistance were already well above the OECD average percentage PSE to begin with. Policy measures which reduce farmers' input costs or raise their returns remain the dominant forms of assistance in all OECD countries except Australia and New Zealand. In 1991, the share of such measures in total assistance remained at around 80 percent. Indeed, their share of assistance tends to increase as the rate of assistance rises.

Results of the Study

The trend to increase rates of assistance and the dominance of assistance measures linked to agricultural output or inputs mean that the economic incentives for extending and intensifying agricultural production have increased substantially since 1979. This is true for most OECD countries but is particularly pronounced for the European members. As we have seen, recent structural changes in many OECD countries have been associated with increased use of agricultural inputs and practices which are associated with the adverse environmental impacts outlined in the first section of this paper. Both microeconomic theory and a casual comparison of the data in Tables 7 and 8 with that in Table 5, suggest that the intensity of the usage of farm inputs is likely to vary with the level of assistance provided to agriculture.

Empirical evidence of a link between producer assistance and environmentally risky inputs is illustrated in Figures 1 to 4. These Figures are based upon preliminary work underway, but not yet completed, in the OECD Secretariat on environmental externalities and public goods associated with agriculture in OECD countries. As part of this preliminary work, the OECD Secretariat has

91

undertaken an analysis of the relationship between rates of assistance, as measured by the percentage PSE, and the usage of various environmentally sensitive inputs in member countries. This work has yielded positive statistical correlations between producer assistance and: fertilizer application (Figure 1), pesticide usage (Figure 2), energy consumption (Figure 3), and farm mechanization (Figure 4).

One of the most striking aspects of these results is the exponential nature of each of the statistical relationships which were estimated by this analysis (11). If confirmed, it implies that the risks of environmental damage, due to intensification of input usage, increase exponentially with the rate of assistance. When allowance is made for the likely geographical extension of agricultural production (and of any environmental impacts associated with that production) due to rising assistance, the aggregate environmental damage is likely to be even greater.

Evidence from New Zealand on the environmental effects associated with a dramatic reduction in assistance is consistent with these results. Since 1984, the rate of assistance in New Zealand has been reduced by more than 90 percent and application rates of both fertilizers and pesticides has also been cut back in parallel (12). On the other hand, the reduction of assistance to New Zealand agriculture has had some negative environmental impacts. Soil conservation and risk management for adverse climatic events seem to have suffered in that there has been a cutback in investment in soil conservation and the conversion of marginal pasture into forestry (13).

The Integration of Agricultural and Environmental Policies

The failure of agricultural production systems to adequately reflect the value of the environmental resources which they utilize or degrade arises because market prices do not fully reflect the environmental costs and benefits of agricultural activities. Hence, achievement of a better integration of environmental and agricultural policies requires both the internalization of the externalities involved (14) and the provision of appropriate mechanisms to encourage the supply of the public goods associated with agriculture (15). In the absence of such intervention, markets can fail to provide socially adequate amounts of the activities in question. (However, the intervention in question has to be able to lessen the extent of failure to make it worthwhile.) For these reasons, a good deal of recent work in the OECD has concentrated upon the need for and the practical means of better integrating agricultural and environmental policies in member countries (16).

OECD Research on Agricultural and Environmental Policies

In 1989, the OECD published <u>Agricultural and Environmental Policies: Opportunities for Integration</u> (OECD, 1989a), the first comprehensive examination of the relationship between agricultural and environmental issues in OECD countries. In framing agricultural and related policies, this report concluded that consideration should be given to:
- enhancement of the positive environmental contribution agriculture can make;
- reduction of agricultural sources of pollution; and
- adaptation of agricultural policies that take account of environmental considerations.

<u>Opportunities for Integration</u> went on to identify possibilities for the better harmonization of agricultural and environmental policies. At the time, some of these had been well recognized, but others were only just emerging (17).

An update of <u>Opportunities for Integration</u> has only just been published as <u>Agricultural and Environmental Policy Integration: Recent Progress and New Directions</u> (OECD, 1992a), which noted that some progress towards better integration had been made by OECD countries but that new directions and priorities were necessary if future effort is to be productive. In particular, the report noted that the issue of environmental sustainability had emerged in the meantime as a central national and international goal for public policy. Sustainable agriculture was identified as having four facets: ongoing economic viability for agriculture;

maintenance of its natural resource base; maintenance of other ecosystems affected by agriculture; and the provision of natural amenity and aesthetic values. The new directions for better policy integration include to:

- ensure agricultural output and input prices are not distorted by producer assistance or the underpricing of environmental assets;
- integrate environmental values into farm research, education and extension services;
- define criteria for defining and pricing externalities and public goods;
- facilitate the transition to sustainable and lower input agriculture with non-distorting measures; and
- apply the Polluter Pays Principle to agricultural sources of pollution as far as is practicable.

In the wake of Opportunities for Integration, the OECD Ministerial Council agreed that the monitoring of agricultural policy reform should include an examination of the relationship between agriculture and the environment (OECD, 1989c). At that time, the Ministerial Council also reaffirmed the critical importance of integrating environmental and economic decision making more systematically and more effectively, as a means of contributing to sustainable economic development. Consequently, the past three Monitoring and Outlook Reports (OECD, 1990a, 1991a and 1992b) have given greater attention to these relationships.

New Policies in OECD Countries

In OECD countries, a wide range of measures have recently been introduced to protect the environment in the course of agricultural production. All countries are now placing more emphasis on the effects of agricultural policies on the environment and are increasingly implementing measures which better protect the environment. The number of policy measures with an explicit or indirect environmental objective has increased. Some have attempted to build an environmental component into agricultural measures, while others have addressed environmental problems such as soil erosion or water pollution more directly.

Environmental considerations have become an increasingly familiar element in structural policies and the concepts of sustainable agriculture and sustainable development are receiving growing attention.

OECD Agriculture Ministers recently met to consider progress and future directions for the better integration of agriculture and environmental policies (OECD, 1992d). While endorsing the need for further analysis by the organization, OECD Agriculture Ministers agreed that:

- agricultural policy reform directed at greater market orientation and lower assistance could be beneficial for the environment;
- a new set of policy responses may be needed to internalize environmental costs and benefits into agricultural decision-making;
- the Polluter Pays Principle should be applied to the extent possible, as indicated by OECD Environment Ministers, among others (OECD 1991c); and
- the international dimensions of environmental impacts or the policy response to them can best be addressed through multilateral approaches.

Policies Should Include Regulatory and Market-Based Solutions

In enumerating the new set of policy responses to internalize environmental costs and benefits, OECD Agriculture Ministers saw that they encompassed both regulatory and market-based solutions. The range of possible measures included environmental management agreements, financial measures, research and development initiatives, and the pricing of previously unpriced services (e.g. redefining property rights to environmental assets).

The possible use of financial measures to enhance agriculture's positive contribution to the environment raises the issue of the role of direct income support (i.e. budgetary payments not linked to agricultural outputs or inputs). These could be used to compensate farmers for the pecuniary losses involved in producing positive environmental externalities as well as public goods, such as rural amenity, which benefit the wider community. Work is being undertaken in OECD to clarify the role that direct income support could play in the context of the overall reform of agricultural policies.

Some preliminary results from this work were published in Reforming Agricultural Policies: Quantitative Restrictions on Production, Direct Income Support (OECD, 1990d). This preliminary work concluded that direct income support could be used to compensate farmers for providing environmental public goods and externalities. Certain characteristics were identified which would help to ensure that such measures are less economically distorting than existing measures of farm income support. These were that:
- payments should be for specifically defined public goods;
- they should not be based on farmers producing specific farm commodities;
- they should reflect the social value of the public goods produced; and
- participation should be voluntary and available to all eligible farmers.

At the present time, work is continuing within OECD to elaborate the use of direct income support to further agricultural reform and to achieve a better balance of environmental and other public goods.

Table 1. **Land Use, OECD Countries**

	State 1989				Changes 1970-1989 (%)		
	Land Area[a] 1000 km²	Agricultural Land		Forests and Woodland %	Agricultural Land		Forests and Woodland
		Arable and Cropland %	Meadows and Pastures %		Arable and Cropland	Meadows and Pastures	
Canada	9 221	5	4	49	10	46	2
USA	9 167	21	26	32	0	-1	-4
Japan	377	12	2	67	-16	122	0
Australia[c]	7 618	6	55	14	17	-5	13
New Zealand[c]	268	2	51	27	-12	8	2
France	550	35	21	28	0	-13	8
Germany	349	36	16	30	0	-15	2
Italy	294	41	17	23	-19	-7	9
Netherlands	34	28	32	10	8	-10	12
Portugal	92	41	8	34	-5	0	11
Spain	499	41	20	31	-1	-12	10
Turkey	770	36	11	26	1	-21	0
UK	241	29	48	10	-3	-1	38
Finland	305	8	0	77	-8	-21	0
Norway	307	29	0	31	8	-22	5
Sweden	412	7	1	68	-7	-20	1
North America	18 388	13	15	41	1	3	0
OECD Europe	4 350	29	17	33	3	-10	5
OECD	31 000	14	25	33	3	-3	2
World	104 731	11	25	36	-19	-21	-12

Note: a) Excludes major lakes and rivers.
Source: OECD

Table 2. **Water Withdrawal in OECD Countries**

Water Withdrawal by Major Uses[a], late 1980s

	Total Water Withdrawal million m³	Public Water Supply %	Irrigation %	Industry No Cooling %	Electrical Cooling %
Canada	43 888	11.3	7.1	9.1	55.6
USA[c]	467 000	10.8	40.5	7.4	38.8
Japan[b]	84 831	16.1	66.8	15.7	1.0
France[c]	43 273	13.7	9.7	10.4	51.9
Germany[d]	44 390	11.1	0.5	5.0	67.6
Italy[b]	56 200	14.2	57.3	14.2	12.5
Spain	45 845	11.6	65.5	22.9	..
Turkey	29 600	12.8	79.1	9.8	..
UK [c,e]	13 221	48.6	0.3	10.8	18.8
Finland	4 000	10.6	0.5	37.5	3.5
Sweden	2 996	32.4	3.1	40.2	0.3

Notes:
a) The four sectors do not necessarily add up to 100%, since "other agricultural uses than irrigation," "industrial cooling," and "other uses" are not covered in this table.
b) 1980.
c) Industry includes industrial cooling.
d) Includes western Germany only.
e) Irrigation: total agricultural water withdrawal.

Source: OECD, OECD Environmental Data Compendium, Paris, 1991.

Table 3. **Protected Areas and Wet Lands**

Countries	Major Protected Areas			Wet Lands[a]		
	1980 '000 ha	1989 '000 ha	Change %	1980 '000 ha	1989 '000 ha	Change %
Canada	56 964.0	70 125.5	+23.1	165 924.0	127 194.0	-23.3
United States	47 391.4	98 297.4	+107.4	38 000.0	--	--
Japan	2 132.1	2 402.3	+12.7	--	--	--
Australia	25 069.1	45 654.4	+82.1	--	--	--
New Zealand	2 619.5	2839.1	+8.4	1 040.0	--	--
EC-12	5 503.8	18 673.2	+239.3	--	--	--
Belgium	82.3	126.1[b]	+53.2	--	--	--
Denmark	8.4	422.5	+4 929.8	340.0	--	--
France	1 281.3	4 778.7	+273.0	278.0	254.5[c]	-8.5
Germany[d]	290.6	2 955.9	+917.2	117.4	91.3	-22.2
Greece	63.1	103.7	+40.6	--	--	--
Ireland	10.7	26.8	+150.5	--	--	--
Italy	410.6	1 300.6	+216.8	--	--	--
Netherlands	110.7	355.0	+220.7	73.7[e]	65.0	-11.8
Portugal	251.1	453.6	+80.6	--	--	--
Spain	1 675.9	3 511.1	+109.5	1 085.3	1 083.0[c]	-0.2
United Kingdom	1 319.1	4 639.2	+251.7	--	--	--
Austria	258.7	1 593.9	+516.1	9.3	7.0	-24.7
Finland	484.8	807.3	+66.5	2 090.0	2 070.8	-0.9
Norway	3 788.3	4 762.4	+25.7	2 030.0[f]	--	--
Sweden	1 058.9	1 758.4	+66.1	2 440.0	2 383.7[b]	-2.3
Switzerland	17.9	111.2	+521.2	5.7	5.8[b]	+1.8

Notes: (For more detailed notes refer to the source cited below).

(a)   Wetlands refer to bogs, fens, marshes and wet tundras.
(b)   1985.
(c)   1988.
(d)   Data refers to western Germany.
(e)   1979.
(f)   1983.

Source: OECD, <u>OECD Environmental Data Compendium 1991</u>, Paris, 1991.

Table 4. **Endangered and Vulnerable Wildlife Species,** OECD Countries

Proportion of known species threatened, late 1980s

Countries	Mammals	Birds	Fish	Reptiles & Amphibians	Vascular Plants
Canada	6.6	3.5	1.9	7.2	1.5
United States	10.5	7.2	2.4	5.8	0.5
Japan	7.4	8.1	10.6	5.0	10.2
Australia	13.4	3.3	--	2.1	12.3
New Zealand	20.3	5.7	0.4	--	4.8
EC-12					
Belgium	21.5[a]	29.0[a]	--	92.0[a]	24.0[a]
Denmark	28.6	17.4	7.8	15.8	13.7
France	52.2	39.8	18.6	49.2	8.4
Germany[b]	39.4	25.6	70.0	64.5	24.3
Greece	--	--	--	--	--
Ireland	16.1	23.7	--	25.0	--
Italy	13.4	14.3	13.9	50.0	10.0
Netherlands	48.3	33.1	22.4	72.7	--
Portugal	51.2	39.6	28.2	32.7	--
Spain	14.8	14.5	18.2	11.4	2.5
United Kingdom	31.2	15.0	3.4	41.2	9.6
Austria	29.4	28.4	35.2	25.0	15.9
Finland	11.3	6.0	12.1	20.0	5.6
Norway	7.4	10.2	1.2	30.0	4.5
Sweden	15.4	6.8	4.6	26.3	8.2
Switzerland	44.7	57.7	78.8	82.4	28.6

Notes: (For more detailed notes refer to the source cited below).

(a)   Brussels region only.
(b)   Data refers to western Germany.

Source: OECD, <u>OECD Environmental Data Compendium 1991</u>, Paris, 1991.

Table 5. Agriculture and the Environment : Selected indicators

		Canada	USA	Japan	France	Germany[b]	Italy	UK	North America	OECD Europe	OECD	World
Agricultural land area	1 000 km²	785	4 314	313	119	171	185	53	5 099	1 858	11 872	46 874
of which:												
Arable and crop land	%	59	44	62	63	71	38	88	46	62	34	31
Permanent grass land	%	41	56	38	37	29	62	12	54	38	66	69
Manpower	1 000 persons	556	3 326	1 437	1 085	2 058	581	4 740	3 882	18 814	28 023	1 082 920
	% change	-8	-7	-48	-52	-47	-26	-47	-7	-29	-30	23
Farm machinery	1 000 machines	913	5 310	1 670	1 600	1 408	573	3 228	6 223	8 824	18 746	29 872
	% change	20	-1	22	4	122	12	819	2	47	45	65
Energy consumption	MTOE[c]	3	17	3	2	3	1	6	20	22	49	..
	% change	..	-	25	7	65	-22	167	17	54	41	..
Nitrogenous fertilizer use on arable and crop land	Tonnes/km²	3	5	13	21	8	21	14	5	10	6	5
	% change	271	32	66	38	82	69	9	40	72	50	142
Pesticide use on arable and crop land	Tonnes/km²	0.09	0.18	0.44	0.42	..	0.58	1.77[a]	0.16	0.45	0.26	..
Irrigated area	1 000 km²	8	181	14	3	31	2	29	189	135	375	2 287
	% change	95	14	83	15	20	76	-15	16	38	20	37

Notes: "% change" data refer to the period 1970-1988: all other data refer to 1988 or the latest available year.
(a) Great Britain only.   (b) Western Germany only.   (c) Million tonnes oil equivalent.

Source: OECD, State of the Environment, Paris, 1991.

Table 6. **Agricultural Land and Irrigated Areas**

	Agricultural Land				Irrigated Areas			
	1 000 km²			% Change	1 000 km²			% Change
	1970	1980	1988	1970-88	1970	1980	1988	1970-88
Canada	645	730	785	22	4.2	5.8	8.2	95
USA	4 350	4 282	4 314	-1	159.0	205.8	181.0	14
Japan	58	55	53	-8	34.2	30.6	28.6	-15
France	320	318	313	-2	7.5	10.9	13.7	83
Germany (a)	131	122	119	-9	2.8	3.2	3.3	15
Italy	194	176	171	-12	25.6	28.7	30.8	20
Netherlands	22	20	20	-9	3.8	4.8	5.5	43
Spain	328	312	306	-7	23.8	30.3	33.2	40
UK	189	185	185	-2	0.9	1.4	1.6	76
North America	4 995	5 012	5 099	2	163.2	211.6	189.2	16
OECD Pacific	5 064	4 973	4 916	-3	50.0	47.4	50.1	0
OECD Europe	1 958	1 903	1 858	-5	98.0	122.1	135.3	38
OECD	12 016	11 887	11 872	-1	311.3	381.1	374.7	20
World	45 903	46 649	46 874	2	1 674.0	2 104.4	2 286.7	37

Note: (a) Includes western Germany only.
Source: OECD, <u>State of the Environment</u>, Paris, 1991.

Table 7. **Percentage Producer Subsidy Equivalents, OECD Countries**

	Average 1979-81	Average 1982-84	Average 1985-87	Average 1988-90(e)	1991(p)
Canada	26	29	46	41	45
United States	21	28	38	30	30
Japan	62	64	73	70	66
Australia	9	12	14	11	15
New Zealand	18	27	23	6	4
European Community	35	33	46	45	49
Austria	29	29	44	47	52
Finland	53	56	67	71	71
Norway	70	69	74	75	77
Sweden	42	38	56	55	59
Switzerland	65	67	77	77	80
OECD	32	34	47	43	45

Notes: EC-10 for 1979-85, EC-12 from 1986.
e : Estimate p : Provisional
Source: OECD

Table 8. **Producer Nominal Assistance Coefficients, OECD Countries**

	Average 1979-81	Average 1982-84	Average 1985-87	Average 1988-90(e)	1991(p)
Canada	1.31	1.36	1.72	1.58	1.69
United States	1.25	1.36	1.54	1.39	1.39
Japan	2.34	2.52	3.23	2.93	2.67
Australia	1.09	1.12	1.14	1.12	1.16
New Zealand	1.19	1.32	1.26	1.06	1.04
European Community	1.52	1.47	1.87	1.80	1.94
Austria	1.40	1.39	1.81	1.89	2.09
Finland	2.22	2.47	3.77	4.00	4.41
Norway	3.21	3.31	4.68	4.69	5.18
Sweden	1.70	1.61	2.45	2.37	2.55
Switzerland	2.69	2.80	4.00	4.02	4.44
OECD	1.45	1.49	1.83	1.71	1.78

Notes: EC-10 for 1979-85, EC-12 from 1986.
e : Estimate p : Provisional
Source: OECD

Figure 1: Fertiliser application and producer assistance in OECD countries
Average 1986-89

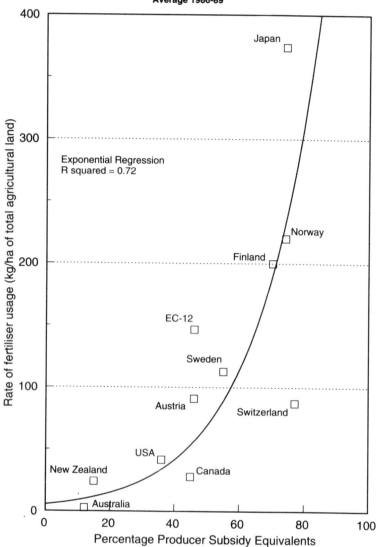

Source: OECD Secretariat

Figure 2: Pesticide usage and producer assistance in OECD countries
Average 1986-89

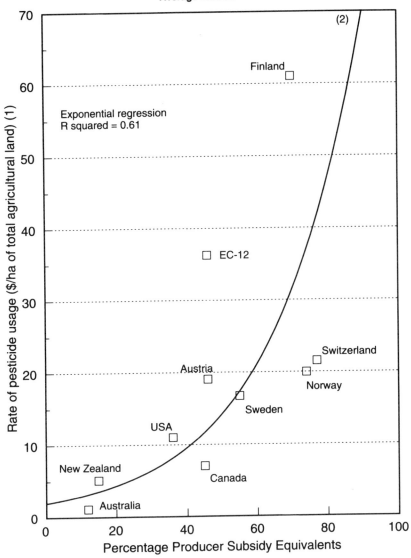

Notes: (1) Expenditures taken from OECD (1991). National currencies have been converted to US dollars by OECD's Purchasing Power Parities.
(2) Japan is included in the analysis but not shown. The relevant values are $378/ha and a PSE of 74%.

Source: OECD Secretariat

Figure 3: Energy consumption and producer assistance in OECD countries
Average 1986-89

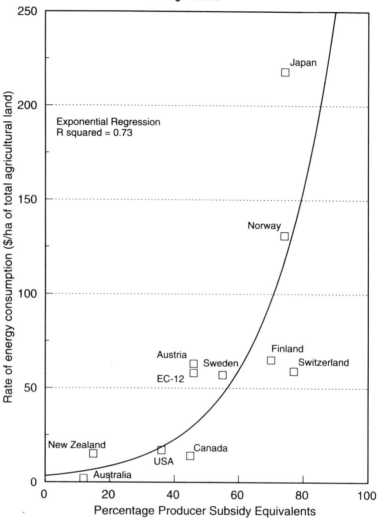

Notes: (1) Expenditures taken from OECD (1991). National currencies have been
converted to US dollars by OECD's Purchasing Power Parities.

Source: OECD Secretariat

Figure 4: Mechanisation and producer assistance in OECD countries
Average 1986-89

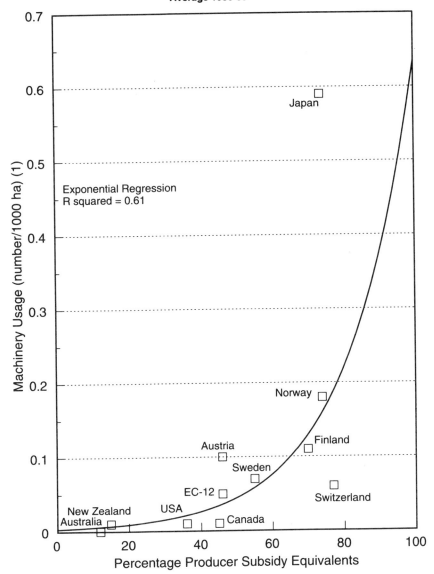

Notes: (1) Machinery usage measured in number/1000ha of total agricultural land

Source: OECD Secretariat

Notes

(1)   The commodities are fruit and vegetables, maize, cotton, rice, soya beans, wheat and sugar beet.

(2)   The definitions of the different agricultural land categories used in the analyses reported in this paper are those used by FAO: **arable land,** denotes temporary crops, temporary pastures, temporary fallow and kitchen gardens; **permanent crops** includes land cultivated with crops that occupy land for long periods and need not be annually replanted, such as fruit trees and vines; and **permanent pasture** covers pasture either cultivated or grazing land.

(3)   Case studies on Australia (OECD, 1987c), Austria (OECD, 1987d), Canada (OECD, 1987e), the European Community (OECD, 1987f), Japan (OECD, 1987g), New Zealand (OECD, 1987h) and the United States (OECD, 1987i) were published with National Policies and Agricultural Trade (OECD, 1987b). Since then further case studies have been published on Sweden (OECD, 1988b), Finland (OECD, 1989d), Norway (OECD, 1990b) and Switzerland (OECD, 1990c).

(4)   For a full explanation of the PSE and CSE methodology and its application to OECD agriculture, the reader is referred to CAHILL AND LEGG, 1990.

(5)   See OECD, 1988, 1989b, 1990a, 1991a and 1992b.

(6)   PSEs and CSEs are calculated for the production or consumption of 13 commodities: wheat, coarse grains, rice, oilseeds (soya beans, sunflower and rapeseed), sugar (in refined equivalents), milk, beef and veal, pig meat, poultry, eggs, sheep meat and wool.

(7) The Percentage PSE measures total assistance as a proportion of the farm gate value of agricultural production valued at domestic prices. It is an indicator of the **income transfer** caused by policy.

(8) The Producer Nominal Assistance Co-efficient is the border price plus the unit PSE (i.e. the value of assistance per unit of output volume) expressed as a ratio of the border price. It is an indicator of the **economic distortion** caused by policy.

(9) In these categories, by far the most popular of the individual measures used by OECD countries at the present are: **market price support** which is maintained by border measures (i.e. tariffs, import quotas, variable import levies, etc.); and **deficiency payments** (budgetary subsidies on output volume). Together they accounted for .. percent of total OECD assistance in 1991.

(10) The central explanation for these increases in total OECD assistance lies in: (a) increases in administered prices and in other forms of output related assistance measures: and (b) a fall in the world prices of PSE commodities. Since 1979, these declines in world prices were largely a reflection of the effects of the additional output associated with high and increasing levels of assistance.

(11) In the case of the estimated relationship involving the rate of fertilizer application, the actual application rate per hectare might be considerably higher than shown in Figure 1. This could be because the share of uncultivated grazing land in the total agricultural land area is relatively high (e.g. in Australia and the United States). However, the statistical correlation between the percentage PSE and fertilizer use per hectare of arable land (i.e. excluding land permanently under horticulture and permanent pasture) is also high according to the preliminary work by the OECD Secretariat.

(12) Between 1984 and 1991, the percentage PSE in New Zealand was reduced from 36 to only 4 percent, which is the lowest rate of agricultural assistance for any country in the OECD. The New Zealand experience in reducing agricultural support and the impacts this has had on the environment are reported in OECD (1992b).

(13) To a large extent, however, these problems were inherited from the period of high levels of agricultural support in New Zealand (viz. 1981-83). It was during this period that the expansion onto environmentally fragile land occurred, the consequences of which are only now beginning to be addressed. However, due to inadequate monitoring and too short a time lapse it has so far been difficult to quantify these effects on the environment.

(14) **Externalities** are positive or negative "spillover effects" of market transactions which affect the economic welfare of producers or consumers who are not parties to those transactions. Such spillovers are not themselves the object of market transactions as there is no monetary compensation for the gains or losses in welfare. As externalities are generated incidentally or externally to market activities they do not appear in the revenue and cost account for with the activity which generates them. However, for the individuals or firms affected by such spillovers or for society as a whole they represent real costs and benefits.

(15) **"Pure" public goods** are a product or service which, having been provided to one individual, must be consumed equally by all members of a community. The term does not imply that either the product or service in question is owned or provided by the state or that it is inherently beneficial or positive. A national defence system and the atmosphere are examples of pure public goods.

(16) An exposition of the issues associated with agricultural policies, farm incomes and the supply of environmental externalities and public goods may be found in OECD, 1992c.

(17) The opportunities in <u>Opportunities for Integration</u> identified included:
- Giving greater emphasis to environmental objectives in farm research and development, extension and advisory services;
- Improving the use of farm inputs and practices through education, advisory services, farm management plans and the introduction of charges;
- Using management agreements and other arrangements to improve landscape amenity and nature conservation;
- Enforcing environmental regulations more stringently and harmonizing regulatory standards and procedures;
- Making taxation measures more neutral between environmental and agricultural objectives;
- Making farm support conditional on farmers compiling with certain land-use conditions;
- Selective use of land set-aside policies.

References

Cahill, C. AND W. Legg (1990) "The Estimation of Agricultural Assistance Using Producer and Consumer Subsidy Equivalents: Theory and Practice." OECD Economic Studies, 13, Winter 1989-90.

OECD. Agricultural and Environmental Policy Integration: Recent Progress and New Directions. Paris: OECD, 1992.

OECD. Agricultural and Environmental Policies: Opportunities for Integration. Paris: OECD, 1989.

OECD. Agricultural Policies, Markets and Trade: Monitoring and Outlook 1988. Paris: OECD, 1988.

OECD. Agricultural Policies, Markets and Trade: Monitoring and Outlook 1989. Paris: OECD, 1989.

OECD. Agricultural Policies, Markets and Trade: Monitoring and Outlook 1990. Paris: OECD, 1990.

OECD. Agricultural Policies, Markets and Trade: Monitoring and Outlook 1991. Paris: OECD, 1991.

OECD. Agricultural Policies, Markets and Trade: Monitoring and Outlook 1992. Paris: OECD, 1992.

OECD. Agricultural Policy Reform and Public Goods. OECD/GD(92)56. Paris: OECD, 1992.

OECD. Communique: Committee for Agriculture at Ministerial Level. 27 March, SG/PRESS(92)27. Paris: OECD, 1992.

OECD. Communique: Environment Committee at Ministerial Level. 31 January, SG/PRESS(91)9. Paris: OECD, 1991.

OECD. Communique: OECD Council at Ministerial Level. 13 May, PRESS/A(87)27. Paris: OECD, 1987.

OECD. Communique: OECD Council at Ministerial Level. 1 June, PRESS/A(89)26. Paris: OECD, 1989.

OECD. Economic Accounts for Agriculture 1976-1989. Paris: OECD, 1991.

OECD. Environmental Indicators: A Preliminary Set. Paris: OECD, 1991.

OECD. National Policies and Agricultural Trade. Paris: OECD, 1987.

OECD. National Policies and Agricultural Trade: Country Study -- Australia. Paris: OECD, 1987.

OECD. National Policies and Agricultural Trade: Country Study -- Austria. Paris: OECD, 1987.

OECD. National Policies and Agricultural Trade: Country Study -- Canada. Paris: OECD, 1987.

OECD. National Policies and Agricultural Trade: Country Study -- European Community. Paris: OECD, 1987.

OECD. National Policies and Agricultural Trade: Country Study -- Finland. Paris: OECD, 1989.

OECD. National Policies and Agricultural Trade: Country Study -- Japan. Paris: OECD, 1987.

OECD. National Policies and Agricultural Trade: Country Study -- New Zealand. Paris: OECD, 1987.

OECD. National Policies and Agricultural Trade: Country Study -- Norway. Paris: OECD, 1990.

OECD. National Policies and Agricultural Trade: Country Study --
    Sweden. Paris: OECD, 1988.

OECD. National Policies and Agricultural Trade: Country Study --
    Switzerland. Paris: OECD, 1990.

OECD. National Policies and Agricultural Trade: Country Study --
    United States. Paris: OECD, 1987.

OECD. OECD Environmental Data Compendium 1991. Paris:
    OECD, 1991.

OECD. Reforming Agricultural Policies: Quantitative Restrictions
    on Production, Direct Income Support. Paris: OECD, 1990.

OECD. The State of the Environment. Paris: OECD, 1991.

Chapter 8

Effects of Agricultural Policies and Practices on the Environment in Developing Countries

Liberty Mhlanga

Africa, Latin America, and Latin America

Similarities and Differences

Agricultural policies in Africa, Asia, and Latin America have a number of similarities, based largely on their colonial past. They are high in plant productivity, have comparatively abundant water and solar radiation, high temperatures, and short periods of growth, all of which favor abundant biomass and high insect build-up. Furthermore, these regions' economies are characterized, on the whole, by producing what they do not consume and consuming what they do not produce. Their exports of tobacco, coffee, cocoa, tea, sugar, bananas, and many minerals and imports of wheat, corn maize, beans, wines, and other commodities tell part of the story. There are also many external factors which have fashioned agricultural policy-making. Differences arise mainly from factors like geographical location, culture, soil, climate, and flora and fauna on which these countries depend.

Factors that Impact Agricultural Production and Environmental Degradation

1. **Population.** In the coming forty years the world's population will expand to nine billion. Food consumption will nearly double worldwide, particularly in developing countries. To provide for this population explosion, world grain output will have to grow by about one and one-half percent each year, a formidable task considering that during the past thirty years a two percent increase per year has been achieved with difficulty. Grain accounts for three quarters of food crops consumed in developing countries. Demand for grain and other foods, fuel and fibre will greatly strain natural resources (e.g. soil, water, fish, and timber).

2. **Natural Resources**. Since natural resources have generally been undervalued, the management and accounting of these natural resources have to be done carefully. They need protection from the inadequate stewardship which is a result of poverty, ignorance, population pressure, and, in some cases, corruption. Many countries' policies inadequately recognize scarcity in the natural world, do not ensure that institutions managing natural resources are accountable, and fail to mobilize adequate knowledge for managing environmental problems. However, the United Nations Conference on Environment and Development (Rio, Brazil, June 1992) has given impetus to the notion of linking economic efficiency, income growth and environmental protection, and to breaking down the negative links between economic activity and the environment. This is a welcome development.

3. **Farmers**. Farmers have had to either expand the land mass they use for increased food production or intensify production areas already in use. The past two and a half decades demonstrate that increases in yields have accounted for a ninety-two percent increase in food production and area expansion for only eight percent of such increases. The main factors here have been use of chemicals and irrigation, both of which create problems elsewhere in the ecological system (e.g. environmental pollution and use of nonrenewable energy). These phenomena have been observed

particularly in Asia and Latin America where the "Green Revolution" has been experienced. Asia has also been hit by natural disasters.

4. **Technology.** In most developing regions, western type agriculture, with its high input technology, was predominate during post colonial times. However, in the 1980s, better knowledge of past failures, deep recession, and food scarcity gave rise to a search for alternatives and different approaches to agricultural development. The role of traditional farming practices was re-examined, resulting in the start of improvising and the creation of innovative "user-friendly" technologies. Developing countries have been sharing this knowledge during the last decade in order to find 1) new plant strains with a natural resistance to pests, drought and disease; and 2) ways to increase crop yields without further damaging and polluting land and water resources. Examples include the research being under taken by the International Rice Research Institute (IRRI) and the International Maize and Wheat Improvement Center (CIMMYI) in Mexico (which is breeding varieties more resistant to the borer, the main maize pest).

Africa

Richly Endowed Yet Constantly in Crisis

Africa is in many ways a richly endowed continent. It has vast soil reserves, water, superb flora and fauna, and a mosaic of human populations with cultures and histories as vibrant as any worldwide.

However, in spite of massive infusions of aid and the adoption of countless new strategies for development and policies, Africa suffers from a food crisis, a poverty crisis, a debt crisis, and an environmental crisis. The poignancy of hunger and suffering is constantly present. Thousands of learned reports and expert analyses pinpoint widespread ecological disasters across large tracts of the continent. Bankers wrestle, unsuccessfully, with its debt crisis. Wars and civil wars reinforce environmental breakdown, creating a situation where almost one African in every one hundred is a refugee. The more than seventy-five coups since 1945 and political instability make it seemingly risky for capital investment. Meanwhile, Africa's population is increasing rapidly. Because of these crises, unlike the rest of the third world which is developing, Africa is regressing.

The Recurring Drought

Africa has had droughts historically. Droughts do not automatically lead to famine. Some experts state that when growth based on exploitation supersedes prudence, good husbandry and the recycling of local resources, communities living at the margins cannot survive. This seems to be the case in many parts of Africa.

When the 1983-85 drought hit thirty African countries, human suffering caught the attention of the West as never before. For the continent, the immediate crisis was an apocalyptic upheaval that left almost no aspect of life untouched. Despite reminders from the Sahelian drought in the 1970s, no policy planners had anticipated such a situation. In Niger, the land was stripped bare when the Harmattan wind blew south from the Sahara. For the first time in living memory, the Niger River dried to a string of pools. Half a million nomads had moved into the cities by 1985. In Ethiopia, eight million people were affected. As the price of scarce grain trebled, farmers sold their sheep, goats, young cattle, mules, asses, cows and draft oxen at half the normal price. Then people sold their ploughs, hoes, and seed for the following year, turned to boiled roots and leaves, and sent off husbands and sons in search of work or help. In the Sudan, the Nile recorded the lowest flood in 350 years. Ten million people were adversely affected. Zimbabwe's maize harvest in 1982 and 1984 was down by a third of the 1981 yield and more than two thirds down by 1983. Zimbabwe prides itself for prudence, proper agricultural policies and efficiency in food production technology.

By 1985-86, the immediate danger had receded and less concern was felt in the North and in Africa. It should be noted that the famines of 1983-85 were not a sudden isolated disaster, but the visible signs of a deeper malady. The return of rainfall allowed the more sensational symptoms to recede. Droughts will certainly erupt again and again until the underlying syndrome is treated. No amount of policies, it seems, will pull Africa out of these crises immediately. A great deal of damage has already been done and the task of repairing it is that much harder. However, solutions have to be evolved to pull the continent out of the crises.

Zimbabwe

Zimbabwe is not necessarily unique but it has shown a few hopeful signs. Between 1980 and 1985 many of Zimbabwe's peasants moved from subsistence to dynamic commercial farming and from yields far below the low continental average to yields in some cases ahead of large scale white commercial farmers. Availability of improved seed, market, credit, and transportation, fair pricing of maize, and good rains were partly responsible for the increased production by Zimbabwean peasants.

Land Settlement

This progress, however, was not achieved without difficulty or pitfalls though. During the late nineteenth century, white settlers began seizing vast tracts of the best land in Zimbabwe and by the 1930s controlled half the country. This division was formalized in 1969 with the Land Tenure Act which gave 16 million hectares of prime agricultural land to 6,700 white farmers. The same amount of land, three quarters of which was marginally suitable for pasture in the so-called communal areas, was allocated to 100 times as many black farmers. This land division still persists today with very little modification. The transition on the ground between these black and white areas is often as distinct as a boundary on a map, especially during the dry season.

A number of policies were initiated by the former governments of what is now Zimbabwe to reinforce land division.

The Land Apportionment Act alienated land in the 1930s. The Native Land Husbandry Act was promulgated in 1951 supposedly to improve natural resources conservation and agricultural productivity in the communal areas. In order to put the burden of supervising conservation under traditional leaders, the Tribal Trust Lands Act was promulgated in 1967 and the Land Husbandry Act in 1970. These measures were harsh and very unpopular with the blacks and have made it difficult for the proper resource conservation measures to be fully accepted today among the communal area people.

As a result, new land resettlement policies in Zimbabwe function under the psychology that peasants are unconvinced that they should really be concerned with environmental conservation. However, the Zimbabwean Government now says that projects of any significant size, including agricultural ones, need an environmental impact study component in order to be accepted for execution.

Agricultural Methods

The Zimbabwean peasant has at his/her disposal the white farmer's modern methods of farm operations. However, their agricultural practices are dependent on high inputs of chemical fertilizer, insecticides, fungicides, and herbicides and on heavy machinery dependent on fossil fuel. In the long run, this path of agricultural development and policies is not sustainable.

Missing Linkages

In Zimbabwe, as in many other countries, there is a heavy dependence on policies which look at individual sectors which do not link up with other sectors or activities. Research for the commercial farming sector does not provide a basis that can be easily linked to the requirements of the peasant. Linkages are also missing, for instance, in research on seed (what areas it is suited for, storage methods, transport to the market, and relationship with nutrition for humans and livestock).

The Way Ahead for Sustainable African Agriculture

Combining Research and Project Studies

For proper, environmentally useful agricultural policies, both at national and international levels, systems of crops, livestock, trees, forestry, and horticulture should be linked. In reality, however, the research stations for each of these are separate. Although projects on livestock (in Ethiopia), agro-forestry (in Kenya), and crop research (in Nigeria), are done in separate countries, they could be combined to produce useful and demonstrable examples of what a farmer/peasant deals with on a day-to-day basis. There are very few African farmers who deal only with monocultural crops or just one crop. Many peasant farmers will keep livestock and grow food crops, fruit trees, fodder crops, and trees, even on small land holdings. Research and policies should be structured to help farmers and preserve the environment and should study systems similar to what the farmer grapples with daily.

Developing Coherent Agricultural Policies

Most developing countries lack coherent agricultural policies. Changing governments, who in many cases fight to keep power by military might rather than by delivering those factors which help the man-in-the-street, further hinders policy continuity. Good governance is therefore an important prerequisite to sustained agriculture.

Eliminating the Conflict Between Modern and Traditional Agriculture

Where there are scarce resources (e.g. inputs to increase corp production), the environment is sacrificed. Where there are ample inputs (e.g. chemicals, draught power, transportation, finance), the application of these on the environment is usually detrimental. There need not be this conflict between modern and traditional agriculture. This is especially so if there is careful observation of some of the traditional means of food production which have stood the test of time but have not been fully explored for use under present extremely demanding circumstance, especially as a result of high population.

Improving Access to International Markets

When it comes to international trade, some of the products from developing countries certainly need ready access to these markets via GATT. Many agricultural raw materials coming from developing countries do not have value added to them by way of processing before they are exported to developed countries. This obviously deprives developing countries of a source that could be quite lucrative to their economies.

Managing Local Resource Bases

The solution in all regions lies, partly, in the evolution of policies which make it possible for individual farmers and communities to be in charge of managing their local resource bases. This means, for the most part, the empowerment of women, who produce up to 80 percent of agricultural commodities, so they can own and protect their local environments.

Conclusion

Changes in many policy areas are necessary in order to promote agricultural growth based on environmentally sound principles. Good governance is essential both within Africa and globally. Global equity based on economic opportunity through fair pricing is important in this regard. Redress must be had of the sometimes deliberate neglect of the indigenous management techniques of local resource bases. Greater efforts at harmonizing the positive practices of indigenous agriculture and environmentally benign practices from western-based agriculture are needed.

Sharing resources between the West and Africa is an important prerequisite. It is also assumed that African governments are willing to recognize the value of local knowledge and resources and the public is clearly accountable. Moreover, serious efforts must be made to make policies that are implementable.

The one issue that is of paramount importance is that the small producer must remain the center piece of agricultural production in Africa. National policy that ignores this situation will not promote sustained agricultural production that is in harmony with sound environmental principles.

Chapter 9

Response to Section II Speakers

Jan Sonneveld

(Transcribed from conference tapes.)

Agricultural Commodities Are Subjected to Different Policies

I have noticed that not all participants have the same ideas about what agricultural policies are related to what kinds of commodities. Not all commodities are subjected to the same agricultural policy.

Extensive farm agricultural commodities, arable crops, and milk are subjected to rather stringent agricultural policies. On the other hand, the higher value and higher input commodities like animal husbandry and horticultural products are rather free and are not subjected to agricultural policies (certainly not to market and price policies). If you are asked then, how do agricultural policies affect the environment, you should know at least what kind of commodities are subjected to what kinds of policies.

Market and Price Policies Are Environmentally Blind

I agree with one of the previous speakers that market and price policies and international trade are blind as far as the environment is concerned for they cannot distinguish between commodities which are produced in an environmental friendly way or not. The market and price policies which prevail in the

Community are not responsible for the environmental problems, nor can they be used to solve them.

On the other hand, in my country we have major environmental problems with the intensive farming system (e.g. horticulture and animal husbandry). In these sectors, we do not even have policies to guide the market price. So, here we have to take specific measures. As specific measures are certainly not blind, they have been pointedly directed towards the environmental problems.

The ambition of the Commission was to change market price policies, among others, in order to have a better environmental affect on production. That was far too ambitious. Although some measures were proposed, they did not materialize and we are left with a set of policy instruments which will not improve very much the environmental conditions of production. The only one I can remember is the slaughter premium which will be connected and commissioned by the number of cows per hectare.

Income Transfer Policies

Income transfer policies are compensation for lower prices. The question is whether those policies are also blind. Not necessarily (as Minister Bukman said). This might be the policy instrument which could be used to improve the environmental conditions of the production. I am in favor of that approach, but we are not at all ready to do this at this moment nor will we be ready to set up a set of acceptable criteria with which we can agree for international trade. If that is true, then at this very moment, we should not quarrel much longer about the green box measures. This income subsidy will go into the green box. But how green is the green box? We have to decide later. There is ample time.

Uruguay Round Should Be Concluded Now

I was also a little surprised that the United States was pressing too much for a one time solution. Here we have a good example of why we should take more time. I think now is the time to conclude the Uruguay Round. Things are moving and we have a nice issue on our agenda for the next round. What should we do with the income measures for instance? To what extent should they serve the purpose of the environment? These kinds of measures should be handled by ministries of agriculture or else impractical practices might be developed.

Section III: Reforming Agricultural Practices and Policies to Protect the Environment

An Outline of the Issues

A number of countries are exploring ways to reform their agricultural policies in order to make them less environmentally damaging. The speakers in this session discussed ways Germany, Japan, and the Republic of South Africa have shifted their agricultural policies and made recommendations for other countries. The important role that farmers may play in this reformation was also illuminated.

In addressing these issues, the speakers answered the following questions:
- What kinds of policy tools are being employed as a means to achieve environmental goals and to address environmental problems?
- What effect will these reforms have on farmers, agribusiness, and consumers?
- What roles should farmers, governments, and agribusiness play in enforcing sustainable farming and agribusiness practices?
- How can and should the costs of complying with environmentally conscious policies and regulations be distributed?
- How far should one go in introducing environmental criteria into agricultural policies?
- Should the goal be the same in all countries or should a differential be established between developed and developing countries?

Chapter 10

Assisting Farmers in Meeting the Challenges of the Market and the Environment

H.O.A. Kjeldsen

Introduction

Thank you for the invitation to speak at this conference on a theme which probably contains the biggest challenge to farming for the years to come, namely to adjust itself both to the market and to the environment without losing income and potential for further development.

I am a farmer from Denmark, a country that has had agricultural traditions for centuries. Furthermore, Denmark is one of the leading countries as regards environmental protection and environmental regulations on agriculture and is a major food-exporting country. Therefore, I believe I have some personal experience on this subject.

But, today, I am speaking as the President of the International Federation of Agricultural Producers (IFAP). Our federation represents 500 million farmers from 80 national organizations, half of which are in developing countries.

Farmers Are The Guardians of the Earth

Agriculture is a basic economic activity for a lot of people worldwide and a precondition for the development of a sustainable society in all countries. More than any other profession, farming takes place in close contact with nature. Farmers produce renewable resources using solar energy as input.

For centuries, the family farmer has been the effective guardian and steward of much of the earth's natural resources. Farmers all over the world have to conserve their environment because they are dependent upon it for their livelihood. Every farmer wishes to leave an enhanced resource base for the future.

Agriculture Can Adversely Effect the Environment

However, agriculture inevitably effects its surroundings. Agriculture and all other human activities are in themselves a disturbance of the natural ecosystems. The important matter is to assure that this influence is the least possible.

Agriculture is never the less a must when taking care of the need for food, feed, and clothing. Certain imbalances in intensive farming systems need to be corrected, but one must not go to extremes. We must face reality. By the turn of the century, there will be 900 million more people to feed. The proper application of agro-chemicals to avoid a substantial drop in yields and considerable losses in storage is therefore necessary, but it has to be on a sustainable level. I believe that most farmers are aware of their responsibilities both to nature and to the coming generations.

In agriculture, as in all other businesses, the awareness of the adverse effects of human activities on the environment has evolved gradually. Until adverse effects on natural ecosystems or other surroundings have been observed, actions will be necessary to prevent these effects.

However, there are very large differences as regards the vulnerability of the ecosystems and landscapes in different parts of the world. In some countries, the risks of water pollution, erosion, and desertification are higher than in others. Therefore, it would be most expedient to move production from highly vulnerable to less vulnerable places. This, however, is not possible. The need for food and, therefore, production is worldwide. Low income countries are very often living on the edge of sustainability as regards both agricultural production and economic stability. The need for food and foodstuffs is prior to all other needs. Hence, in these countries, poverty is the root cause of environmental degradation.

How Practices Should Be Reformed

A shift towards environmentally sound technology, education, and training in using this technology is essential. For example, research and extension of Food for Help programs is one way in which industrialized countries can (or rather should) be committed to making agriculture sustainable in those countries.

Farming practices, respecting the environment, require not only accurate and reliable techniques, education, research and development but favorable economic and social frameworks as well. These policies must be in harmony with each other.

Agricultural Policies and the Environment

As agricultural practices effect the environment, so do agricultural policies. Lack of a good price policy in developing countries is impeding a shift from subsistence farming to commercial farming. Poverty is forcing some farmers even to eat the seed needed for next year's crop or to let their cattle graze where there is little grass left. The debt burden is pushing developing countries to produce more and more coffee and cocoa for export, even though the prices of coffee and cocoa are at the lowest level in 18 years. This pressure from debt and low export prices has serious environmental consequences and leads to both over-exploitation of the land and to farmers abandoning the land.

The aim of a future agricultural policy must be to ensure needed food supplies and reasonable incomes for farmers and to minimize the effects on the surrounding environment. Within the agricultural policies of industrialized countries, there are a number of actions to ensure the protection of the environment, such as regulations on the use of fertilizers and pesticides and programs for extensification of the most vulnerable areas.

Fertilizers and pesticides are important for food production in sufficient quantities and of quality. It is, of course, in the interest of the environmental groups and countries' environmental departments that only pesticides with little or no adverse effects on the surroundings are used in the agricultural sector. It is also in the interest of the farmers themselves; if the pesticides pollute the ecosystems, they also destroy the farmer's production system and, hence, his way of earning an income. They also destroy his health and that of his family.

However, it is highly important for farmers to have equal opportunities of earning and income. Therefore, very strict environmental legislation may adversely effect farm incomes. If farmers in one country cannot use the optimal pesticides, they are not able to compete with other farmers. This is an essential problem, which only can be solved by international initiatives.

If strict environmental regulations are enforced, farmers may consequently not be able to keep their farms economically sustainable. This leads to a decrease in the number of farms and farmers and effects the whole socio-economic structure. The single farmer cannot pass on his expenditures for environmental regulations to consumers, since farm prices are fixed eternally.

The Optimal Solution

The optimal solution would be if consumers were willing to pay production costs, including environmental costs, at the farm level. But, unfortunately, I regard this only as theoretical. The only possible way, therefore, is to compensate the farmer for income loss due to environmental regulations in general.

Farming practices are altered with agricultural policy reforms, and technological developments. However, changes in agricultural policy often lead to very rapid changes in production conditions. If there is no room for economic adjustments, farms shut down.

Farmers Are Willing to Change Practices

Farmers are willing to change their practices if at all possible. There is, however, a lag: if a farmer has invested in one production system, he cannot buy a new one until the investment has been paid back. Political demands for radical changes in agricultural production therefore need to allow the farmer sufficient time to make the necessary adjustments.

Where intensive farming methods are used, efforts are needed to move towards integrated systems, a more careful use of agro-chemicals, more diversification in crop growing, greater emphasis on mechanical weed control, and well balanced use of manure, fertilizers, and pesticides.

Especially as regards pesticides, it is very important that farmers and employees are well educated. Improper and excessive use may lead to the destruction of ecosystems, such as can be seen now in the former Soviet Union and in some developing countries. Also, we in the industrialized countries must not export to the developing countries pesticides and herbicides which we have banned at home.

Environmental Issues Deserve International Attention

The possibilities for producing non-food agricultural products on areas which are set aside in the new Common Agricultural Policy can offer an important environmental improvement.

It is most important for the farmers that environmental issues are incorporated in future GATT negotiations, especially the issues of usage of pesticides or fertilizers, desertification, deforestation, and erosion. Without international regulation, distorted competition will be witnessed. Production will be moved to those parts of the world where regulation is absent.

The Relationship Between Urban and Rural Areas

Farmers are not only producers of food but also the custodians of natural resources. The efforts of the farmers on behalf of the environment are not rewarded in the product's price. Farmers also need to be rewarded for their countryside management roles, including preservation of wildlife, habitats, and endangered species and the maintenance of genitive resources, recreation, and leisure facilities. The use of clean sewage sludge from cities on crop land illustrates very clearly the interdependence of urban and rural areas in the recycling of resources.

Insufficient attention is given to the fact that agriculture itself is often the victim of environmental degradation such as acid rain, industrial pollution, and damages caused by visitors to the countryside.

Sustainable Development Is a Shared Endeavor

IFAP recognizes that each farmer is responsible individually for the effects of his farming activities on the environment. However, it is the responsibility of firms supplying agricultural inputs as well to develop ecologically adapted technology. It is the responsibility of governments not to force the pace of change of adjusting to new conservation requirements at a speed which is faster than technical innovation and financial possibilities permit. And, it is up to the EC and GATT to see that environmental regulations do not lead to distortions in competition.

Mutual cooperation is essential; the adoption of sustainable practices cannot be successfully imposed from above. Farmers participation is crucial. The general public must come to recognize that the farmer is the key to the development of an ecologically sustainable society based upon renewable resources.

Solutions must be global. Environmental issues know no boundaries. Hunger, poverty, third world debt, instability of farm commodity prices, rules for fair competition, and harmonization of legislation on food safety can have dramatic effects on the environment in which farmers operate. There is a need to establish international rules for the protection of the environment, particularly where these effect world trade. Therefore, environmental questions have to form a strong component of the next GATT round.

Finally, you do not help the environment by squeezing the farmers economically. It must be clearly understood that only an economically viable agriculture is capable of achieving the objectives of environmental sustainability. Therefore, farmers need fair prices for their products, fair trading conditions which include environmental considerations, a sound infrastructure, and secure land tenure.

Chapter 11

Reforming Agricultural Policies and Practices in Germany

Walter Kittel

(Transcribed from conference tapes.)

I would like to briefly touch upon the following items: 1) the importance of environmental aspects in farm policy; 2) present instruments; 3) outlook, the so-called new approach; and 4) allocation of costs. I do so not to differ from any Minister or anyone here but to explain the decisions of the European Community. The Netherlands played a very constructive role in advancing these decisions and, as any other member country, is bound by them. I speak as an economist who spent more years in Brussels than in Bonn and more years in trade policy than I will ever be able in agriculture.

Importance of Environmental Issues in Agricultural Policy

The landmark decisions of the European Communities on CAP reform contain *inter alia* incentives for less intensive, more extensive farming, acreage and headage premiums, and set-aside. Our set-aside scheme is a bit different from that in the United States as we simultaneously introduce that system on a practically mandatory basis and we decrease our prices by 30 percent. We also have accompanying policies that represent very positive incentives, especially for forestation, ecological zones, special extensification, and an early retirement scheme.

On the national level, the Federal Republic is a highly developed, densely populated, industrial country, even after the reunification. We appreciate very much our partner's contribution to that historic event. We have 220 inhabitants per square kilometer. In the Netherlands the rate is 350, even a little bit more. But please, gentlemen from around the globe, look at your figures and then you will see that even the conditions of agriculture and of agricultural production are very much influenced by figures like that. In national agricultural policy, the farming sector has to meet increasing demands of the modern, industrialized, and recreational society, such as protection of the environment, conservation of species and natural resources, and preservation and management of varied, attractive man-made landscapes.

The specific measures in the EC scheme have a very important effect in directing the scheme we are discussing. But, they are not compensation for income transfers which have another reason, the historical price reduction within three years. So, we should not mix both events together.

Conservation and development of natural resources is as important as the other three priority aims of my government's agricultural policy: equal participation in general income development; secure supply with high quality food; and contribution to the solution of problems in the world farm trade and food sector (including GATT).

Environmental policy for the farm sector has two aims: a positive one and another preventive one. First, it aims to avoid future social costs and to reduce existent environmental problems caused by intensification and specialization, costs that are transferred to certain parties. Secondly, it aims to create social benefits -- active support of the contribution by the farm sector to the rest of the society, the preservation of man-made landscapes, and the creation of habitats for many species of life, flora, and fauna.

Instruments of Environmental Policies in Agriculture

Environmental policy in the agricultural sector has hitherto been based on the national and regional levels on the following measures:
- legal provisions, like imposing limits on the use of organic fertilizers (at the regional level, we already have some experience with that scheme) and on the type of farm management near drinking water sources;
- financial incentives like regional nature conservation programs;
- voluntary participation on the part of farmers in training, advisory services, research and development;
- undertaking by farmers to control the use of fertilizers and pesticides in an economically sensible and ecologically acceptable way;
- the idea to convince the farmers what is useful in their own interests, but sometimes they do not see it that way.

Measures have started to show an impact but there are still a lot of problems, like the accumulation of nitrates in groundwater and the decline in the number of wildlife species.

New Approaches to Promote Environmentally Benign Farming

For Environmental Policies

Environmental policies should live up to the following criteria:
- achieve environmental aims in the best way economically possible;
- avoid distortion of competition and other problems in international trade;
- be easily administered and enforced;
- restrict entrepreneurial decisions of farmers as little as possible; and

- take account of farmers' income situations.

Basic principles should be as market-oriented as possible and require as much government intervention as necessary.

For Government

The government's policies should go in the following direction:
- In the field of agricultural market policy, measures must be taken to reach a better market equilibrium by means of supply management and price control. This is why the CAP reform of May 1992 goes in the right direction.
- Environmental legislation should be applied to those cases in which it is indispensable to immediately, directly, and safely avoid environmental damage. If, in individual cases, this goes beyond the requirement of good agricultural practice, farmers must receive suitable compensatory payments (e.g. in areas in which no fertilizers and pesticides are allowed).
- Grant programs must be widened, particularly in granting premiums for active countryside management for farmers. Examples are the already mentioned policies that accompany CAP reform and the pilot project in the federal state of Baden-Würtenberg for market relief and to maintain landscapes.
- In the future, attention must also be paid to taxing yield increasing inputs. But, there is still a need for further research on the economic impact depending on location and type of crop and solution of income and income distribution problems. In addition, one must take into consideration distortion of competition on national and international levels. Support will be given from our side to a Dutch initiative with the EC Commission that proposes to examine that question. I think it is also important to develop a good cost/benefit analysis, to include organic fertilizers in that exercise, and to promote training and advisory services.

For Farmers

The farmers options are:
- to follow the principle of sustainability. We are convinced that in the long run you can only obtain economic benefits if you conserve natural resources.
- to limit the use of yield increasing inputs through the economic optimum. In doing so, they should make use of tools like the threshold principle in plant protection and, therefore, strictly adhere to the principle of commensurability and techniques to measure the nitrogen content of the soil.
- to undertake controls on their own.

For Agribusiness

Agribusiness options include:
- The pesticide industry should produce environmentally friendly pesticides.
- Plant breeders should breed plants with a natural resistance to harmful organisms.
- Agricultural machinery should concentrate on equipment suitable to the location and the environment.
- Traders should be active to improve the marketing of green products.

Distribution of costs

As a rule, the polluters principle should also be applied to farming. But there are some limits to the application of this principle: 1) it is often difficult or costly to measure environmental damage; 2) often the polluter cannot be identified clearly; and 3) the assessment of environmental damage is difficult (e.g. the loss of an extinct species).

Furthermore, one must take into consideration the income distribution inside the farming sector. Farm policy is for man and for the man-made landscape and, of course, policy is always to find the right balance between different and sometimes divergent positions. Therefore, grant schemes in the environmental sector must be extended. One advantage of subsidies not related to production is that they make it easier to compensate farmers for losses resulting from legal obligations in the environmental field. So, we are in a better situation now in the Community.

In the context of GATT, it is necessary that environmental policy gets a higher rank and priority. So far, I recommend Minister Bukman's idea of code of conduct in the environmental field in order to avoid distortion of competition at the international level.

In conclusion, I think we in the EC are on the way and moving in the right direction. I do regret that there was no spokesman from the European Commission to explain that better than I am able to do. I think that what we need is to use and apply our decision and to gain public acceptance inside and outside the Community. It is certainly not the moment to discuss changes of the new system of income transfers.

Chapter 12

Reforming Japan's Agricultural Policies

Jiro Shiwaku

(Transcribed from conference tapes.)

I would like to focus my presentation on sustainable development and agricultural policies in Japan by dividing the agenda into three parts. First, I would like to take up how Japanese agriculture has traditionally been relatively sustainable. Secondly, I would like to explain how events, particularly during the 1960s and 1970s when we experienced rapid economic growth, have brought about conflict between agriculture and environment. Thirdly, I would like to speak about the development of a new set of policies which we are now developing, particularly in relation to sustainable agriculture policy.

The Sustainability of Japanese Agriculture

Japan is located in the northeastern region of the Asian monsoon zone. The climate is warm and rainfall is frequent, about three times as heavy as in many European countries and on the west coast of the United States. Seventy percent of Japan's land is mountainous and, as a result of the high rainfall, is vulnerable to soil erosion.

In such a climate, the Japanese have developed a unique style of agriculture with rice farming as its core. The paddy fields, which account for nearly half of the arable land in Japan, are generally terraced in small embankments. These terraces help to retain water for irrigation and to regulate the flow when rainfall is heavy. Thus, they control flooding and prevent soil erosion. The soil in paddy fields is saturated under the water, thereby helping to kill bugs and pests and allowing rice cultivation year after year on the same fields. Oxidation is also slow under the water, so fewer nutrients are required. The multifunctional aspects of paddy field farming have allowed the Japanese to enjoy an uninterrupted history of more than 2,000 years of rice cultivation.

These factors mean that Japanese agriculture is generally more sustainable than agriculture in the West. With its agriculture centered around rice farming, the rural community of Japan plays multifaceted roles in providing the public with a wide range of benefits, including: flood control and the prevention of landslides and soil erosion, the provision of ground water supply, the preservation of biodiversity, the maintenance and enhancement of greenery and natural environment, and the provision of areas in which urban dwellers can come to relax. Farming areas are also characterized by the traditional culture represented by seasonal festivals and the sense of unity that has its origins in rice farming traditions.

Rice farming is based on irrigation which is only successful with the cooperation of all farmers in a given area. Even now that many of the members of traditional farm households have migrated to the cities, this sense of unity still lives deep in the hearts of the people and strengthens urban-rural relationships that may otherwise be tense. This can be considered one of the reasons why there have not been many conflicts between agriculture and the environment in Japan. Although recently the populations in farming communities have increasingly become a mix of urban and rural workers, many traditions are still maintained and constitute a feature of rural life.

Events During the 1960s and 1970s

During periods of economic growth, significant structural changes have occurred in Japanese agriculture. As peoples' tastes have been westernized, livestock farming and horticulture have increased, while rice farming has shrunk in contrast. The need to boost productivity in order to compete with other industries has changed agriculture. Manpower has been replaced by greater capital expenditure and agro-chemicals, thus contributing to environmental problems.

During the 1960s, Japan experienced a period of rapid economic growth. Along with its benefits, it also brought environmental deterioration, and water for agricultural irrigation was polluted by household and industrial waste water. One result was a reduction in agricultural output. Another was the contamination of farmer and agricultural products by pollutants, such as heavy metals. For example, we have experienced contamination by cadmium and other industrial chemicals. Since those times, however, the situation has improved somewhat through the enforcement of emission control legislation and the development of waste-water treatment technologies. Contaminated agricultural soil has also been replaced in some areas.

Changes in Japanese Agriculture

Under traditional Japanese agriculture practices, crop residues (such as rice stalks) and manure were always recycled locally. As agricultural technology has progressed, however, significant changes have occurred:
- Agriculture has become more dependent on chemical fertilizers and pesticides. As agro-chemicals have become more readily available, farmers have started to use them as either precautionary or safety measures rather than in response to an actual threat from pests or crop nutrient demand.
- As farmers have become increasingly specialized in either livestock or crop farming, fewer crop residues and less animal wastes have been recycled on farms.
- Yet, another change has been in the composition of rural populations. Increasing numbers of non-farmers have been moving into the rural communities, where naturally they live near the farms. This has brought out into the open such problems as smells from livestock farms, water

144

pollution from animal waste, and environmental pollution from pesticides. More recently, fertilizer has been cited as one of the contributory factors in the eutrophication of inland bodies of water in certain areas.

Counter Measures

Some measures are being taken to counter these problems. For livestock farming, measures include legislation such as the Water Pollution Act to regulate the emission of waste water and the Maloder Prevention Act to control the emission of smells from stockyards and to provide specification for the construction of cow shacks and the like. Loans are also available to build waste water treatment plants or to facilitate the relocation of stockyards to more remote areas.

For pesticides, measures include the Pesticide Act which allows the cancellation of legislation of pesticides such as DDT that have a serious impact on the environment. Alternatively, the use of such pesticides can be restricted. Also, pest forecasting is facilitating a more precise and timely application of pesticides while environmentally friendly pest management technologies, such as the use of natural predators or less harmful viruses, is also being developed.

For fertilizers, measures include legislation to enforce the appropriate use of fertilizers in lake basins that are threatened with eutrophication. Methods that prevent fertilizer from entering the water supply are also being promoted. Deep soil application and paste fertilizers are just two of the methods in use.

A New Set of Policies

Peoples' interest has been shifting recently from quantitative satisfaction to the quality of life and spiritual fulfillment. Nowadays, values that cannot be measured in terms of money or efficiency -- values such as culture or greenery -- are being

145

reevaluated. Against this background, there is growing concern to make agricultural areas viable.

Conversely, Japanese agriculture and rural areas are in decline. The aging of rural inhabitants, the depopulation of rural areas, the lack of successors, increased tracks of abundant farm land, and reduced income as a result of either market destabilization or cuts in support prices are some of the many reasons for this decline. If the decline in Japanese agriculture is ignored, then there is a possibility that not only the security of the food supply but also the many other functions of agriculture, such as the maintenance of rural landscape and flood control, will be lost.

MAFF's Initiatives

The Ministry of Agriculture, Forestry and Fisheries (MAFF) initiated a study to identify the direction that agriculture should take into the 21st century. After a year of discussions that took into account not only the views of agricultural parties but also of the general public, we finalized a report in June 1992. The report is titled <u>The Basic Direction of New Policies for Food, Agriculture, and Rural Areas</u>. The report offers suggestions on the fostering of viable farm successors, expanding the scale of farming operations, making a clear distinction between land for agricultural and other uses to avoid sprawl and inefficiency, improving the infrastructure for agricultural production and rural life, developing rural industries, promoting green tourism, and so on. In addition to these objectives, the report gives high priority to environmental issues and the need to develop and implement environmentally friendly agricultural methods.

More specifically, the three priority areas identified as regards environmentally friendly agriculture are:
- Lower the input of pesticides and fertilizers and bring agriculture into harmony with the environment without compromising productivity. To make this possible, levels of use for agricultural chemicals will be reviewed and environmentally friendly technologies for input materials,

crop varieties, and farming methods will be researched and developed.
- Promote the recycling of animal and other wastes. To make this possible, animal waste composting and deodorizing technologies will be developed and the recycling of industrial waste from sectors such as the food processing industry will be promoted.
- Enhance public awareness of the many and varied functions of agriculture and rural areas, including the maintenance of natural landscapes and traditional cultures and flood control. A national consensus will be sought to gain widespread support for these functions. In addition, aesthetic quality and ecological preservation will be pursued in improving the rural infrastructure.

Chapter 13

A South African Perspective

A. I. van Niekerk

Plants, animals, soil, water, and air are natural resources which serve mankind. When properly managed by agriculture and industry, they perform well; but when abused, a dear price is paid in terms of our social and economic well-being and environmental quality.

There is no quick fix to right an environmental wrong. Even the most stringent policy cannot prevent a deterioration of resources if a number of factors or conditions not only coincide but cooperate in a conservation based action.

Any reformative or preventative policy can only be successful when it is backed by a suitable advisory and research capacity. Since such reform implies new actions and approaches, it has to be guided and pampered by incentives and rewards.

Furthermore, reform can only take effect if the people on all levels of society are concerned and involved, accept the reforms, and are capable of handling and managing the problems. In the African context, reformative agricultural policy should also be in line with cultural and economic realities to be successful. Knowledge and training increase the acceptance of implementing the right actions and maintaining the momentum of reform policies. Therefore, effective training is seen as part of reform and as an important prerequisite.

The more reform policies are implemented, the more training facilities and opportunities will have to be established. This is the starting point of reformative agricultural policy in Africa if we are to solve the problems of rural and, particularly, communal land use. The extent and vision of training the trainers will determine the success of any policy regardless of how well structured it is or how morally acceptable that policy or action might be.

The Realities of South Africa

South Africa has a unique, diverse, and vulnerable natural resource base:

- Total size is 120 million hectares, of which 95 million hectares are available for *agriculture.
- 35 million people with an annual population growth rate of 2.8 percent per annum.
- The present population density per hectare of arable land is approximately 2.5 or 0.4 hectare of arable land per capita.
- Climate varies from sub-tropical to semi-arid conditions.
- Only 13 percent of the land is suitable for crop production. Only about four percent of the land is of high potential, of which one million hectares are irrigated.
- The important livestock industry is supported dominantly by natural vegetation, mostly of a low grazing capacity.
- The economy, in general, and agricultural industry, in particular, are dualistic in character, with commercial and noncommercial or subsistence sectors.
- The Republic of South Africa (RSA) is comprised of developed and developing sectors. Each sector poses its own demands in terms of resource allocation, infrastructure, research, support services, and social or cultural problems.
- The land is characterized by a soil type highly susceptible to wind and water erosion and subjected to extremes in climatic conditions.

Yet, South Africa is able to produce enough basic agricultural products to export and to supply the nation with high quality nutritious food.

Policy Tools Employed to Address Environmental Problems

Service Structures

A strong agricultural service structure for research and extension is needed (approximately 3,000 qualified researchers at ten research institutes and more than 10,000 qualified and dedicated workers involved in extension).

Research actions aimed at improving environmental quality include the biological control of pests and alien plant species (Acacia, Hakea, Prosopis, Pereskia); plant breeding aimed at resistance against diseases and pests and for tolerance to physiological stress, such as droughts; the optimal use of fertilizer; the optimal use of water for irrigation; and preservation of soil quality.

Agricultural extension and training should incorporate 65 experimental stations; a holistic approach through agricultural advisory centers (where a number of public and private agriculture-related disciplines confer to find and prescribe a holistic based policy and advisory service aimed at sustainable resource utilization); and six agricultural colleges at which prospective commercial and subsistence farmers are trained.

Farmer Support Policies

Over the past few years, we have significantly adapted our farmer support policies and systems. The whole structure of the technology transfer and extension service has been adapted to focus on and flow out from the Agricultural Development Centers (ADC). All of these centers, of which we already have ten in operation and another 20 in the planning stages, are based on well manned and funded experiment stations.

In the stations, multidisciplinary teams of scientists and technicians are in the process of developing area-specific sustainable production systems and practices. These have to conform to three main criteria:

150

- production goals must be determined within limits set by climate and soil potential;
- production practices should not be detrimental to the natural resources; and
- production systems should be economically and financially sustainable within a free market environment.

The ADCs are linked on the one hand to the research institutes of the recently established Agricultural Research Council (ARC) and on the other hand to the extension services. Technology development, effective technology transfer, and training the trainer at the grass roots level are essential elements of our system, which can cover the entire spectrum of farming in South Africa from the highly developed commercial sector to the emerging sector of subsistence and small farmers.

Several initiatives, with government financial support, have been taken to lead the way to more sustainable farming systems. In the Land Conversion Scheme, dry land grain farmers are supported technically and financially to convert at least one million hectares of marginal crop land back to low cost grazing. For participation in the Drought Aid Scheme for stock farmers, proof is required that livestock numbers on the farm have been maintained within the long term carrying capacity of the farm over the previous twelve months. This is to ensure that production goals are set within the natural constraints and that production practices are not detrimental to natural resources.

Government Initiatives

Legislation is the most important policy instrument to effect environmental protection in South Africa. Over 50 legislative acts exist to guide agriculture. All of these are environmentally conscious and friendly. Legislation covers *inter alia* soil conservation, pollution prevention, protection of high potential agricultural land, registration of agro-chemicals and pesticides, phytosanitory standards, subdivision of agricultural land, and marketing.

A financial assistance policy exists for soil conservation works relating to irrigation, drainage, contour, fencing, and water infrastructure.

The great demand for wood fuel and resultant resource degradation and depletion has prompted a Biomass Initiative as part of an overall energy provision strategy. This coordinated program will promote "social" forestry with the full participation of rural communities.

Rural development assistance includes infrastructure creation in terms of manpower and extension, a policy encouraging private ownership of land, and assistance of approximately 300,000 subsistence farmers with workable technological packages for finance and extension.

Effects of Reforms on Farmers, Agribusiness and the Environment

The availability of the formerly mentioned policy tools on ground level means:
- enhanced profitability for farmers and better quality of life;
- a decrease in the occurrence and probability of resource degradation through exploitation;
- increased level of expertise and independence of farmers through education and training;
- increased availability of alternative commodity and production methods through adapted technology;
- increased ability of farmers to survive natural disasters (droughts and floods);
- increased sustainability of the environment;
- promotion of private enterprise/ownership and consequently farmer/landowner responsibility for sustainable resource utilization;
- decreased pollution;
- safe food and fodder for man and beast;
- elimination and prevention of the use of harmful pesticides, hormones, and agro-chemicals; and

152

- economic growth and stability for the country as a whole.

The Role of Government, Farmers, and Agribusiness

Government

Government should facilitate a favorable agro-economic environment for farmers and industry through: sound economic policy based on free market or market-related principles; funding for research and extension; creating infrastructure for education; and environmentally conscious policies and legislation.

Agribusiness

Agribusiness should develop and supply farmers and the industry with their requisites in a responsible and not exploitative way and should strive for environmentally friendly product development and train users in the correct application thereof.

Farmers

The farmer should live as if he is to die tomorrow; should farm as if he is to live forever; and should utilize and have access to sound agricultural practices and extension aimed at enhancing (or at least not decreasing) the potential of natural resources.

Cost Distribution

Government should take responsibility for basic research; for adapting research results and technology to function in local conditions; and for the cost of basic training and creating educational infrastructure, economic infrastructure, and support services.

Agribusiness should take responsibility for the development of technology; for the implementation of research results; and for training the end user.

The farmer must foot part, if not all, of the bill for agricultural support services which contribute directly to profitability and must bear part of the financial burden of education and training. A more lenient approach should be followed towards the subsistence farmer and the total community should contribute towards the funding of support services for this category.

Conclusion

Guided by these principles and striving towards sustainable utilization of our natural agricultural resources, the RSA is one of the few countries in the world which can be regarded as a net exporter of basic foods. In terms of the African continent, South Africa covers less than 4 percent of the continent's area, has about 7 percent of the arable land, and accommodates approximately 5 percent of the population. However, it produces 45 percent of the maize, 31 percent of the sugar, 27 percent of the wheat, 17 percent of the red meat, and 54 percent of the wool.

Africa's main potential lies in its human and natural resources. The developed world has a stake in the conservation of these resources. If their responsibility in terms of investment and development projects is ignored, they will not escape the result and consequences of exploiting the continent's natural resources. They should create room and space for the products of commercially driven agriculture in Africa.

Theorists and naturalists should take note of the specific problems of Africa. First world principles, which serve developed countries, are also applicable to Africa, but the plans to implement them should be adapted to function in African conditions. Secondly, these principles can only bear fruit in Africa if the first world is willing to facilitate the development of Africa, to help in training, to adapt technology to function in Africa, and, most importantly, to create economic advantages and enumeration for the products and people of Africa. In the end, all environmentally favorable or friendly policies and procedures will be governed and guided in terms of economic realities. The hungry and the poor cannot reform and will remain indifferent towards the environment as long as they are without the necessary sustenance or financial means to encourage them.

Section IV: Agribusiness - Protector or Polluter?

An Outline of the Issues

Agribusiness contributes to the environment in both positive and negative ways. Regulation of companies that use agricultural products, however, can also have positive and negative results.

The speakers in this session explored the following issues:
- What is the relationship between agribusiness and the environment?
- How do regulations aimed at agro-chemical and biotechnology companies improve or undermine environmental quality?
- What role can and does agribusiness play in improving the environment?
- What potential exists for developing new technologies which replace non-renewable and highly polluting resources?
- What prospects does biotechnology offer for creating new, more resistant strains of plants and animals which require fewer chemicals?
- How can we market environmental stewardship?
- Should the same regulations and goals be applied to developed and developing countries alike?
- Do regulations help or harm agribusiness?

Chapter 14

Agribusiness and the Environment in the United States Corn Belt

Charles S. Johnson

Pioneer Hi-Bred International is the world's largest agricultural seed company with product sales last year to farmers in more than 100 countries. The heart of our North American business is row crop agriculture (i.e. the intense production of corn and soybeans stretching across the Corn Belt of the United States). Today, I will focus my comments on agribusiness and agriculture as it relates to the United States Corn Belt.

To those of us at Pioneer, this conference is even more timely than its organizers could have imagined. We are nearing the end of a one year process of evaluating how Pioneer should deal with environmental issues. Last October, Pioneer brought together a group of experts from both inside and outside the company to look at environmental issues, particularly the relationship between row crop agriculture and the environment in the United States Corn Belt. This process, which is not yet completed, has left me with three major impressions.

Agriculture Is a Major Health Risk to Farmers

First, the major human health risk from production agriculture is to the farmer, his family, and others in the rural community. Farmers are exposed daily to hazardous chemicals and machinery. An apparent hazard is the loss of limbs, while less apparent occupational hazards include skin cancers from too much sun;

lungs damaged by grain dust, mold spores, or gases from hog confinement operations; and the increased risk of being poisoned by mishandling agricultural chemicals.

To decrease personal health risks, farmers must do a careful job of regularly cleaning and calibrating the equipment they use to spray chemicals; they must practice proper cleaning and disposal of their pesticide containers. Too many farmers are still handling these chores near their wells, where contamination is virtually assured over time either by accident or by accumulation. An important component of environmental stewardship will be seeing that farmers receive the management information necessary to properly and safely handle chemicals. Agribusiness firms are and must continue to be significant sources of this information.

The Consequences of Excessive Nitrogen Use

We also looked at fertilizers and chemicals and their impact on our surface and ground water. We found that the most significant human health problem caused by nitrogen is with a very narrowly defined but critical segment of the population. Many experts feel the nitrate problem lies primarily in the area of infants younger than six months of age. They develop a condition known as "blue baby syndrome." First discovered in 1945, there have been 2000 reported incidents of the syndrome world-wide, of which ten percent resulted in death. The last reported death from blue baby syndrome was in South Dakota in 1986.

As adults, 70 percent of our total dietary nitrate intake is from vegetables. Most babies are not fed vegetables until they are more than six months old. Since there is no evidence that mothers pass nitrate through breast milk, water then becomes the major source of nitrate for babies. In cases of severe nitrate contamination, bottled water may be a temporary answer to the problem until more permanent solutions can be found. But bottled water can be hard to find or too expensive for many people, particularly those living in rural areas. That is why nitrogen fertilizer use has caught the public's attention in many parts of the United States, and it is one reason why many of us in production agriculture are working hard to find ways of using less nitrogen.

Another significant environmental problem caused by excessive nitrogen is that it stimulates the growth of algae in standing or slow-moving water, such as lakes and ponds. Nitrates can be deadly for fish and other elements of the marine ecosystem.

In addition, excess nitrogen use is expensive for farmers. It is simply not good economics to buy nitrogen fertilizer and allow it to leach into the groundwater or out of reach of the plants.

Chemical Pesticides

As for chemical pesticides, I was not able to find any documented cases of food safety problems from agricultural pesticides currently registered in the United States and used in the Corn Belt when applied at label rates. Clearly, one dilemma is our inability to prove a negative. That is, we can never be absolutely sure that some long-term negative effect will not turn up in the future.

A significant challenge for agribusiness or other research entities is to understand the nitrogen uptake pattern of the plant and balance that with appropriate nitrogen application technologies. This research should be encouraged.

All of this does not mean that we should simply forget about nitrate and require all infants to have bottled water. Nor does it mean we should not be concerned about agricultural chemicals turning up in our water supplies or threatening wildlife. What it does mean, however, is that based on our present knowledge these problems currently appear to be manageable.

Crops Must Be Produced in Sustainable Areas

My second impression is that to sustain the world's ecosystem, our major grains, and oil seed crops must be produced in those areas conducive to sustainable agriculture. The world simply cannot continue to break up fragile soils, raze rain forests, and pour tons of scarce water on arid land in the nationalistic name of food security. One cannot extract gold from rock that does not contain much gold without expensive and environmentally damaging processes. The same statement can be made about trying to grow crops under inappropriate conditions.

Let me hasten to add that the agricultural policies of the United States have been as damaging as those of almost any other nation. We have paid farmers to produce surplus crops on fragile land, abandon crop rotations, and use scarce water resources. Farmers have also used higher rates of fertilizers and pesticides in pursuit of higher yields, so that they would qualify for greater subsidies. While these were not the intentions of United States farm programs, they are certainly among the results.

Many feel that farmers would never do anything to harm the environment because they live where they work. I believe the vast majority of farmers care deeply for the environment and want very much to protect it. But it is not the job of the farmer to watch over a wilderness. The farmer must find ways to make a living from the land. While it certainly benefits the farmer to preserve the resources with which that living is made, the combined effect of individual actions by many farmers may cause unexpected damage.

Environmentalists and farmers often view the world through different eyes. Environmentalists want to preserve, conserve, and enhance natural resources. Farmers are not opposed to that, but they seek to maximize the utilization of those same natural resources.

In the process, farmers have done things that seemed fine at first but turned out to be problematic. When DDT was first used, who knew that it would harm eagles as well as kill insects? When "drainage wells" were dug on flat land to remove excess water, farmers did not realize the water they were injecting into the aquifer could be laced with fertilizers and pesticides. However, since the mid-1980s, the United States has done an effective job of incorporating environmental stewardship into its farm programs.

The world's major grain and oil seed crops can be met without resorting to the exploitation of lands inappropriate for high-technology and sustainable agriculture. We must develop global agricultural awareness and policies to allow us to do that. At the same time, trade policies are needed to ensure that food and feed can be adequately distributed from those countries able to produce them to those countries who need more than they can produce. A critical issue continues to be the ability of many consuming nations to generate the resources necessary to purchase their food and feed needs.

Sustainable Agriculture Is Consistent with Environmental Stewardship

That brings me to my third impression. I am absolutely convinced that a sustainable, productive and profitable agriculture is consistent with good environmental stewardship.

I believe this for two reasons. First, if those of us who are involved in production agriculture are not also good environmental stewards, both our livelihoods and our lives will ultimately be threatened. Second, there is evidence that sound production practices, good management skills, and emerging technologies provide the ways to achieve environmental stewardship.

Examples of Stewardship

As a group, farmers in the United States Corn Belt are using significantly less nitrogen today than several years ago without a reduction in yield. Farmers are looking for any means to lower their cost of production. They are establishing more realistic corn yield goals, which call for lower rates of nitrogen, and they are using soil and plant testing methods to help reduce the guesswork when selecting the best rate of nitrogen. This is both economically and environmentally sound.

With a look to the future, a new satellite tracking system, called the "Global Positioning System," could make it possible for farmers to apply precise amounts of fertilizer based on the soil types and nutrient needs in a field. Currently, this new technology is too expensive for most farmers. In the future, however, this satellite technology could eventually have a significant impact by allowing more precise chemical application.

Integrated pest management is another environmentally friendly practice of modern agriculture. Farmers do not apply a chemical treatment unless enough pests are found to cause economic damage. Through this simple yet effective method, farmers save money and protect the environment.

Biotechnology

Another area that holds tremendous potential is plant biotechnology. As a company, Pioneer has gone to considerable effort and expense to help preserve germplasm in our product crops. It has always been important to our business to have access to as much of this germplasm as possible, wherever it exists in the world. With the new sciences, advances in technology will allow scientists to transfer genes from one species to another, thus making the conservation of all gene sources even more important. After all, who would have suspected that a gene from a tropical nut would improve the protein quality of soybeans? But it does.

The new sciences will mean higher yields from lower amounts of fertilizers, pesticides, and other inputs. That means the end products should be more plentiful, less expensive, and less damaging to the environment.

Biotechnology offers yet another way for agriculture to be more environmentally friendly. Plants genetically altered to ward off insects may replace or reduce the need to apply synthetic chemical pesticides. About 30 percent of the corn ground in North America (nearly 10 million hectares) was treated this year with a chemical insecticide. Such altered plants may some day cut that number dramatically.

Biotechnology also offers potential solutions to particular disease problems, such as the need to protect against viruses. This could lead to simple answers to diseases in developing countries or minor crops, where it is difficult to attract research funding for traditional breeding. By correcting problems in the plant, farmers in developing countries will not have to cope with the new management skills and additional exposure risk that comes with chemicals.

Herbicide Resistant Plants

Herbicide resistant plants are often positioned in debates as a negative result of plant biotechnology. Some people think they will prompt farmers to use excessive amounts of chemical herbicides because the crop is resistant. My experience is that farmers are looking for every opportunity to use fewer chemicals and at lower amounts. That means less cost and less risk for farmers.

There are also many strong arguments that herbicide resistant plants offer some very real environmental advantages. As a rule, the new classes of chemicals to which plants will be resistant are much safer to mammals (i.e. less toxic than table salt). Farmers apply significantly less active ingredient (grams instead of kilograms per hectare). The new compounds degrade quickly and adhere to soil particles; thus they do not leach through the soil.

There is another possible environmental advantage for herbicide resistant plants. While some farmers may be reluctant to use cultivation for weed control because they cannot be sure they will be able to get into the field at the right time, a herbicide resistant crop provides a backup system for farmers who want to cultivate for weed control. If they cannot get equipment into the field at the right time, farmers can apply the chemical. Herbicide resistant crops should, therefore, encourage more farmers to use cultivation for weed control.

There is a need to be concerned about putting herbicide resistant genes in crops that have close relatives that are weeds in the same growing areas. Plant breeders are very aware of this and are sensitive to the concern.

Suggestions for Regulations

Regulations impacting the use of plants developed by biotechnology should also be science-based, easy to read and understand, and have clearly defined objectives. They should not overlap or impose conflicting or varying standards upon companies. Furthermore, regulations should be concise, consistent, and internationally harmonized. We must always seek to balance potential risk with appropriate regulatory hurdles.

Finally, these new, environmentally friendly products will be nothing but a dream unless they can be protected. Companies cannot and will not invest millions of dollars in product research and development unless there is the opportunity to recoup that investment.

Chapter 15

Marketing Environmental Stewardship: A Policy Framework for Agriculture and Agribusiness

Kenneth A. Cook

(Transcribed from conference tapes.)

Questions To Be Answered

The question before us is "Agribusiness: Protector or Polluter?" My answer is "yes." Having thus discharged the bulk of my official responsibilities for the panel, I am now going tackle two bonus questions and use them to frame my remarks today.

The first question is this: can anyone seriously believe that we can hope to improve agriculture's environmental performance in an efficient and timely manner and on the sufficiently large scale that we need within the OECD countries without the active involvement of agribusiness, its technical capacity, its scientific knowledge, and its marketing know-how? Is that thinkable?

Secondly, can anyone seriously believe that we can solve the agriculture sector's environmental problems through voluntary and market means alone? Or that taxpayers can, should, or will offer to purchase through direct payments or other means every single environmental improvement that will be required, even ones that end up saving farmers money?

My personal answer to the first question is that it is impractical and undesirable to ignore the potential of agribusiness to protect the environment, even if, as I suggested in my ambiguous and very clear answer at the outset, agribusiness can also play a role as a polluter.

As for the second question, my answer again is "no." Much, if not most, of what we need to and can accomplish to resolve the wide range of agriculture's problems with the environment and natural resources can be achieved through voluntary means. This can be realized if farmers are given education, technical assistance, and the right incentives. But, at some point, regulations do become necessary. A minority of farmers, some for very good and fair reasons, others for no reason at all, will not respond adequately to the carrots or the technical advice about a particular problem. Whether it is protection of ground and surface water; the conservation of erodible lands, wetlands, or wildlife habitats; or the preservation of the health of farmers or others, there is going to be some role for regulation.

Progress Has Been Made

I realize that perhaps this is not the most welcome message to bring to this audience. After all, we have made considerable progress in our general understanding of the nature of the problem and what needs to be done and have even seen a measure of agreement between agriculture and environmentalists.

Many in agriculture used to deny the existence of the very problems that, according to many previous speakers, society is now going to provide income payments to solve. The very continuation of income transfers for agriculture in Europe seems dependent on what one speaker called the creation of a "green box," a new rationale for income transfer to agriculture. Those arguments were very actively raised in the debates in 1985 and 1990 over the farm legislation that was passed by the United States Congress. In a sense, a kind of market process is at work. Incentives produce problems to fit solutions and regulations produce solutions to fit problems; often they are in a dead heat for competition for which can be the least efficient.

Many in the environmental movement have learned a great deal too, speaking at least for the United States' experience. What we have learned is that very significant changes are possible in the agriculture sector to deal with resource conservation and environmental problems if the changes make economic sense to farmers and if the public and the majority of farmers are behind the changes.

The United States' Experience

Let me elaborate a little bit on the United States' experience with broad based requirements and incentives for farmers, which were first instituted in the area of erosion control in 1985. Basically and in a nut shell, the story is this: from the mid-1930s until the mid-1980s, we had an exclusively voluntary approach to controlling soil erosion on crop land in the United States. It was very successful in many locations for many farmers. Millions of farmers spent a great deal of their own time and money improving their land and protecting it from erosion.

Still, we came to 1985 with several government resource inventories, conducted by the Soil Conservation Service, which showed fairly dramatically that there was still a large area of crop land that was not only very prone to erosion but which, despite years of technical and financial assistance, did not have a single soil conservation measure on it. Some of this was the legacy of the great "plow out" of the 1970s, when grain prices skyrocketed. Some of it was a result of farmers not fully realizing that they had an erosion problem because it is often manifested in very subtle ways. (In Iowa and Missouri and elsewhere, you can have a very high soil erosion rate and yet not see very clear evidence of it when you look at your field.)

But, in 1985, Congress and the Administration decided to draw the line. Basically, conservation became a *quid pro quo* for receiving a wide range of farm program payments (i.e. everything from the overall commodity program benefits to crop insurance, government farm loans, and other provisions of federal assistance to agriculture). In 1990, the list was expanded. The lesson that was drawn was that the time had come to mix some carrots and sticks together.

Another program instituted at that same time, the Conservation Reserve Program, has enrolled 36 million acres of highly erodible land. Farmers are given rental payments to keep their land in grass or tree cover for ten years. We now spend $1.6 billion per year on that program, making it one of the major environmental items in the U.S. budget.

The Conservation Compliance Policy applies to highly erodible crop land that is currently in production. The United States government and farmers prepared 1.3 million soil conservation plans between 1986 and the end of 1989. Preparing these plans occupied the time and resources of over 6,000 full time equivalent employees of the Soil Conservation Service each and every year on average for four years. A like amount of effort is now going into monitoring the implementation of those plans, which are to be fully implemented by farmers by the end of 1994.

Here, I think, is the key. If you phase in the right mix of requirements, have adequate flexibility, offer incentives over the initial period and plenty of education, you have a winning formula for making very substantial changes over a reasonably short period of time in a wide range of agricultural and environmental issues.

Marketing Environmental Stewardship

This brings me to the theme of my talk, which is marketing environmental stewardship. It is in this way that I have tried to think of what the opportunities will be in the future for taxpayers to invest in an agriculture that is devoted directly to promoting the environment, while the market provides the signals for production. In addition, it will be an agriculture and an agribusiness that also sees a great many new opportunities for protecting the environment, opportunities of the sort that we have seen in other industries.

Bill Reilly, Administrator of the Environmental Protection Agency, in his comments to the National Press Club a few months ago pointed out that the OECD estimate of $200 billion currently in international trade of environmental goods has been projected by the Office of Technology Assessment to grow to about $300 billion per year by the turn of the century. He noted that the United States has a 40 percent share of the current market by Commerce Department estimates. This is the kind of substantial growth we can see in the agriculture sector both in terms of traditional productivity measures and of providing additional environmental services and amenities.

Key Elements of a Policy Framework

Here are the general elements of what I think a policy framework will have be in order to achieve this potential. My limited knowledge forces me to consider only the United States and the European Community.

Commitment to Cope with Agriculture's Environmental Problems

The first framework element is a commitment to cope with agriculture's environmental problems. Whether this comes from concern about the impacts of agriculture or whether it comes from economic necessity, political necessity, or a combination, I am not fussy. As long as we have it, and I think we now do have it on both sides of the Atlantic, we have the starting point for this new approach to agricultural policy.

Knowledge of Problems

A defensible, general knowledge of the location and nature of specific problems is required to begin to design some broad policy instruments. For example, in the United States, there was a general working understanding of where we had soil erosion problems, how serious they were, and what it would take to solve them. This can really only be derived from fairly intensive country level studies, which need to be upgraded regularly as advances in science allow. These studies should furthermore proffer some fairly tangible goals for environmental protection as a result of the analysis. Where can we go in terms of reducing the pollutant loadings, lowering soil erosion, and improving wildlife habitat, and so forth? This is not unlike the concept of targets and timetables in international agreements and in various national laws.

Technical Capacity

One must have a developing, if not existent, capable technical capacity in the private or the public sector. You need people who can identify problems in the field and provide very good advice for how to deal with them. That is a major issue and, I think, a major opportunity for agribusiness.

Farm Level View

I think the most relevant unit of analysis of all of this is to develop a farm level view. A very clear farm level framework should include an assessment inventory of resources, an evaluation of problems, a description of the commodities produced and the cultural practices that produce them, and an appraisal of the potential for restoring ecosystems where that potential exists. It has to be flexible, site specific, sensitive to prevailing farming conditions and traditions, and environmentally rigorous. By definition, this means the plans have to be developed locally. Therefore, there has to be a substantial amount of local capacity to understand problems, to decipher them, to identify them in the field, and so forth. Ideally, the plans have to first be implemented in a voluntary, incentives-based environment.

How much time one allows for such an implementation process depends on the problem, the money available, and politics. There needs to be a phase-in period where incentives are the chief measure. Long term agreements make sense as the instruments -- at least three years, ideally, five years; in the case of other contracts for purposes of ecological restoration, ten years or even permanent easements where it is obvious that land should be protected for the long term. Once those are in place, then one can consider phasing in requirements, if any. No problems, no requirements, and no payments; that would be the formula.

Agribusiness

We have spent a considerable amount of time during the last year at the Center for Resource Economics looking at opportunities for agribusiness in the upper Midwest, particularly agri-chemical dealerships.

Wendy Hoffman, an agricultural economist on staff, has been looking at six agribusiness firms that sell agricultural chemicals. Perhaps you can appreciate that this is an unusual undertaking for an environmental group. Our view in doing it was we felt fairly strongly that what we were reading in the farm magazines and in the trade magazines seemed to make some sense. More and more progressive agri-chemical dealers were saying their future was in services. They were going to continue to make a good deal of money in the sale of materials as they always have (pesticides, fertilizers). But, increasingly we heard from leaders in the industry about the ability to sell services and information. This information input was going to be what separated prosperous dealers from the rest of the pack, a pack that is getting smaller and more fiercely competitive every day. We see considerable opportunity in the right policy framework for that kind of agribusiness ethic and incentive system to thrive.

There is no question that agribusiness will continue to thrive in the high tech direction, which is the kind of image that a lot of people have of agribusiness. But there is also this vital service component. There is a lot of new technology needed for services such as soil and tissue testing for nutrients, weed and insect scouting prior to spray, reduced application rates, and banding herbicides instead of broadcast application. These are all things, of course, that farmers can do for themselves and many of them do. But, it is also the kind of information and service that agribusiness can provide. I think this could be a growth area for agribusiness.

Conclusion

Finally, I would like to mention a couple of items that indicate the polar extremes of agricultural technology and its impact on the environment.

About a week ago, there was a story that appeared in the Washington Post. It had to do with corn plants, caterpillars, and wasps. A couple of scientists from the Department of Agriculture discovered that certain plants, including corn plants, emit aromatic compounds when they are being chewed on by a caterpillar, and the aromatics attract predatory wasps. These tiny wasps attack the caterpillars and immediately lay their eggs in them. The caterpillar's feeding rate is reduced by about 90 percent. As the larvae hatch within the caterpillar, things get even bleaker for it. What the researchers had in mind was to find other plants (like lima beans) that had this trait and attempt to selectively breed them in such a way as to perhaps produce plants with a great capacity to repel insects. Therefore, they would need less insecticide. When environmentalists think about the future of agriculture, technology, and agribusiness, we struggle most with those kinds of questions where biological control leads into the potential for biotechnology.

The other end of the spectrum deals with tractor tires. An article in the most recent issue of Farm Journal pointed out a very simple fact. For the second year in a row, the Journal held a series of very small field trials in which farmers were asked to operate their tractors with the minimum amount of tire pressure that was recommended, or even a little bit below. Low and behold, they experienced about a nine percent improvement in efficiency on two farms and a 25 percent improvement in energy efficiency on another simply by this lower tire pressure.

I would suggest that we are going to see examples of environmental progress from both ends of the spectrum. We will see a substantial improvement in the environment from agribusiness' provision of information, from simple things like reducing tire pressure to extraordinary things such as multi-species bio control. We are going to see major changes and agribusiness will play a key role. Remembering these tractor tires, environmentalists and agribusiness interests should probably try and focus on some common sense ways to lower the pressure.

Chapter 16

Opportunities for
Healthy and Sustainable Agriculture

P.J. Strijkert

Prospects for Biotechnology

The quantitative development of the world population and its scientific, technological, and economic progress has led to today's mechanized agriculture with its tremendous environmental problems caused by overfertilization, over-use of pesticides, and waste production. As with many other world problems, there will ultimately be no solution unless we solve the catastrophic growth of the world population, which is today about 100 million people per year.

However, the solution for this problem lies beyond the scope of just biotechnology. If we suppose that a solution will be found, then biotechnology offers lots of opportunities for creating a healthy and sustainable agriculture. In fact, many environmental problems today are strongly enhanced by overproduction caused by subvention mechanisms. A restoration of the equilibrium of elemental cycles (e.g. carbon, nitrogen, phosphorous) is needed in combination with a responsible and moderate use of crop protection agents.

Although Western agriculture is presently overproducing certain primary products, it is an illusion to think that large scale production has become obsolete and can generally be abandoned. The degree of urbanization and the organization of our society cannot be sustained without applying the principle of economies of scale to agriculture and associated industries.

Necessity of an Economic Agriculture

The gradual erosion of subvention and other supporting measures will cause agriculture to face the full impact of free market trade. This will bring a new element; namely, the necessity of an economic agriculture. In other words, agriculture will change from production oriented to product oriented. Although this could mean a considerable extension of the number of crops, it surely does not mean a move away from high-density agriculture (see horticulture).

The basic requirement for an economic agriculture is that it provides the farmer with an acceptable sustainable income without inducing overproduction of products and waste. The mere setting aside of valuable soil will not contribute to the competitiveness of European agriculture. Other ways of adding value to this land need to be developed (e.g. by introducing new crops for industrial or energy purposes or by using existing crops for new applications).

However, these changes do not solve agriculture's basic problem; being the local overproducer of waste or, in other words, the local exhauster of nature's recycling capacities. In searching for a solution, one has to keep in mind that only highly concentrated waste streams will allow viable recycling or re-use.

Ways to Cope with Waste

Basically, there are eight ways to cope with the waste problem:

1. Ignore
2. Hide
3. Wait
4. Cure
5. Dilute
6. Transform
7. Prevent
8. Improve

Ignore and Hide essentially mean leaving the problem for the next generation. They should be considered unacceptable, although at this moment they seem to be most widely practiced. Waiting may be an instinctive human reaction to a seemingly insoluble problem, but it is only acceptable in those cases where an affordable solution is within reach. Cure is an obvious action but a very costly approach. Dilute is a marginally acceptable and only in those situations where nature's recycling capacities can cope with the level of waste offered. Transforming a waste stream into valuable products is a combination of two things. Environmental requirements could be met while at the same time as a product is manufactured, resulting in the prevention of waste elsewhere. (Table 1) Prevent definitely ends up in a clean environment; but if it means stopping production, costs may be very high. Improve means a clean environment and an improved product/process. Molasses presents a specific problem. In fact, here the fermentation industry has to solve a tremendous environmental problem of the sugar industry, a factor that has so far never been accounted for in the molasses price.

Table 1

PROCESS	WASTE	NEW PRODUCT	APPLICATION
Slaughter Houses	Carcasses Bones	Animal flour Gelatin Phosphate	Feed Ingredient Food Ingredient Feed Ingredient
Cheese	Whey	Whey Powder Drinkbase	Food Food
Sugar	Mother liquor Pulp	Molasses Silage	Fermentation, Feed Feed
Beer	Spent grain		Feed
Potatoes	Proteins, fibers	Protamylasse	Feed

It is evident that the efforts and technological input required will increase in the order they have been mentioned. From the point of view of sustainable agriculture, only the last three options are viable, although they may initially require considerable

178

investment. However, compared to the environmental costs that may be attributed to the other methods, they will be more economical in the long run. It is especially in those areas that biotechnology provides powerful tools for solutions.

Biotech Options

Agricultural-Nitrogen Cycle

The agricultural-nitrogen cycle provides an excellent analysis as a starting point to design valuable technical solutions. A more detailed picture unveils that nitrogen is mainly applied in animal husbandry, especially where milk and meat production from cows shows very low yields (nine percent). The low yields may be explained by the fact that the production process optimizes costs and does not reflect any environmental effects. This is further illustrated in bio-farming where the same process is optimized on such parameters as fertilizer use, non-use of pesticides, and no additional feeding. A yield of approximately 30 percent may be reached, however, at much higher product costs. Nevertheless, this may serve as an indication that from an environmental point of view, there is room for improvement.

Relatively simple mechanical means like injecting nitrogen into soil rather than dumping it on the soil in combination with a dosage scheme based on the real need of the crops will provide considerable improvement. The latter principle applied to animal feeding schemes rather than an *ad libitum* scheme also reduces waste.

Biotechnology becomes prominent when the overall production efficiency of the animal itself is improved. This may be achieved through improvement of the digestibility of feed (i.e. by adding enzymes like Phytase which result in better conversion and less waste).

Another opportunity is by adding amino acids produced from fermentation to the feed, increasing its nutritional value and reducing waste. The next step is to produce these amino acids from manure, which in essence means closing the circle.

Although controversial, it is worth mentioning the application of hormones. Provided they are safe for both man and animal, they offer opportunities for increased feed conversion and better product yield, which result in a lower cost price of the products and less waste.

Analogons

A different approach made possible through biotechnology is the production of milk and meat (analogons) from plants and micro-organisms.

Substrate technology in horticulture has made production virtually independent from soil and climate and comes very close to preventing waste by carefully controlling nutrients, protective agents, etc. This sector has proven to be very capable in overcoming crises. In the early seventies, the aftermath of the oil crisis was overcome. The same holds true for the environmental crisis of the last few years (i.e. prohibition of a number of crop protection agents and the development of very strict environmental regulations). In fact horticulture has emerged stronger after each of these catastrophes.

Adapting to Extreme Conditions

A step further away is the adaption of crops to saline, drought, or other extreme conditions. From an environmental point of view, this may help spread agricultural production and thus reduce the density of local waste streams elsewhere.

Regulations

Regulations play a key role in whether these opportunities will be realized or remain utopian. For the purpose of this lecture, two types of regulation affecting the future of these solutions may be distinguished: product oriented and process oriented.

Product Oriented

Regulatory requirements for products in food, feed, or industrial production are increasing to such an extent that they may soon prohibit further development. This is especially true for products derived from modern biotechnology.

A major cause of this development is the tendency of governments to give in to the political fashion of the day. It may seem odd but environmental requirements for certain products or production methods may postpone or even prohibit the introduction of products that may improve the environment. In this respect, consumer reservations about biotechnology are a good example. A hesitant government, unwilling or unable to take a clear position and to address every issue raised, stimulates neither the further development of nor public confidence in biotechnology. A more positive approach is absolutely necessary.

Process Oriented

Process oriented regulations aim to limit or reduce negative environmental aspects of agriculture. However, different approaches are possible. A negative approach is an undifferentiated levy on waste, as is now the case in the Netherlands where excess nitrogen, phosphorous, and potassium are charged. This approach invites dumping, hiding, or generally evasive behavior. A positive approach would invite solution oriented behavior and stimulation of research for Prevent, Transform, or Improve actions. A way to achieve this would be a Value Added Tax Type Levy paid by the originator of the pollution (importer, producer, etc.).

The tax could be on energy content or pollution resulting from raw materials. This would stimulate either reuse, a search for alternatives, or improvement of the specific raw material. It is essential that the waste inducing behavior is exposed at the beginning of the chain, not at the end. For example, if there was a tax on phosphor as feed ingredient, then the application of Phytase would allow the farmer to avoid the tax but also to improve the environmental balance of his animal production chain.

Conclusion

There are a number of approaches for achieving healthy, sustainable, and environmentally acceptable agriculture. The further development and application of biotechnology is an essential part of that.

We are losing valuable time and opportunities because of the hurdles that are put up by society. There is an unavoidable responsibility for agriculture, industry, and government together with opinion leaders to do their utmost to grasp the opportunities in this field now.

Chapter 17

Agribusiness: Protector or Polluter?

C. Peter Johnson

It is with some trepidation that an agriculturalist whose experience in a highly regulated and over supplied temperate market on a crowded isle and with a business size unremarkable in world terms addresses such an international gathering. However, I look forward to sharing with you some of the factors which shape our actions and influence the direction of our progress. It will not surprise you when I conclude that I believe the ability of agribusiness to do good far outweighs any negative contribution to life on this planet but the need exists to retain our watchfulness.

My approach is that of the corporate rather than private family farmer, a concept in contrast with much of European agriculture. My company owns no land and its performance has to satisfy the aspirations of the professional public shareholders in our parent company. The circumstances which bring landlords to do business with us are extremely varied and our arrangements flexible to match. There is a wide range of requirements. That we can please both our landlords and our owners gives me confidence in addressing this subject. Both share an interest in the stewardship we apply to the land in our care. Increasingly well informed, they expect us to lead rather than lag on environmental matters and the practical application of them to their property. Without success in this area we would have neither land to farm nor capital to risk whatever our financial performance. The disciplinary pressure thus exerted by our structure is considerable and quite different from the pressure exerted on (the normal) family occupation. We really do need to be on the side of the angels.

A formal agricultural education a quarter of a century old hardly included any reference to an environmentally friendly approach since it was not deemed necessary in a temperate zone. After all how could farming harm its natural home? The awareness that it might not be so benign was slower in coming to this industry than to many others, but the attack on farming methods and the aggressiveness with which it has been pursued has been quite a shock and, as I shall hope to show, not all well directed or informed.

Change in Public Perception

Passive public acceptance of new farm buildings, the noises and smells of farms, and changes in landscape, drainage, and reclamation and their effects on wildlife is no longer available. What was formerly unquestioned is now regarded as polluting. The change in attitude has resulted from the mobility of an educated public, the availability of a full diet, and an awareness of the ludicrous costs and wasteful surpluses generated by an outdated Common Agricultural Policy (CAP).

In the case of the United Kingdom, the consumer was also used to accessing cheap and competitive food sources worldwide. This consumer has now, on the facts before him, been led to the conclusion that his agriculture cannot compete without financial subsidy (a characteristic he vigorously demands of the suppliers of all his other worldly requirements) and is therefore less important. This may turn out to have been a major disservice of the CAP. It is in this climate of disbelief that I shall attempt to show how agribusiness can be competitive, profitable, and environmentally acceptable. I believe that it has to be all of these together.

From the viewpoint of a producer operating in a highly regulated industry, there is a danger of reliance on artificial supports which diminish the commercial nature of food production and drive it into a fairy land of make believe. The flow of funds is associated with the fickleness of administrations and the public mood. I have already indicated how the low standing of agriculture arises. Additionally, the allocation of hard cash for purely environmental matters will, I believe, always be small and much less than the level of publicity might appear to indicate. For example, less than one percent of the United Kingdom's agricultural expenditure is currently so directed. Such expenditure will be increasingly scrutinized for its effectiveness and cautious businessmen would reflect before depending on it. Reliance will continue to be placed on farming's committed stewardship and self interest in conservation with most public payment continuing to be through the product price.

This change in public mood towards agricultural support and practice has been constructive in the raising of environmental matters. Care must, however, be taken to differentiate this from the misuse of the political base by some activists who have an impractical agenda affecting the ordering of modern society and its "return to nature." For these latter, commercial considerations are always suspect and their analyses are often selective and unsound. Their creed is that the market economy is inimical to the achievement of environmental objectives.

The Regulation of Agro-chemicals and Biotechnology

Let me be unequivocal; sound and increased regulation of what is a relatively new, applied agro-chemistry will inevitably benefit environmental quality. The removal of long life organochlorine products from use in the United Kingdom has been an outstanding example. In the Netherlands and the United Kingdom, the banning of certain products led to the collection and destruction of tons of chemicals from farms. The majority of these were long outdated, seldom used, and often stored inadequately. The stimulus to remove them from circulation and temptation has been invaluable.

Regulation Benefits Enterprise

We have found it possible to turn new regulation to our advantage. The dual introductions in the United Kingdom of controls on the use of substances potentially hazardous to health and tests of operator competence were initially seen as a burden. They encouraged us to extend special training and education in the use and supplication of agro-chemicals to a level never previously contemplated and to staff who directly influence events in the field. As a result of greater understanding and transferred responsibility, we have achieved economies in rates of use, better timing, and targeting. Less wastage and supervision requirements have been recorded. Costs are less and the field is better tended.

But caution on increased regulation is required. Regulation must be accompanied locally by improved resources necessary for monitoring and approval. Otherwise, a competitive introduction may be thwarted to a trading disadvantage. This is correctly an investment by the taxpayer. Similarly, possible new developments representing an environmental advance (for example, fungal, or viral controls on pests) could be frustrated or delayed. Any lack of resource commitment by the regulating authority is not compatible with the world's increasing need for development in this sector.

Most importantly, regulation must have an authentic scientific or medical foundation. Failure to observe this rule must surely lead to a lack of investment in agriculture by chemical or biotechnical companies, who have other customers, fearing that an expensively developed product could be unpredictably banned on non-scientific grounds before a return was earned.

International Regulation and Competitiveness

Attempting to impose strict limits on pollution always risks directing scarce resources from activities which might be valued more highly by society than the elimination of a marginal unit of pollution or damage. The interpretation of this balance varies between nations. There are some success stories like the soundly based agreement to restrict the use of chloramphenicol for livestock. However, in terms of international competition, unilateral and falsely based restrictions will lead to almost insoluble difficulties in the negotiations for freer trade in GATT.

Calls of regulation develop at various paces in different economies, due to diverse national sensibilities. Welfare sympathetic animal husbandry systems are considerably advanced in the United Kingdom but the moral and ethical concerns have to be balanced against competitive demands. In countries with good communication systems, an over- sensitivity can readily develop. The emotional and altogether hasty banning of ALAR contributed to a demise in apple sales. It does not take long for five supermarket owners supplying over one third of the United Kingdom's food to withdraw an item about which they have doubts. The damage to a long developed market or product is immediate and lasting.

Without pesticides, crop yields in the United Kingdom would, it is estimated by Rothamsted Research Station, be reduced by between one third and one half. So, it is vital to boost consumer confidence by the <u>universal</u> introduction of such measures as Maximum Residue Levels. The record is good. In the United Kingdom, during 1989-90 no pesticide residues were found by the Ministry of Agriculture in 72 percent of the samples and in only three percent were residues above M.R.L. But, we are also faced with a lack of public understanding that the natural world contains toxins which are often more lethal than those chemicals applied in agriculture.

Unfortunately, some regulation has, I fear, rather more to do with beating agricultural surpluses on the head than environmental protection. This is a dangerous practice. On the EC's banning the use of naturally occurring and synthetic anabolic steroids and growth promoting agents, the United Kingdom's Food and Surveillance Agency continues to report that it was made on non-scientific grounds and not based on adverse toxicity data. To the satisfaction of the United Kingdom's Royal Commission on Environmental Pollution (1992), the use of current nitrate limits in drinking water is unjustified by any medical reasoning. Enforced absolutely, it alone would end world competitive farming in England's breadbasket.

Investment and trade flows are sometimes affected in unexpected ways by new regulation. The preoccupation with meat hygiene in the EC has resulted in the closure of local facilities and the transportation for slaughter of many hundreds of thousands of animals for substantial distances often over national borders. Quite apart from the redestination of the value added contribution, agribusiness has missed an opportunity to distance itself from the negative welfare aspects of a trade which will eventually reduce sales to a sensitive public.

The Contribution to Improving the Environment

Urban pressure has for reasons both financial and related to improved distribution inevitably pushed agriculture to use land less well suited. Worldwide, the area of arable tillage has increased by 70 percent in the last century. The contribution from agribusiness can be seen in the World Bank's estimate that 90 percent of the doubling in world food production in the past 25 years came form higher yields and only 10 percent from extra lands. In the United Kingdom, the area of crop and temporary grassland is now 90 percent of the level in 1960. These higher yields in the United Kingdom have actually improved organic matter and, hence, soil fertility and structure.

So, through increased productivity, agribusiness has preserved valuable forests, wetlands, and grasslands and prevented further degradation of unstable soils. In developed economies it has yielded land to urban and leisure requirements. As a continuation of these achievements is required, there can be no lessening of our commitment to advancing technology. The wholehearted pursuit of the correct technology, refined for environmental protection, is not compatible with calls for restriction on production inputs. They are, in reality, calls for less of a commitment to the new level of world population and mean raising the costs of production often by raising the costs of entry. The United Kingdom's Agriculture and

Food Research Council, for instance, has estimated that over the longer term a 30 percent reduction in nitrogen fertilizer would reduce wheat yields by 22 percent, but profits by 112 percent. Nitrogen alone is responsible for 60 percent of crop yield.

I indicated earlier that the current position often influences a country's regulatory policy. Since arable and field crops in the United Kingdom receive only one third of the weight of pesticide per acre currently used in the Netherlands, the compulsory halving adopted in that country would be totally inappropriate for the United Kingdom's conditions. While continuing the search for economy in agro-chemical, I believe we must accept that there will always be a case for a well judged prophylactic application in order to protect the major investment of a maturing crop.

Good Agro-chemical Housekeeping

Influenced by national policies, the relationship of farming to the environment is one of constant change. Sometimes the policies change more rapidly than the appreciation of the changes they induce. Fertilizer applications are a case in point. Overall in the United Kingdom, application rates of nitrogen and phosphate have declined by five percent over the last five years. Our own farm record is of faster change. Nitrogen applications on cereals are now three quarters of the levels in the mid-1980s and, together with even greater phosphate reduction, we are achieving improved retrieval rates and not building leachable reserves. Further improvement in crop spacing and timing of applications is expected to lead to further fertilizer economies. It is well, however, to emphasize what is not possible. It is probably 150 years too late to lower, even if it was desirable, the phosphate levels in many United Kingdom soils.

We have a similar experience with pesticides. Our farm use of organophosphorus based chemicals is now rare as reliance is placed on pirimicarb and pyrethroids. The use of the toxic but degradable aldicarb is restrained by careful preliminary soil assessment and rotation.

Examples of Changing Practices

The application of good husbandry practices as well as reducing food production costs have been simultaneously developed with environmental care as a necessary component.

In Booker's fish farming operation, tightened margins through inadequate growth and survival performance have led (rather unsuprisingly you may think) to reduced stocking and fallowing of cropping areas. Together these have had the effect of dramatically lowering the antibiotic and parasite treatments used even two years ago. Low phosphate feeds have been introduced to lessen fresh water enrichment and the level of sedimentation has been shown to be insignificant and lowered even further by tidal flushing during fallowing. It will be interesting to see if the fish breeders can mirror the continuing progress in food conversion rations as led by the poultry industry.

Likewise, modern forestry design and practice with sympathetic contouring, ploughing well short of watercourses together with species and open space mixtures leads, in our experience, to lowered soil erosion and a greater diversity of wildlife. Fortunately, soils at risk from erosion in the United Kingdom are limited by macro-policies and have contributed to the loss of some land by overgrazing in pursuit of headage payments. A reversal of this process is difficult for the now accepted treeless landscape receives protection on account of its open vista whenever a return to woodlands is contemplated. Further damage may be anticipated following the major change of emphasis authorized by the EC towards headage and area payments rather than product price which will encourage the maintenance of cropping on marginal and fragile soils at the same time as the idling of more stable and productive land. This will tend to perpetuate the extension of farming on the less viable area to which it was stimulated to intrude by earlier excessive price incentives.

The agricultural reaction to such policy signals causes not only changes in land use but also husbandry practice (drainage, crop colors, increased field size, etc.) the landscape acceptability of which, like a reversion to woodland, will always be subjective and polluting to some. It is important that agribusiness points out to the legislators the environmental effect of such signals.

New Technology Replacing Non-Renewable Resources

In its quest to capture more solar energy, world agriculture is responsible for some three and one half percent of fossil fuel consumption. For such a vital task, it is surely difficult to argue that this represents an excessive prioritization. Much more is used, especially in developed countries, for the further preparation, packaging, and distribution required to service modern urban life styles. However, primary usage can still be targeted for a reduction. There is potential both to fix nitrogen from the air without using fuel energy (currently one-third of agriculture's energy use is for fertilizer manufacture) and, as price thresholds rise, to use agriculture as a renewable energy source.

Bacterial assistance for natural nitrogen fixation has already reduced the need for nitrogen fertilizer in some South American soya bean and sugar cane cropping. The change to biomass production would, because of its likely scale, need public acceptance in our situation for new techniques and naturally emphasize the need to increase the intensity of food cropping on the remaining land.

So, the potential for these developments is uncertain and the time scale quite long. While we await them, down on the farm we can benefit both the environment and our pockets by pursuing opportunities for a more rapid payback. Training in new cultivation techniques, tractor fuel economy, and the precision targeting of inputs yields early measurable gains. With our investment at field operator level, we are sure of a sensible interpretation of pest threshold levels where they matter -- at the point of application. This added to improving pest monitoring and forecasting skills coupled with greater knowledge about response levels gives us financially attractive savings. I would emphasize that here we are only at the beginning of mining a really rich seam. The much greater precision that I believe is possible in resource application needs a much better understanding of soil and climate science at the individual field level.

Alternatives to High Farming

Unsaid, but implied by this part of my brief, is the consideration of the future for low input "organic" type agriculture. At its peak this provides a low output solution even with husbandry of the highest class. The financial implications for the consumer and farmer are often disregarded by advocates. In Denmark, applications for organic aid and licensing have fallen to one-third of previous levels and the country is awash with eco-milk which is unwanted and sold at a loss. In the United Kingdom, .2 percent of the farmed area is "organic" and no longer increasing. If it were to do so, there could be significant effects on the livestock industry through the additional numbers needed to maintain "organic" fertility and on soil water from the ploughing out of temporary grassland. Even the attractive extensification of outdoor pig production has been shown to be a significant contributor to nitrate leaching on the soils utilized for this purpose.

I was asked the potential for replacing "highly polluting" resources. This is a difficult phrase and badly defined. I have already referred to the elimination of organochlorines and I am confident any substance similarly damaging should and would be quickly removed. Equally, point source discharges such as the application of fertilizer into field verges and waterways or the escape of silage or slurry waste are indefensible. They are in no sense essential for yields or profits and must therefore be categorized differently than some of the other environmental effects of agriculture that must be continually addressed. Such incidents are a poor basis for introducing wider legislation.

There is no room for agricultural complacency. While the wartime ploughing of grassland led to the higher nitrate in United Kingdom groundwater, the levels are now falling. However, new agricultural practices are still losing excessive amounts of ammonia to the atmosphere. In the United Kingdom they are the major contributor to an aerial deposition of 40 kilograms of nitrogen per hectare each year in Southern England (despite which we are still a net exporter). The loss to the atmosphere is from animal excreta rather than fertilizer and from processes that must and can be rapidly modified.

In 1990, 36 percent of major water pollution incidents in the United Kingdom originated from farms. There is a growing acceptance that action against such polluters should be as severe as is applied to other forms of industry. But this leads to an important point for those framing legislation. Would-be polluters need financial and managerial resources in order to take up and install safe facilities and regimes. Many legal requirements, if enforced, will be beyond the reach of the small scale agriculture encouraged in some EC thinking. And it is no use relying on the converse. In my experience, the small farm operator is every bit as likely to cause pollution as a more frequently inspected large neighbor who has more to lose by civil disregard. In this area, small is not necessarily environmentally friendly. Closely related to this, I believe the sophistication of certification of food production origins and treatment required by our consumers indicates further difficulty for the small, poorly organized, and uncommitted producer exposed to market forces.

Conclusion

By definition, agriculture modifies the natural state, but the rapidity of the up-take of new science by agribusiness is at once an advantage and a disadvantage environmentally. Often a new approach is applied on an untested scale and of a visibility resulting in a detrimental effect. Effective environmental regulation can, however, provide the necessary stimulus to the beneficial refinement of new introductions in the field; ineffective regulation will diminish innovation and profitability in the food production process, the dynamo of general economic development.

With its massive contribution a matter of record, agribusiness remains the sole repository of the skills and means of executing policies which sustain food and fiber production and the appearance of the landscape. Disciplined by the need to maintain profitability and to reduce production costs and resource use, it is also in the interests of agribusiness to improve its practice of environmental care. We must also remain on guard to prevent over-reliance on nature's resilience especially in the maintenance of biodiversity. Human dependence on increasingly sophisticated technology, inevitably taken up on a large scale, has to be accompanied by professional skills of a high order. The competitiveness of the industry and benefit to consumers rely on it. Agribusiness, backed by alert shareholders who are also consumers, has the resources, expertise, and will to ensure that the best environmental practice accompanies plentiful production.

Chapter 18

Agribusiness: Not a Problem in Zimbabwe

Kumbirai Kangai

When people in the developed world discuss the role of the agribusiness sector, they tend to think of the processing of farm products as an activity that takes place in their part of the world. The conventional wisdom is that the less developed countries export primary products in their crude or unprocessed forms to the developed countries, where they are processed for the final consumer.

Like many of our beliefs about the nature of the less developed world, this issue has some validity but, in many ways, oversimplifies reality. In my own country, Zimbabwe, we have a very well developed and flourishing agribusiness sector. It provides a wide range of processed foods, both for our own domestic population and for export. Indeed, the agro-processing sector is the major component of our entire manufacturing industry. Sixty percent of our manufacturing industry is concerned with either processing farm products or producing inputs for farm use.

Questions for Less Developed Countries

For the less developed world, the question of whether agribusiness is a protector or a polluter has to be set in the proper context. This involves two issues.

1) Does the development of our agro-industrial sector create any major environmental problems?

2) Are any environmental problems that come from agro-industry in the less developed world really of serious concern when related to the major problems for our

environment which arise from badly managed farm production systems?

These questions almost dictate their own answers. In Africa, we must develop our agro-industrial sector. We must develop our exports of value added products. There have been no major environmental problems from our industry in Zimbabwe, and we are as well developed as most African countries in this regard. It may be a heresy at this conference, but I wish our agro-industrial sector was so developed and had such a large output that we began to worry about the effects on our environment. But, that is far from the case.

Nor do we have to worry about problems of nitrates and other nutrients in our water supplies. It is the water we worry about, at least in our major towns and more developed farming areas. In places where water has become extremely scarce, and there are a growing number of these, the quality of water is becoming a serious problem. However, this is not caused by agribusiness; it is a consequence of the catastrophic drought we have faced during the past year.

Agribusiness Is Not Major Concern Now

I do not see the development of agribusiness causing environmental damage for many decades to come in the developing world. We have many more immediate problems with which to contend, including the effects of population pressures, the shortage of capital, and the lack of skilled professional people. If we can help to alleviate concerns of the developed world in terms of the effects of agribusiness on their environment, then please accept our invitation to come and work in Zimbabwe. We have many hard working people who would only be too glad to help you develop agribusiness.

Certainly, we must address the problem of damage to the environment of our farms, which has been caused by badly designed crop production systems, over grazing, and population pressures. This is a very serious and urgent matter for us, for which there are no short term solutions. Perhaps if we can develop our agribusiness sector a great deal faster, it would make the basic farm resources of land and people far more valuable in economic terms. That (not the consequences of a rapidly growing agribusiness) is the challenge we must face. For us, agribusiness is a potential protector, not a serious polluter. It is a potential we need to turn into reality.

Section V: How Will Environmental Concerns Affect Trade? Do We Need a "Green Round?"

An Outline of the Issues

As countries lower trade barriers, they may be tempted to use environmental standards as a new way to protect domestic agriculture and to create barriers to trade. Presently, no institutions exist which can monitor agri-environmental policies or settle policy disputes. Therefore, the GATT, which only recently brought agriculture under its umbrella, is now being pressured to also take on environmental issues.

Questions:
- What is the GATT's role in agriculture, the environment, and trade?
- Is the GATT the appropriate forum for monitoring agri-environmental trade or for settling policy disputes?
- Should there be a "Green Round" of the GATT or should the current round be "greened?"
- How can trade and the environment be mutually supportive?
- What was the message of the Rio Treaty and how can it be applied to the future?
- How can environmental concerns be accounted for in trading block agreements?
- What role should other international institutions play in monitoring policies?
- What are the various approaches for resolving environmental problems between countries?
- Should standards for environmental quality be harmonized?

Chapter 19

The GATT's Role in Agriculture, the Environment, and Trade

Richard Eglin

The need to protect the environment better, both at a national and an international level, is creating strong pressures on governments to quickly put together a comprehensive policy response. The potential for using trade policies in this context has attracted a large share of attention. In the process, the multilateral trade rules and disciplines of the GATT and the anticipated results of the Uruguay Round negotiations have come under scrutiny from what is, by and large, an entirely new perspective. How well do they stand up?

Conclusions of the UNCED Conference

At the UNCED Conference in June 1992, governments delivered a strong vote of confidence for an open, non-discriminatory trading system and an early conclusion to the Uruguay Round negotiations. Both are viewed as prerequisites for effective action to protect the environment and to generate sustainable development in the developing countries.

One factor supporting such a conclusion is the potential for competitive trade opportunities to generate wealth and, thereby, to contribute to the expansion of the economic resource base. Cleaning up and protecting the environment is an expensive affair, and governments cannot afford to turn their backs lightly on any source of income generation that can contribute to the task.

A more important factor is that reducing trade restrictions and distortions encourages a more efficient use of resources found around the world. That goes for environmental resources as much as for any others, but it is important to be clear about the meaning of the term "efficient" in this context. It hinges on the powerful role played by prices in the market economy. That is a fundamental yardstick of the GATT trading system, and one which is at the center of the Uruguay Round negotiations. Putting the market back in place in several key areas of world trade, such as agriculture and textiles and clothing, is a fundamental objective of the negotiations.

However, the GATT does not stand for free trade at any cost, a point which particularly needs to be stressed in the context of trade and the environment. There are examples in all countries where governments intervene and set prices to capture social, rather than purely economic values, and allocate resources accordingly. Doing so can be a priority for public policymaking in particular where the free market mechanism is perceived to fail regularly, as, for instance, when dealing with resource allocation over the very long-term, or with common resources that have no evident commercial value, or with the very poor sections of society. All three examples are relevant to the discussion of environmental protection and sustainable development.

Correcting the Market's Misallocations

One of the keys to effective environmental protection lies in correcting the failure of markets to assign realistic values to environmental resources. Public policy intervention is called for, but this is not a task that is well-suited to trade policymaking, at least not on its own. Appropriate environmental and resource management policies are needed first and foremost. Even in a completely closed economy, cut off from trade with the rest of the world, environmental protection will not be assured. But equally, open trade on the basis of the wrong environmental prices can lead to unacceptable levels of resource exploitation and environmental damage. The policy challenge, then, is to get environmental prices right while interfering as little as possible with the allocative efficiency of the market mechanism.

Examples of policy tools that can do the job are sales taxes on products that create pollution, favorable tax treatment of environmentally friendly production processes, and technical regulations and standards. The GATT is a flexible instrument. When policies such as these affect imports as well as domestic products, as they inevitably will, it need not get in the way. What the GATT does demand, however, is that policies do not discriminate against imports, from whatever source, and that the legitimate trade interests of other countries are safeguarded in the process.

It should be emphasized that the concern of the GATT in this regard is limited to the trade-related aspects of environmental policies. The Contracting Parties have made it clear that they see no role for the GATT in environmental policymaking *per se*. Even so, the task of ensuring multilateral policy cooperation between environmental and trade policies is not an easy one.

One government's legitimate environmental objective may be seen by another as a case of disguised protectionism; or there may be fears that national environmental standards could be challenged for purely commercial reasons by a party that would suffer no direct consequences from having the standard degraded. Multilateral cooperation in this context involves developing a common understanding on the legitimacy of the objectives being sought and the proportionality of the policy instruments being used.

Understanding Different Value Judgements

The exercise is laden with value judgements. The current approach of the GATT, evident in the Tokyo Round Agreement on Technical Barriers to Trade (TBT) and in the draft Uruguay Round Agreements on TBT and on Sanitary and Phytosanitary Measures (SPS), is to accept international environmental or health standards as *prima facie*, not trade-distorting, and to examine national standards from the viewpoint of whether they are no more trade restrictive than necessary to achieve the objective in question.

To date, there have been no direct challenges under the TBT Agreement of any government's national standards. Yet, this is an area where environmental policymaking is rapidly becoming more sophisticated (e.g. in the fields of packaging and labelling requirements). It is an area where more work may need to be done by GATT's Contracting Parties to ensure that unnecessary clashes between environmental regulations and the rules of the trading system are avoided.

When it comes to valuing and protecting domestic environmental resources, the GATT places essentially no constraints on a government's course of action, subject to the rule of non-discrimination and the already mentioned requirements of legitimacy and proportionality. But, the values assigned to environmental resources will not necessarily, or even probably, be the same in every country. It is in this context that some of the most difficult issues relating trade to the environment arise.

Causes of Trade Friction

Claiming Jurisdiction Over Another Country's Resources

Trade friction can develop in several ways. One that we have had recent experience of in GATT involves the claim by one country of jurisdiction over the environmental resources of another and the use of a trade restriction to give force to that claim. The case in point was a trade embargo imposed by the United States on tuna imports from Mexico on the grounds that Mexico's incidental dolphin catch was too high. The dispute panel which examined the case concluded that the GATT does not permit the use of trade measures to achieve extraterritorial objectives, in this case saving dolphins outside US territorial waters.

That result was hardly surprising, given the historical role of the GATT in endorsing multilateral policy cooperation as the most effective means of achieving orderly international relations.

Allowing GATT's member countries to dictate, under threat of trade reprisals, any policies and practices of their trading partners which they happen not to agree with would start the trading system down a long, slippery slope. The rule of law would degenerate into the rule of might. No country is immune to the threat of capricious trade actions by its biggest trading partners.

The tuna/dolphin dispute illustrated an important element of many current environmental concerns. Rightly or wrongly, it has become harder to limit to a purely domestic context the value placed on environmental resources. This is obviously so in the case of the ozone layer, the oceans, or the world's climate, which have to be shared internationally. It has increasingly become the case with tropical forests, whose services are valued by the rest of the world for absorbing carbon dioxide and for providing a source of biodiversity. Finally, it is clearly felt to be the case, in some circles at least, with resources such as dolphins or the pollution of a natural environment within another country even though the pollution remains entirely within its borders.

It should hardly come as a surprise to hear from the GATT the suggestion that multilateral cooperation is the preferred course of action to find solutions to protect the resources in question. The fact that there are over 120 multilateral environmental agreements in existence should give cause for optimism in this regard. Indeed, the United States and Mexico, along with several other countries, are moving quickly in this direction to resolve their conflict over tuna/dolphin. Trade measures are unlikely to be the key policy instrument in such cases, but they may well be felt to have an important role to play. The control of trade in endangered species and in toxic wastes, for example, was clearly considered important by the governments which negotiated the CITES and the Basel Convention.

As long as the trade measures in question are not discriminatory, which of course they will not be if all countries sign an international environmental agreement, there is basically no cause for concern under the GATT. However, experience shows that some environmental agreements with limited membership have incorporated discriminatory trade restrictions against non-signatories. The purpose is not always the same, but it appears

205

often to be designed to prevent circumvention of the agreement or to create an inducement to non-signatories to join.

Given the central role assigned to non-discrimination in the GATT, some of these trade provisions may raise awkward questions. I say only "may," because no such case has ever come up for dispute settlement. The Contracting Parties have therefore never taken a view in this regard. The matter is under examination in GATT at present in the Group on Environmental Measures and International Trade.

In the meantime, the UNCED process has forcefully reconfirmed governments' commitment to a truly multilateral process of cooperation in the field of environmental protection. GATT rules will never block the adoption of environmental policies which have broad support in the world community. What they do constrain is attempts by one or a small number of countries to influence environmental policies abroad not by persuasion and negotiation but by unilateral reductions in access to markets.

Internalizing Environmental Costs

The most worrying of the potential areas of trade friction is the issue of international competitiveness. Pressure to internalize environmental costs is increasing, and the OECD countries have already endorsed the application nationally of the Polluter Pays Principle. This, however, will inevitably have an impact upon production costs in an economy. When the products concerned compete with imports or find their way into world markets as exports, changes in competitiveness as a result of the change in environmental policies are brought forcefully home.

One result may be pressure to make other countries harmonize up to one's own domestic environmental standards, so that production costs abroad also rise. If this can be done cooperatively with other nations, fine; but I have already explained the GATT's opposition to threatening to use unilateral trade restrictions if they do not comply.

A second reaction may be demands for higher import protection against foreign products considered to be benefiting from an unfair competitive advantage because they are produced in "environmentally dirty" ways or for production and export subsidies to compensate for the added costs of meeting higher domestic environmental standards.

From the point of view of someone concerned about the proper functioning of the trading system, neither of these claims is valid. It is normal that environmental resources are valued differently around the world. There is nothing inherently wrong in finding that the price of a good varies from one country to another because of a difference in the value placed on environmental protection and conservation, any more than it varies because of differences in wage levels or corporate tax rates.

Maintaining competitive market conditions has always been a major concern of the GATT. The rules on non-discrimination are part of a broader concern with the security and predictability of market access and the need to ensure that trade can take place in an undistorted manner. That is why the "unfair trade" controversy is so destructive for the multilateral trading system, no matter what the reason for labelling trade as "unfair".

Sorting out the genuine cases of injurious dumping or subsidization from the spurious claims of uncompetitive producers has no simple solution. Part of the answer lies in agreeing as specifically as possible upon what standards governments should respect in sensitive areas of domestic policymaking, so that trade distorting actions are avoided as far as possible and, where unavoidable, are nevertheless kept to a minimum. Part lies in agreeing upon what recourse should be available to a country that suffers economic injury from the policy actions of its trading partners. In GATT, this approach has touched only tangentially so far upon the linkages between trade and environmental policymaking. But the real problems emerging in this regard today make it possible that it will be central to GATT's work on environment-related trade measures in the future.

Agriculture and the GATT

Having analyzed the general concerns of the GATT in the area of trade and the environment, let me turn to apply the analysis to the specific case of agriculture.

Relationship with the Environment

First, can we be confident that the kind of policy reforms envisaged in the draft agreement on agriculture will not be damaging to the environment? Concerns have been voiced in this regard about the environmental consequences of the perceived message to farmers in the industrialized countries of "get bigger or get out" that reducing border protection and domestic support policies are likely to entail. There are also concerns about the environmental consequences of the shift of more intensive agricultural production to developing countries, involving potentially an acceleration of tropical deforestation to make available more cropping and grazing land and the more intensive use of chemical fertilizers and pesticides.

Recent analysis by Tyers and Anderson suggests that the concerns are exaggerated on both counts, since they conclude that both the aggregate output effect and the production relocation involved in implementation of the draft Uruguay Round results would be smaller than is commonly presumed. They also point out the importance of taking into account the benefits that would accrue, through more efficient resource allocation, in the form of economic welfare. With agricultural subsidies and transfers in the industrialized countries accounting for $300 billion a year or more, according to OECD estimates, the potential for releasing resources to pay for better environmental protection is clearly considerable.

But even that is only part of the story. Reforming agricultural trade policies on its own cannot be expected to resolve at the same time the environmental problems associated with intensive agricultural production. Proper environmental and resource management policies are needed as well. These may take many forms, and they lie generally outside the competence of the GATT.

However, the provision in the draft Uruguay Round agreement permitting environmental subsidies to be excluded from the commitments to reduce domestic agricultural support provides an important means of coordinating the environmental and trade objectives of the reform package.

Sanitary and Phytosanitary Measures

The inclusion in the draft Uruguay Round agreement on agriculture of an agreement on the use of Sanitary and Phytosanitary Measures is an indication of the importance governments attach to ensuring that as border restrictions and domestic support policies for agriculture are reduced, agro-environmental standards do not take their place as a new way to protect domestic agriculture and create barriers to trade.

The SPS Agreement is built on the basic GATT principles of non-discrimination and transparency, and it reflects also the principle of encouraging international harmonization of standards where these threaten otherwise to create unwarranted barriers to trade. Its key provisions, however, relate to the setting of national SPS standards which differ from international standards, and here the criteria of legitimacy and proportionality become all important. As with the existing TBT Agreement, difficult value judgements are involved on both counts, and considerable concern has been expressed by environmental groups that those judgements will be biased in favor of free trade and at the expense of national food and health standards, leading to pressure for the downward harmonization of such standards.

Since there is no case history yet to turn to for inspiration on how the SPS Agreement might be applied in practice, assurances cannot be given one way or the other. Experience with the TBT Agreement suggests, however, that these fears are exaggerated. Of over 250 notifications of national environmental standards made in the past ten years, not one has been
challenged on commercial grounds for failing to meet the tests of legitimacy or proportionality. The possibility cannot, of course, be discounted in the future. If cases do arise, objective scientific opinion will play an important role in resolving differences, but

nothing can avoid the need for governments to interpret collectively, as time passes, whether the right balance has been struck between respecting national environmental policy objectives in the SPS area and protecting adequately the trade interests of GATT Contracting Parties.

Future Agenda for the GATT

The most provocative question raised by the title of this session is whether there will be a need for a "Green Round" in GATT in the future. The honest answer it would seem is that it is too soon to tell. For one thing, we need first to finish the Uruguay Round. For another, governments domestically have quite evidently not yet reached clear conclusions on the extent to which their domestic and international environmental objectives require them to use trade policies in ways that are incompatible with their current GATT or post Uruguay Round obligations.

In parallel with the domestic policy debate on these issues, GATT's Contracting Parties are examining certain key issues in the Group on Environmental Measures and International Trade. Their discussions are, at present, focused on three points: trade provisions contained in multilateral environmental agreements; the transparency of trade-related environmental measures; and the trade effects of new forms of packaging and labelling requirements. Each of those points is raising issues that will most probably require clarification in the context of the post Uruguay Round trading system. Their agenda may well need to be broadened as time passes.

If further negotiations do prove necessary to resolve problems caused by the overlap of environmental and trade policies, the indications at present are that the following four principles can and should guide policymakers towards finding the right kind of accommodation with the multilateral trading system:
- keep markets open and competitive;
- feed in proper environmental prices to ensure the full benefits of the market mechanism are realized;

- respect the fact that environmental standards will not, and should not necessarily, be the same in all countries;
- and resolve international environmental disputes through cooperative, multilateral action, not through unilateral resort to punitive trade restrictions.

Chapter 20

A Trader's View on the Environment

Michael Smith

(Transcribed from conference tapes.)

Environment is The Trade Issue

This afternoon I speak as a trade "guru." I am not a professional environmentalist but view myself as one with an abiding interest in the environment <u>and</u> the trading system. As a "trader," I happen to think that the environment is a great issue for us traders if for no other reason than to keep the bureaucrats busy for the next ten years when and if the Uruguay Round is ever finished!

In addition, the environment is <u>the</u> trade issue of this decade and likely to be, perhaps with competition policy, the two major issues of the next decade in trade terms. At least in my country, the environment is no longer a question for the tree huggers or for the smokestack lovers. It is an issue, as we would say, for Middle America. It is an issue that has arrived as a growing, day-to-day concern for the vast majority of the American people.

Conflict Exists Between Trade and the Environment

Now, some of us believe that there is no conflict between trade and the environment. Actually though, at least intellectually in the United States, there is. The traders would say that by definition the GATT says that the fundamental objective of trade is to seek the most efficient allocation of resources. The environmentalists will say that is precisely the problem; that this drive for the most efficient use of resources leads to the degradation of the environment. Ergo, the environmentalists reject that. I believe that this issue is so important that if we traders ignore it, we do so at our own peril.

We have talked about the tuna/dolphin decision. Perhaps, you here in Europe do not quite appreciate it. There was a firestorm of criticism in the United States when the GATT rightly made the decision that it did. I say rightly from a legal point of view. Morally, I think they were wrong. Nonetheless, the GATT ruled as it had to given the parameters in which it was then working. Shortly thereafter, on the lamp posts of Washington and on the doors of the USTR appeared these posters called "GATTsilla is coming." An artist created either a dragon or a gorilla, which said that "GATTsilla is coming to Washington on November 14. What you don't know will hurt you."

Environmentalists Are Better Organized Than Traders

In the United States (I do not know if it is true in Europe or in Asia), the environmentalists are today better organized politically in the Congress than the traders. We saw that in the "fast track" legislation for the North American Free Trade Agreement (NAFTA). I would submit that the battle is not yet over, even though the negotiations are allegedly concluded between Canada, the United States, and Mexico. It, of course, has to be ratified by the United States Congress, which has made it very clear that it wants to see a satisfactory environmental something -- law, agreement, understanding -- between the three countries. This is the first time, certainly in my experience in trade, that we have seen the environmentalists mobilized in a very effective way. Indeed, they caught the administration flat-footed.

GATT Must Evolutionize

In terms of the GATT, it must evolutionize its thinking about the environment or it will be revolutionized. On the one hand, we must avoid what I would call environmental imperialism, which is the want of some of the more radical tree-hugging, berry-eating elements of the environmental movement. Yet, at the same time, we cannot be oblivious to the fact that a great number of people, who are otherwise strong believers in free trade, are also concerned about the environment.

I would submit, for example, that every time an environmental law is suggested in the United States or in any national parliament, it should be accompanied by a trade impact statement, just like in many cases we are being asked now to have environmental impact statements accompany trade legislation. Indeed, if you want to build a plant or to do something, you have to have an environmental impact statement. I think the turn-about is fair play. It is good ole GATT reciprocity and we ought to have trade impact statements so that politicians at least have some idea of what the costs are going be if and when they have to make choices between the environment, on the one hand, and trade, on the other. Mark my words; they will have to make choices sometimes.

We have seen this in the north western part of the United States in the spotted owl debate. There are choices -- either you are in favor of the spotted owl or you are in favor of the forests. A satisfactory compromise has not been reached and politicians are being faced, cruelly in a way, with having to make decisions about which they know very little. Unless and until they have such sorts of impact statements, our political processes are going to suffer.

The Trade/Environment Dilemma

There are some real problems, however, in the environment and trade dilemma. One is to use trade as an environmental enforcer. Traders tend to shudder from that; except we do have the cases (27 of 137 treaties) which have trade enforcement mechanisms to protect something dealing with the environment, especially species.

Going beyond the protection problem, using pure trade agreements as a way to save the environment is another matter and is something which the GATT is not easily equipped to do under its present provisions.

There are, for example, key questions of standards. Can you legitimately use trade measures to enforce standards? There is no question that a GATT member can take trade measures against a non-GATT member and escape relatively scott free, unless that particular country wishes to retaliate. But, the question of a GATT member taking trade measures against another GATT member because the one is a member of an international agreement and the other is not is a very difficult question.

There is also a question of what is called "sound science." We have heard talk about the sanitary and phytosanitary negotiations going on. In California, and this was a very, very scary thing in the United States in 1990, there was a thing called "Proposition 65," in which the standards of the state of California were going to be mandated on all products being sold in California (whether made in California or not). By and large, these standards rejected the notion of sound science. In many instances, the people who were determining what you could eat or not eat were not scientists or doctors but Jane Fonda and Tom Hayden. Hollywood was telling you what they would do if they had their way. Fortunately, for a change, California voted wisely and rejected Proposition 65.

We have a problem in the United States, which perhaps is seen also in Canada and maybe in some of the European countries like France with its *departementes* and Germany with its *lander*, in which there are certain powers that are derived to local authorities as opposed to the federal or central authority. In the United States, that has been a particular problem, because, for example, the Reagan/Bush administration has embraced a doctrine which is known as federalism. It does not intervene in certain institutional or governmental matters. So, when you have an administration which says that local communities or states should set

215

environmental standards, how do you think that applies for a foreigner who wants to trade with California, or Massachusetts, or Minnesota or wherever? Had Proposition 65 passed, we could have had the situation of perhaps 19 or 20 other states passing their own and different environmental phytosanitary and sanitary regulations. There is a nightmare prospect to this.

The Developing World

Back on a larger issue, what do we do about the developing world? Let us assume that we all agree that we should do something for trade and the environment. One of the key questions which will surface is how to transfer technology.

Some of you will remember during the Montreal Protocol that for a very long time the Chinese held off adhering to that agreement because they wanted in essence to do what Herbert Hoover had said in the 1920s (i.e. put a chicken in every pot). The Chinese said they wanted to put a refrigerator in every Chinese house. The only problem is the refrigerators were using refrigerants that were going to be outlawed or limited by the Montreal Protocol. So, the Chinese went to the United States government and said, "This is a great idea. We want to get rid of these bad pollutants and stuff. Now, will you tell Dupont to give us the substitute technology to take the place of the freons?" Well, doing so causes a problem in a democracy of a government telling the private sector that it should give technology which it developed at some expense.

Conclusion

There is a role for the GATT. I think it is true that the traders and the environmentalists have perhaps more in common than they do not. But, we should not underestimate the difficulties that this is going to cause for both the environmentalists and the trading community. There are going to be costs for one or the other or both. Anybody who thinks that it is going to be a free lunch -- that the environmentalists are going to be able to get something scott free -- again, you only have to see what happened in the north western United States with the spotted owl debate. Or, if the traders think that they are going to get away scott free, you only have to look at what has happened with either the tuna/dolphin or the Danish bottle decision.

Finally, with regard to the "green round," I do not hesitate in saying that perhaps when the Director General of the GATT and the Ministers convene to wrap up the Uruguay Round, they should then and there say that the next international negotiation that the GATT undertakes will indeed deal uniquely and specifically with the environment. I recognize the fact that if it is a single issue, there is not much to trade off with. But, I do not think we should be putting the GATT in a position of trading off things for the environment. The GATT is a big enough and mature enough organization and the environmental problem is pressing enough an issue that we should be able to take this issue on, even if we do not immediately succeed in coming up with definitive decisions in the course of those negotiations.

Chapter 21

The EC Commission
on Trade and the Environment

Tom Garvey

There is a high level of agreement among developed countries about the importance of environmental considerations for continuing economic growth. The G-7 countries concluded at their Paris Summit of July 1988:

"Environmental protection is integral to such issues as trade, development, energy, transport, agriculture, and economic planning. Therefore, environmental considerations must be taken into account in economic decision making."

So, environmental considerations are part and parcel of the economic relationships between countries, North-South as well as East-West. The causes of environmental degradation are well known and documented. The rate at which this degradation is proceeding is frightening enough to cause 155 Heads of State to come together in Rio to try to develop a global strategy to deal with the problems.

What we need to consider on this occasion are the effects on international trade of existing and future measures to arrest environmental degradation, in particular the effects of trade in agricultural produce. The European Community plays an important role in the agricultural sector globally, both in terms of production and trade.

The Agricultural Sector

Agriculture, together with forestry, occupies more than 80 percent of the territory of the Community. Traditionally, the farmer is the guardian of the soil and the countryside. By careful husbandry, including integrated crop and livestock farming and waste management, farmlands are passed in sound condition from one generation to the next. Agriculture has shaped and indeed continues to shape the European countryside and has set much of the foundation of European culture.

Just as in the case of manufacturing industry and transport, however, the agricultural sector and farming practices have undergone significant modernization and change during this century, especially over the last forty years. Among the factors which have brought change are the drift of rural populations to cities and towns; increased mechanization; improved transport; improvements in seed quality; crop protection and animal strains; and international trade and competition in food products and feed-stuffs.

Against this background, the Community's Common Agricultural Policy (CAP) has been developed and adapted so as to fulfill the objectives of the Treaty of Rome of assuring the availability of food supplies at reasonable prices, the stabilization of markets, and a fair standard of living for the agricultural Community. However, while the achievement of these objectives has been greatly promoted by the CAP's price support mechanisms, the same instruments are now seen to be having some less positive side-effects.

One of these effects has been an over-emphasis in some areas on production levels with consequential over-intensification. This, in turn, is leading to over-exploitation and degradation of the natural resources on which agriculture itself ultimately depends: soil, water, and air. In crop production, systematic use of plant protection products has lead to a relative resistance in parasites, increasing the frequency and the cost of subsequent treatments and causing additional soil and water pollution problems. In certain areas of the Community, large quantities of fertile topsoil are lost every year because of erosion due to inappropriate land management. In livestock farming, animal diseases have become more difficult to deal with as genetic uniformity and concentration in space of holdings have increased. Animal wastes create more and more problems of water and soil pollution. Ground clearance and drainage are causing depletion of wetlands and reducing biodiversity. Excessive use of nitrogenous and phosphate fertilizers causes eutrophication in surface waters in many regions of the Community; the resulting algal blooms disturb the oxygen levels of the water with dramatic consequences for fish, feeding matter, and the ecosystem in general as well as the use of the water for drinking and recreation purposes.

Even in cases where specific regional or horizontal measures are introduced for soil protection, their success is often compromised under the pressure of other market or structural measures. For example, efforts to protect heatherland and to combat erosion in northern countries can fail because of overgrazing as a result of the headage payment schemes, particularly in the sheep sector.

Given all of these circumstances, it is not only environmentally desirable, but it also makes sound agricultural and economic sense to seek to strike a more sustainable balance between agricultural activity and natural resources.

This appreciation is clearly reflected in the recent reform of the Common Agricultural Policy, which, *inter alia*, recognizes that "producing more" cannot be any longer considered as the central point of Community policy. The Commission's 1991 Reflection Paper on the development and future of the CAP (COM(91) 100 final of 1 February 1991) recognized the need to encourage extensification with the object of not only reducing surplus production but also of contributing to an environmentally sustainable form of agricultural production and food quality and formalizing the dual role of farmers as food producers and guardians of the countryside. The new approach includes an agri-environmental action program which encompasses several types of financial assistance designed to encourage farmers to operate their land holdings in an environmentally friendly way.

The Community as Trading Partner

The identity of the Community is to a large extent determined by its significance as a trading partner in the world: its imports make up a third of world trade, it is the principal market for developing countries as a whole, and it provides a large part of development aid in the world. The Community thus has a fundamental interest in maintaining an open world market and therefore to strengthen the competitiveness of its manufacturing base. Because the Community is dependent on the world market for almost 45 percent of its energy requirement and for almost three quarters of the most needed raw materials, it depends on the export of its processed products.

The main features of the Community's trade policy can be summarized as follows:

a) Liberalization of world trade within the framework of the General Agreement on Tariffs and Trade (GATT), which should be reinforced to enhance its capacity to prevent and solve trade conflicts and expanded to cover areas of growing importance in trade relations (such as services or intellectual property rights).

b) The elimination, as part of the establishment of the internal market, of remaining restrictions to trade within the Community. A large and dynamic single market should be a factor in the expansion of world trade.

c) The establishment or strengthening of close trading links with other countries in Europe (EFTA, Eastern, and Central Europe) as well as with developing countries with which the Community has close historical associations.

d) An active policy to promote the integration of developing countries into the trading system, both through multilateral trade liberalization and the granting of trade preferences.

e) The use of commercial policy instruments to ensure fair conditions of competition.

Environmental Policy with Trade Impacts

In 1990, the Community decided that existing environmental policies, which remain mainly regulatory, needed to be complemented by economic and fiscal instruments. Climate change, solid waste, water, and integration of environment policy into other areas were to be targeted as priorities. Bearing in mind the complex overlaps with economic, energy, taxation, transport, and other policy areas, all work on economic and fiscal instruments must have a significant impact on trade flows within the Community.

It is also fostering self-regulation and voluntary agreements to encourage the productive sector to modify its economic behavior and to conduct its activities in ways which are responsive to environmental concerns. Several schemes already exist to form an embryo program in this field. For example, since 1987 the Community has made a series of environmental awards for industry which recognize the efforts of individual companies. A proposal for a Community eco-labelling system was proposed in 1991 (see Chapter 4). A further proposal, on environmental auditing, is also being prepared. It encourages enterprises to subject their major industrial sites to an evaluation and to publish the results as an environmental statement. The very process of integrating environmental concerns into the fabric of the Community's life will lead to changes in the allocation and use of resources which will inevitably be reflected in trade patterns.

Trade and the Environment

The new priority given worldwide to environmental objectives has brought to light the complex interrelationships between environmental and trade policies. Countries with high standards come under pressure to protect themselves against competitors with lower standards. Their competitive positions will depend on their ability to offer environmentally friendly products which are in accordance with both consumers' demands and the product standards of their trade partners. However, regulatory standards or market-based instruments may have economic effects distinct form their environmental objectives, altering the competitive position of firms and countries and triggering shifts in trade flows which may prompt demands for compensation and protection *vis-a-vis* competitors facing less stringent environmental obligations. In some cases, environmental groups propose the adoption of trade measures as a means to promote better environmental conservation and management policies by third countries.

Several conventions already exist which restrict or prohibit certain forms of trade. One deals with endangered species and three with environmentally dangerous products. The Washington Contention (CITES, chapter 24) prohibits or severely limits the trade of endangered species of fauna and flora. The Montreal Protocols of 1988 and 1991 prohibit the import and export of ozone depleting substances (Chapter 22). Under Community legislation, based on UNEP guidelines, notification procedures are required for the export of a range of dangerous chemicals, coupled with procedures to ensure that the rules applicable to their handling within the Community are also applicable to the importers (Chapter 4). When it comes into force (probably before the end of 1991), the Basel Convention of 1989 on the transfrontier movements of hazardous wastes will restrict and control the export and import of such products.

This overlap between trade and environment policies creates a potential for tension that must be eliminated by reflecting on ways of achieving a suitable balance between securing environmental objectives and preserving the open multilateral trading system. Trade and environment policies need to be mutually supportive in order to enhance their respective efficiency overall. It is particularly important to avoid having trade restrictions used as the substitute for domestic environmental policies or that environmental standards constitute hidden barriers to trade.

Sustainable Development

One issue related to trade and to sustainable development is the use of depletable raw materials in order to earn foreign exchange. Developing countries face the dilemma of having to balance their needs for foreign currency with damage to the environmental resources which supports their growth. Trade can and should help achieve the goals of sustainable development since it generates additional resources through growth and contributes to the more efficient use of available resources, providing a long term incentive for conservation through the valorization of natural resources for a large number of developing countries.

Although a growing number have diversified into manufactured exports, primary commodities other than petroleum continue to account for more than one-third of the export earnings of the group as a whole. The Community gives broad trade opportunities and a generalized system of preferences for many products through the Lomé Convention or the cooperation framework with Mediterranean countries.

On the other hand, the growing number of trade opportunities and economic growth contain a certain risk for the environment. The often urgent need for foreign exchange in developing countries may lead to unsustainable production patterns and an over-exploitation of resources if environmental considerations are not taken into account.

The Community, through the technical and financial assistance it provides to the framework of bilateral cooperation programs as well as its active participation in international environmental agreements, is aiming at the minimization of these negative phenomena, although the primary responsibility lies with the developing countries themselves.

The priority attached to environmental consideration in new orientations of the Community's economic cooperation and development aid and the Community's consistent position in mobilizing appropriate resources to assist developing counties in complying with international environmental requirements are in the right direction of balancing these difficulties.

Common Standards

In the world we live in with its increasingly serious gaps between haves and have nots, globally and within regions, it is difficult to foresee a state of affairs in which levels of concern about climate change, civil liberties, health and safety issues, hygiene, and accidents on the land will be the same in each country. As these levels of concern are translated into regulations and standards governing the composition, sale, and use of products, it is inevitable that in their disparity they will impinge on trade and conditions of competition. There is no reason why countries should not seek to protect their environment by adopting stringent (and differing) national standards and regulations, provided these are applied equally to home produced and imported goods. It is when attempts are made to discriminate in favor of domestic manufacturers and their products that potential conflicts arise. It is therefore desirable that maximum effort be launched to achieve common or harmonized environmental standards, where possible.

Relations with Specific Trade Structures (GATT)

Liberalization of the GATT

The Community supports the further liberalization of world trade within the framework of GATT and expects to bring its single market legislation into line with the agreements reached in the current negotiations. Although the negotiations have not examined the interactions between trade and the environment, a number of issues raised there have a bearing on the subject, in particular those relating to prohibited or severely restricted goods, including hazardous substances. The GATT does not prevent countries from following the policies they believe to be necessary to protect the environment, provided that such measures do not constitute hidden barriers to trade.

However, there is considerable uncertainty as to the relationship between GATT provisions and certain types of trade-related measures that may be adopted for the protection of the environment. Questions arise, for instance, on what might be the rules applicable to environmental production and processing requirements or on how to avoid potential conflict between the GATT and the trade provisions of international environmental agreements. The Community was among the leaders in pressing the GATT to clarify these issues.

In principle, there is nothing environmentally dangerous in the international exchange of agricultural produce. It is unwise to create the impression that environmental prudence when applied to such exchanges constitutes an entirely unprecedented and unmanageable set of problems. The developments which we all hope for in the context of the Uruguay Round will lead to an increase in international trade while developments flowing from, *inter alia*, Rio will lead to an increase in environmental concern and regulation.

In previous GATT Rounds, tariff reductions across the board led to increased international trade at the same time as there were increasing levels of concern in the developed world about health and safety and consumer protection. There is no contradiction between the two tendencies; only the need for careful analysis, consultation, and efficient mechanisms for problem solving. Technical barriers to trade are not new (whatever their source) and the techniques for avoiding or abolishing them are generally known.

The fact is that it is not the increasing or decreasing of trade in agricultural products per se which impacts the environment but the interference in markets by governments through subsidies and other supports which give rise to excess production from increasingly over-exploited natural resources. In order to maximize yields per hectare, increasing inputs of fertilizer and chemicals are resorted to, leading to soil erosion and diminishing water quality, with concentrated livestock production units creating major waste disposal problems.

Community Actions

Of course, as pointed out previously, there has not been any lack of environmental concern in the Community about the effects of intensive agriculture on eco-systems. But, the overwhelming power of direct crop specific subsidies or price interventions have tended to overcome them.

The CAP reform decisions of 21 May 1992 will further enhance the sustainability of Community agriculture and make a valuable contribution to the preservation of the environment and living conditions in rural areas.

The substantial reduction in agricultural support prices will in general lead to a less intensive use of natural resources as well as of agro-chemicals which may affect the environment. This effect will be enhanced by a set-aside of 15 percent of arable land for which direct payments are requested and by a limitation of premiums to a specific number of animals per hectare of forage area. These limitations apply to all but small producers. In addition, premiums are increased for further extensification in the bovine sector.

At the same time, compensation payments and premiums unrelated to production will ensure the viability of the agriculture sector. Early retirement assistance will facilitate the improvement of farm structures and free-up land for other activities such as forestry and leisure. The reform package includes a special program for forestation as an alternative use of agricultural land, as an additional source of farm income, and as a regime that provides for the financial participation of the Community in a wide range of agri-environmental measures to be introduced by Member States.

While the major benefits of the above-mentioned reforms will occur within the Community, there will also be positive transborder effects with regard to water, air, and the global climate. In addition, reduced Community production and exports will contribute to improved world market conditions for third country exporters and to their efforts towards the sustainability of their own agriculture.

As was interestingly demonstrated in a recent study undertaken for OECD, agricultural trade liberalization based on the reduction of price interventions in the production sector will lead to a growth in world trade, which will be more environmentally friendly.

The Role of GATT

The recent publication of the GATT Panel Report on the United States' tuna embargo has reactivated public discussion on the interface between trade and environmental policies. Some have argued that this report highlights concerns that the GATT system may be an obstacle for the implementation of domestic environmental policies or for the efforts to tackle global environmental challenges. A close examination of the Panel report shows that such negative perceptions are far from being justified.

The report contains not only a very positive global message, but it also provides useful pointers for future work to be carried out in the GATT in order to better integrate environmental policies into the multilateral trading system. In order to have a more focused public discussion, it is worth examining the relationships between the GATT and both domestic and global environmental policies. On both accounts, the Panel report introduces a number of valuable clarifications.

Specifics of the Panel Report

The GATT does not challenge the sovereign rights of countries to introduce high standards of environmental protection. The fundamental objective of domestic environmental policies is to achieve sustainable development through the internalization of environmental costs. Instruments of a regulatory or economic kind can be used to achieve these goals. While domestic regulations like standards or taxes may have an impact on trade flows, the GATT has never questioned the right of countries to apply such measures in order to attain high domestic standards of environmental protection. Indeed, the Panel report confirms this principle:

"The provisions of the General Agreement impose few constraints on a contracting party's implementation of domestic environmental policies. . . . A contracting party is free to tax or regulate imported products and like domestic products as long as its taxes or regulations do not discriminate against imported products or afford protection to domestic producers."

There can be therefore no question of a GATT challenge against the sovereign right of countries to introduce domestically high standards of environmental protection. Nor would the GATT require countries to lower their environmental standards. Indeed, the GATT as a trade institution does not have the competence to judge on the appropriateness of conservation policies. This principle is again clearly stated in the Panel report:

"Article XX(b) allows each contracting party to set its human, animal or plant life of health standards. The conditions set out in Article XX(b) which limit resort to this exception, namely that the measure taken must be 'necessary' and not 'constitute a means of arbitrary or unjustifiable discrimination or a disguised restriction on international trade,' refer to the trade measure requiring justification under Article XX(b), not however to the life or health standard chosen by the contracting party."

The GATT would examine trade restrictions adopted for environmental purposes on the basis of the principles of non-discrimination and proportionality. This latter principle is not intended to weigh trade against environmental concerns, but rather to consider whether, for any given environmental goal, the less trade restrictive instrument has been applied. These two principles are sound from both a trade and an environmental perspective. They offer considerable scope for cooperation between trade and environmental exports in order to ensure both the maximum effectiveness of environmental regulations or taxes and the need to avoid unnecessary obstacles to trade. Indeed, it is worth noting that, despite the fact that many countries have given a high priority to environmental protection, GATT challenges against such policies have been extremely rare.

An important feature of environmental policies has been the adoption of measures to reduce the pollution or environmental damage caused by the production process. The panel fully recognized the right of countries to apply any such instrument to domestic production. At the same time, an important clarification is introduced by noting that production requirements may only be applied to imported products if the method of production has a bearing on the final characteristics of the product (i.e. if the product as such is a source of environmental damage when put in the market of the importing country).

The "Golden Rule" --
Unilateralism Versus Multilateral Cooperation

Environmental policy is rapidly evolving into a global policy, which includes a set of multilateral obligations. The Community is firmly committed to enhancing the role of international environmental law, both as regards the implementation of existing multilateral conventions (e.g. Montreal Protocol, CITES, Basel Convention) and the development of new instruments to tackle urgent global challenges (e.g. global warming, biodiversity, and deforestation). The argument that the Tuna Panel report may hinder such efforts is unjustified. Since this is a point of crucial importance, a careful reading of the Panel is necessary.

The Panel establishes a "golden rule" on extraterroriality, which has implications well beyond the environmental field (i.e. that a country may not legislate outside its own jurisdiction and impose unilaterally on other countries rules of behavior, the penalty for non-compliance being a restriction on imports). As the Panel notes, the consequence of accepting such trade restrictions would be that "each contracting party could unilaterally determine the life of health protection policies from which other contracting parties could not deviate without jeopardizing their rights under the General Agreement." Furthermore, the Panel suggests that the United States could have pursued its objectives "through the negotiation of international cooperative arrangements."

The Community believes that in order to tackle global environmental challenges, which go beyond the jurisdiction of any individual country, solutions need to be found which are based on multilateral cooperation. Unilateral trade restrictions would not normally be effective and raise serious equity issues, in particular as regards their impact on developing countries. This point can be illustrated by reference to the Montreal Protocol, which has been a particularly successful example of multilateral cooperation in the environment field. The Protocol recognized that developing countries need certain flexibilities in achieving the targets for phasing-out substances depleting the ozone layer and that resources should be transferred in order to help them meet the costs of environmental protection. The adoption, within this multilateral context, of trade restrictions is fully justified. On the other hand, unilateral trade measures of an extra-jurisdictional nature could easily result in the imposition of excessive burdens on developing countries.

The Panel has, therefore, provided important pointers in the direction that multilateral cooperation is required to address global environmental challenges. In its concluding remarks, the Panel notes that "the adoption of its report would affect neither the rights of individual contracting parties to pursue their internal environmental policies, nor the right of the contracting parties acting jointly to address international environmental problems which can only be resolved through measures in conflict with the present rules of the General Agreement." The Community reads this as an urgent invitation for the collective GATT membership to seek ways to better integrate the global environmental dimension into the multilateral GATT framework. This is a task to which we are fully committed.

If the unilateral approach is ruled out, then we are thrown very largely on international cooperation to achieve agreements and standards which will prevent trade distortions while respecting the urgent need to take action on environmental degradation, an objective which the Commission believes is achievable. The role of GATT in this process is clear.

The Commission is conscious of the fact that the Uruguay Round Final Act has by no means provided a response to all the

231

issues raised by the interface of trade and environmental policies. This is an issue which must now receive a comprehensive examination in its own right. This decision to activate the Group on Environmental Measures and International Trade is welcome. The Community has always pushed for GATT recognition of the importance of the global environmental dimension. The proposal to establish a Multilateral Trade Organization to englobe the GATT is welcome.

A new Commission on Sustainable Development now being constituted under the auspices of the United Nations in follow up to the UNCED Rio Conference will also deal with the question of the environment and trade. The concern for the environment is a global issue. Our future will depend on actions taken or not taken by both North and South.

It is therefore worthwhile in conclusion to recall the conclusions of that conference on this specific topic.

Making Trade and Environment Mutually Supportive

(Extract from Preamble to Agenda 21, Chapter 1 as adopted by the Plenary of the United Nations Conference on Environment & Development on June 14, 1992.)

Basis for Action

Environment and trade policies should be mutually supportive. An open, multilateral trading system makes possible a more efficient allocation and use of resources and thereby contributes to an increase in production and incomes and to lessening demands on the environment. It thus provides additional resources needed for economic growth and development and improved environmental protection. A sound environment, on the other hand, provides the ecological and other resources needed to sustain growth and underpin a continuing expansion of trade. An open, multilateral trading system, supported by the adoption of sound environmental policies, would have a positive impact on the environment and contribute to sustainable development.

International cooperation in the environmental fields is growing, and in a number of cases, trade provisions in multilateral environmental agreements have played a role in tackling global environmental challenges. Trade measures have thus been used in certain specific instances, where considered necessary, to enhance the effectiveness of environmental regulations for the protection of the environment. Such regulations should address the root causes of environmental degradation so as not to result in unjustified restrictions on trade. The challenge is to ensure that trade and environment policies are consistent and reinforce the process of sustainable development. However, account should be taken of the fact that environmental standards valid for developed countries may have unwarranted social and economic costs in developing countries.

Objectives

Governments should strive to meet the following objectives, through relevant multilateral forums, including GATT, UNCTAD and other international organizations:

a) To make international trade and environment policies mutually supportive in favor of sustainable development;

b) To clarify the role of GATT, UNCTAD and other international organizations in dealing with trade and environment-related issues, including, where relevant, conciliation procedure and dispute settlement;

c) To encourage international productivity and competitiveness and encourage a constructive role on the part of industry in dealing with environment and development issues.

Activities: Developing an Environment/Trade and Development Agenda

Governments should encourage GATT, UNCTAD and other relevant international and regional economic institutions to examine, in accordance with their respective mandates and competencies, the following propositions and principles:

a) Elaborate adequate studies for the better understanding of the relationship between trade and environment for the promotion of sustainable development;

b) Promote a dialogue between trade, development and environment communities;

c) In those cases when trade measures related to environment are used, ensure transparency and compatibility with international obligations;

d) Deal with the root causes of environment and development problems in a manner that avoids the adoption of environmental measures resulting in unjustified restrictions on trade;

e) Seek to avoid the use of trade restrictions or distortions as a means to offset differences in cost arising from differences in environmental standards and regulations, since their application could lead to trade distortions and increase protectionist tendencies;

f) Ensure that environment-related regulations or standards, including those related to health and safety standards, do not constitute a means of arbitrary or unjustifiable discrimination or a disguised restriction on trade;

g) Ensure that special factors affecting environment and trade policies in the developing countries are born in mind in the application of environmental standards, as well as in the use of any trade measures. It is worth noting that standards that are valid in the most advanced countries may be inappropriate and of unwarranted social costs for the developing countries;

h) Encourage participation of developing countries in multilateral agreements through such mechanisms as special transitional rules;

i) Avoid unilateral actions to deal with environmental challenges outside the jurisdiction of the importing country. Environmental measures addressing transborder or global environmental problems should, as far as possible, be based on an international consensus. Domestic measures targeted to achieve certain environmental objectives may need trade measures to render them effective. Should trade policy measures be found necessary for the enforcement of environmental policies, certain principles and rules should apply. These could include, *inter alia*, the principle of non-discrimination; the principle that the measure chosen should be the least trade-restrictive necessary to achieve the objectives; an obligation to ensure transparency in the use of trade measures related to the environment and to provide adequate notification of national regulations; and the need to give consideration to the special conditions and developmental requirements of developing countries as they move towards internationally agreed environmental objectives;

j) Develop more precision where necessary, and clarify the relationship between GATT provisions and some of the multilateral measures adopted in the environmental area;

k) Ensure public input in the formation, negotiation and implementation of trade policies as a means of fostering increased transparency in the light of country-specific conditions;

l) Ensure that environmental policies provide the appropriate legal and institutional framework to respond to new needs for the protection of the environment that may result from changes in production and trade specialization.

Chapter 22

UNCED Addresses Trade and the Environment

Tahar Hadj-Sadok

The title of this session includes the question "How will environmental concerns affect trade?" One recent occasion when environmental concerns and threats were discussed by representatives of world governments was the United Nations Conference on Environment and Development (UNCED), which met in June of this year in Rio de Janeiro, Brazil. The primary aim of my presentation today is to inform this meeting on how UNCED addressed the issue of trade and the environment.

Place of Trade and Agriculture in UNCED

First, I would like to clarify two points.

1) UNCED has a broad agenda, dealing with most aspects of the environment and development. In that context, the trade of agricultural products was an important issue, but one among many such issues. Agenda 21, the program of work adopted by UNCED, includes some 800 pages, only a few of which are devoted to agricultural trade.

2) UNCED was not a forum for trade negotiations. It merely envisaged the topic of trade in the context of other development and environment issues. As Mr. Kjeldsen informed the meeting yesterday, Agenda 21 includes a chapter on strengthening the role of farmers. Trade and the environment are addressed in the initial economic chapter of Agenda 21 in two sections respectively dealing with promoting sustainable

development through trade and making trade and the environment mutually supportive.

UNCED's Approach to Trade

Rather than trying to paraphrase or to summarize language adopted by UNCED, I would like to quote passages of the language adopted in Rio. In my opinion, these passages are characteristic of the spirit of the UNCED conference.

Promoting Sustainable Development Through Trade

"The commodity sector dominates the economies of many developing countries in terms of production, employment and export earnings. In the 1980s, very low and declining real prices for most commodities in international markets led to substantial contraction in commodity export earnings for many producing countries. The ability to mobilize, through international trade, the resources needed to finance investments required for sustainable development may be impaired by this decrease in incomes and by tariff and non-tariff impediments, including tariff escalation, limiting their access to export markets. The removal of existing distortions in international trade is essential. In particular, the achievement of this objective requires that there be substantial and progressive reduction in the support and protection of agriculture -- covering internal regimes, market access and export subsidies -- as well as of industry and other sectors, in order to avoid inflicting large losses on the more efficient producers, especially in developing countries."

As far as actions in this regard are concerned, UNCED recommended promoting an international trading system that takes account of the needs of developing countries. Specifically, it should: "halt and reverse protectionism in order to bring about further liberalization and expansion of world trade, to the benefit of all countries, in particular the developing countries;" and "strengthen the international trade policies system through an early, balanced, comprehensive and successful outcome of the Uruguay Round of multilateral trade negotiations."

Trade and the Environment

Regarding the relationship between trade and the environment, UNCED stressed both the importance of an open trading system and that of a sound environment. It recommended an environment, trade, and development agenda, including a series of propositions. The following paragraph characterizes the general orientation:

"Avoid unilateral actions to deal with environmental challenges outside the jurisdiction of the importing country. Environmental measures addressing transborder or global environmental problems should, as far as possible, be based on an international consensus. Domestic measures targeted to achieve certain environmental objectives may need trade measures to render them effective. Should trade policy measures be found necessary for the enforcement of environmental policies, certain principles and rules should apply. These could include, *inter alia*, the principle of non-discrimination; the principle that the trade measure chosen should be the least trade-restrictive necessary to achieve the objectives; an obligation to ensure transparency in the use of trade measures related to the environment and to provide adequate notification of national regulations; and the need to give consideration to the special conditions and developmental requirements of developing countries as they move towards internationally agreed environmental objectives."

Regarding "promoting sustainable development through trade," the message is loud and clear. "Trade liberalization should be pursued on a global basis so as to contribute to sustainable development." It is the development of developing countries that will enable them to act to protect their environment. Access to markets is essential for development.

Regarding "making trade and environment mutually supportive," the message is one of caution, particularly when it comes to the possible use of trade measures for environmental purposes.

In UNCED's perspective, the answer to the initial question "How will environmental concerns affect trade" should, therefore, be: environmental concerns should, in general, not result in barriers to trade and trade measures should only be used for environmental purposes when this is the best way to reach the desired result and is the least disruptive to trade. On balance, environmental concerns should lead to trade liberalization rather than trade restrictions.

Harmonizing Environmental Standards

In order to address the issue of harmonizing environmental standards, I will clarify one point and ask two questions.

The clarification is that environmental standards on products should apply to markets in which products are sold. Environmental standards regarding production processes should be geared to the environment of the production facility. Both types of environmental standards are useful for protecting consumers and the environment. While the case for harmonizing environmental product characteristics in a given market is self-evident, that of international harmonization of environmental standards for production processes is much more dubious.

The two questions are:
1) Trade in agricultural products is characterized by massive interventions (e.g. tariffs, tariff escalation, quotas, price

support, export subsidies and "voluntary" restraints) which greatly affect the competitive positions of various producers. In such a playing field, which is far from level and full of high barriers, what is the significance of offsetting cost differentials that may result from differences in environmental standards before doing away with the barriers?

2) If environmental standards need to be harmonized because they generate differences in production costs, why is the harmonization of other factors that differ greatly from country to country and generate differences in production costs not given consideration? One could mention in this regard factors such as interest rates, salaries, and social benefits.

Chapter 23

Trade and the Environment: New Zealand's Experience

W. Rob Storey

I want to approach this topic from a New Zealander's point of view. Like most countries, our focus on environmental issues has been on the UNCED process leading up to the Earth Summit. At Rio, our delegation consisted of representatives of widely different groups: government, environmental NGOs, industry, and New Zealand's Maori people. This could have been a mix for conflict. But, as the UNCED process evolved, environmentalists and businessmen began to get a better understanding of each others' positions and to identify areas for cooperation towards common goals. I think our UNCED experience may provide a microcosm of the way environmental and economic concerns can and must be reconciled.

New Zealand Has Stake in Trade and Environment

New Zealand has a major stake in both sides of the trade and environment relationship. In an interdependent world, we require the strongest possible protection for the international environment in order to assure our long term economic viability. As a country heavily dependent on trade, we are fully committed to the liberalization of the multilateral trading system.

New Zealand has been at the forefront of much of the environmental debate. We are only too aware of our vulnerability to global environmental threats not of our making. At the same

241

time, our economic growth depends heavily on the sound and forward-looking management of our natural resources in agriculture, forestry, and fisheries. We, therefore, recognize our responsibility to ensure that decisions on trade, agriculture, and the environment take full account of their long term implications.

No Conflict Exists Between Trade and Environment

From a New Zealand perspective then, I do not see any inherent conflict between trade and environmental objectives. On the contrary, I am convinced that trade and environmental policies must be mutually supportive and not antagonistic. Trade promotes economic growth, which gives people a stake in the future and helps provide the technology and wealth required to sustain the environment. But trade can exist only if the environment is protected to ensure that the natural resource base is sustained.

Multilateral Cooperation is Necessary

Moreover, many trade and environmental problems can be solved only through multilateral and global action. Unilateral measures to reconcile trade and environmental objectives are likely to be ineffective or counterproductive. Real solutions on trade and the environment, whether taken together or separately, will be reached only through international cooperation.

That is why the focus of the Rio Summit was on sustainable development, a concept which embraces both economic and environmental imperatives. In New Zealand, the sustainable management of our natural resources has been formally built into Government policy through pioneering legislation introduced in 1991. The Resource Management Act enshrines in law the concept of sustainability and a comprehensive definition of the environment. It focuses on environmental effects with greater freedom for economic and social decision making within that context. The Act also places an obligation on decision makers and developers to anticipate and assess the impacts of their policies and proposals. In short, it ensures that economic development and resource management are sustainable.

The Conflict Over Subsidies

We have learned from our mistakes. A decade ago New Zealand flirted briefly with a system of agricultural subsidies (e.g. loans for the development of hill country farms and guaranteed minimum prices) which encouraged the environmentally unsound exploitation of marginal land. Those subsidies have been abolished. As a result, New Zealand farmers have to make production decisions based on the market. We have recently developed a sustainable agricultural policy which will encourage land users to take account of the longer term effects on resources of their decisions.

On an international scale, the distortions produced by interference in the agricultural market have been vastly more damaging in their consequences. Agricultural subsidies have produced a system driven by large scale inputs of chemicals, fertilizers, and energy rather than one determined by natural endowments and comparative advantage. The result is often erosion, pollution, depleted water resources, and deforestation.

Equally damaging is the way agricultural subsidies distort international trade. The OECD countries are estimated to spend US$350 billion on subsidizing agriculture, six times the amount provided in ODA transfers. The Rio Summit was about economics and politics as much as about the environment. The message from Rio was that we must not allow politics to get in the way of economic and environmental common sense.

Much was said at Rio about the need for increased development assistance. Perhaps more needs to be said about the more fundamental need for access to markets and a more liberalized trading system that will allow market forces to reflect efficiency (including sustainability of resource use) rather than the outcome of subsidy wars. This is where the real challenge lies if

243

the goal of environmentally sound and sustainable development is to be attained.

Efforts to tackle the environmental problems identified at Rio would therefore be significantly advanced by a successful conclusion to the Uruguay Round. Speaker after speaker at the Summit identified the need to bring these negotiations to fruition. Chapter 2 of Agenda 21 strongly endorses the link between an open and nondiscriminatory multilateral trading system and sustainable development to the benefit of both developed and developing countries.

Necessity of a Green Round

Once the Uruguay Round is completed, do we need a "Green Round?" Until the negotiations are satisfactorily resolved, the way ahead will remain uncertain. Without a successful conclusion, we will have no foundation on which to construct an international system which satisfies both environmental and trading needs. The vision at Rio of a new framework for relations between developing and developed countries, of a multilateral system which would integrate environmental concerns into economic and social policies, will otherwise remain an elusive goal.

I, therefore, feel strongly that the first priority is to finish the job in hand. At stake in the Uruguay Round is not only the credibility and indeed the viability of the GATT, but also the effectiveness of multilateral action in dealing with global problems of development and the environment.

The conclusion of the Uruguay Round should give substantial impetus towards a trading system in which the true costs of agricultural production are recognized. This will allow us to move away from the subsidization of inputs which leads to their overuse and to the detriment of the environment. Correcting inappropriate market intervention will encourage greater efficiency with less waste and fewer inputs.

In New Zealand, one of the consequences of removing subsidies has been a reduction in the use of inputs such as chemicals and fertilizers. We are thus harmonizing the goals of environmental enhancement and lower-cost production. In the fisheries sector, we have introduced an innovative quota regime that is designed to ensure that our marine resources are harvested in a sustainable manner. In the important forestry sector, New Zealand's experience in the production and management of commercially-planted forests has highlighted the potential contribution planted forests can make to environmental and economic objectives, as carbon sinks, as soil conservation and water management areas, as recreational facilities, and through providing employment opportunities.

National Policies Should Not Be Barriers

By the same token, the last thing we need is a new system of non-tariff barriers replacing the trade restrictive practices we are just on the point of eliminating. National environmental policies should not act as a barrier to trade by penalizing exports; rather, they should take account of the principles of nondiscrimination, national treatment and transparency. It is just as essential to avoid unnecessary barriers to trade as it is imperative to address the need for improved environmental protection.

For example, the drive by several OECD governments to enact more stringent environmental standards in areas such as packaging and recycling needs to be tempered by the need to ensure these standards are consistent with accepted trade rules.

Environmental problems need to be addressed at source, not by poorly targeted intervention. Invoking trade measures to address environmental concerns is usually a second-best solution and often no solution at all. A root cause of much environmental degradation is the inadequate valuation of environmental costs and benefits. This needs to be redressed. The most effective environmental controls will be those that are levied by the market place rather than by regulation. I have been particularly impressed by the work the Business Council for Sustainable Development has done in demonstrating that environmentally sound policies also open up commercial opportunities.

The Role of GATT

That does not mean that there is no need for further work on environmental matters in the multilateral trade context. There is general recognition of the need for an increasing focus on environmental issues in the GATT.

New Zealand welcomes the working groups that have been set up in the GATT and the OECD to begin to look more closely at the relationship between trade and environmental measures, including the implications of the UNCED outcomes. There is clearly a need for the GATT to be more user-friendly and to help dispel some of the opposition of environmental NGOs, who see trade and the environment as mutually antagonistic. Environmental NGOs need to be vigilant to the danger of manipulation by protectionist sectoral interests, the divergence between the goals of environmental protection, and open trading that is more apparent than real.

There is also scope for involving developing countries to a greater degree and overcoming suspicion of the GATT as a developed country club. I could in this context mention the Cairns Group, which brings together developed and developing countries with shared concerns, as evidence that the North-South division is not unbridgeable.

While I remain cautious about an all-embracing "Green Round," there are actual or potential conflicts between the GATT and environmental measures which will need to be considered on a case-by-case basis. Some countries have expressed concern about the compatibility of parts of the Biodiversity Convention with intellectual property rights. Trade sanction provisions under several other international environment agreements have also been questioned by some. We do not favor reopening debate on existing agreements with broad international support at this stage.

However, we recognize that we need to consider the trade and environment angle very carefully in relation to new agreements.

Another indication of the potential for conflict is the proposed non-binding resolution in the United States Congress that would in effect place domestic environmental law above multilateral obligations such as the GATT. From both the environmental and trade perspectives, we need to avoid getting on such a collision course. As I said earlier, there is no necessary incompatibility between multilateral trade and environmental concerns. The need is for balance between two equally valid perspectives, based on a deeper understanding of the relationship between them, rather than the adoption of doctrinaire positions.

The proliferation of agencies dealing with environmental and trade issues also indicates a need for better communication and cross-referencing. I envisage that the Commission for Sustainable Development, to be established shortly by the United Nations to oversee and promote UNCED follow-up, will have a particular role to play through disseminating information on environmental policy and relevant economic developments.

Consumers Ultimately Decide

My final comment is that we should move beyond the belief that protection of the environment is a barrier to trade or that an open trading system is inimical to sustainable development. In a market system, the consumer ultimately decides, and it is evident nowhere more so than here in Europe that consumers place a high premium on environmentally friendly products. Hopefully, this will become a global trend as the economies of developing countries respond to increased technology transfers and opportunities through trade liberalization.

We in New Zealand therefore see increasing environmental awareness on the part of international consumers as a challenge to which we all need to respond. Our exporters have traditionally enjoyed a competitive advantage through our country's "clean green" image, and we have no fears about consumer demand which is more environmentally sensitive. Our main concern is to ensure that the symbiotic relationship between an open trading system and sustainable development and environmental protection is fully recognized.

Chapter 24

Agriculture and the Environment Without Subsidies

Brian Chamberlin

(Transcribed from conference tapes.)

First of all, I would like to apologize for our Minister, Rob Storey, for not being able to make it at the last minute. He was very much looking forward to this conference, to presenting his paper, and to responding to the views put forward by other participants. In answering the questions that have been put forward for this session, we in New Zealand and our Minister believe very strongly that some of our experiences are certainly worth sharing with this important gathering. I believe that once we have shared these experiences, they may assist you in your decision making. Since time does not permit me to read the whole speech, I intend to pick out a few highlights and read one or two paragraphs.

The Resource Management Act

The Resource Management Act supersedes or overrides any other planning legislation in New Zealand. It was introduced by one government. When they were defeated before the act became law, the incoming government put the bill through Parliament. So, it is something that has the substantial support of the political process in New Zealand.

There have been a number of questions asked at this conference about the meaning of the word "sustainability." This term is very central to the purpose and principles of the Act. If I may quote very briefly from the Act, it reads:

> "In this Act, sustainable management means managing the use, development, and protection of natural and physical resources in a way or at a rate which enables people and communities to provide for their social, economic, and cultural well being and for their safety, while among other things safe-guarding the life supporting capacity of air, water, soil, and ecosystems."

There are many more pages, but I just want to reinforce the point that this Act is central to all planning decisions whether they are made at national or local levels. Anyone who is competing against New Zealand products in the market place can be confident that in environmental terms we have to as farmers in our country comply with very high standards.

New Zealand's Experience with Subsidies

The second point Mr. Storey makes in his speech is that for a period of time in New Zealand we made the mistake of trying to subsidize our farmers with a whole series of input and output subsidies. One really needs two or three hours to go through the process and all the things we did, the mistakes we made, and the good things we found out. We simply do not have that sort of time this afternoon.

Looking specifically at one or two features which impact on the environment, we found out that since we have removed the subsidies, we no longer farm to any extent the erosion prone, fragile land that we encouraged to be developed through the subsidy system. In general terms, those erosion prone, fragile lands are now returning either to native forest vegetation or to commercial forestry.

The other thing that has happened is that we are using many less chemicals and much less artificial fertilizer than we previously used. We may even be using less than we actually should be using. New Zealand's experience is that input usage is very much

250

related to output prices; when our output prices went down, the use of those inputs went down by a very substantial amount.

In addition, people are making much more effective use of the inputs they have available. For example, suppose you subsidize fertilizer but not fencing when in economic terms fencing may actually be a better use of the resource than fertilizer. Farmers being the perverse people they are will use the fertilizer when fencing could be a better investment, especially as far as using the grass that they are actually growing.

Furthermore, farmers are now focusing very clearly on the market place. Since subsidies have been removed on just about everything we produce, there has been a marked improvement in the quality of the product.

We in New Zealand are very happy indeed to respond to the Honorable John Gummer's suggestion that we need to be conscious of what the consumers want and we only hope that he continues to give us that opportunity. We as a country certainly have no fears about consumers becoming more environmentally sensitive because we are already responding to that.

The Cairns Group

Mr. Storey raised the Cairns Group in his address because we see this group of fourteen countries, a mixture of North and South and of developed and developing countries, as a example which shows that countries with very diverse backgrounds can work together for the common good. We think in many international processes, groups similar to the Cairns Group have a very positive contribution to make. We are certainly proud of the contribution that we have made in the GATT negotiations.

The UNCED Conference

New Zealand in a way took a risk when it brought together in one group elected politicians, government officials, nongovernment organizations, environmental groups, indigenous Maori-people, and industry leaders to prepare for the Rio Summit. As Mr. Storey said in his notes, there was great potential for conflict in that group. But, when they got together and as the process evolved, they discovered quite quickly, once they had a better understanding of each other's goals and ambitions, that in many cases their goals were common goals. Therefore, we could work together very satisfactorily for everyone's good.

New Zealand as a country has a major stake in both sides of the trade and environment relationship. Firstly, we need the strongest possible protection for the international environment to actually assure our long term viability. As a country which is heavily dependent on trade, we are fully committed to the liberalization of the multilateral trading system. Our trade is very dependent on natural resources. For us and for countries like New Zealand, it is vital that decisions are made on a multilateral basis. Time after time people in countries like ours find that decisions which are made and actions which are taken in other countries many miles from our shores can actually affect both our environment and our ability to trade. Our Minister and his government believe very strongly that the decisions must be multilateral and not unilateral.

Possibilities for a Green Round

To answer the second question, "Do we need a green round?" I would like to quote directly from Mr. Storey's speech notes. Mr. Storey says that he does not see any conflict between trade and environmental objectives. On the contrary, he is quite convinced that trade and environmental policies must be mutually supportive and not antagonistic. Trade promotes economic growth, which gives people a stake in the future and helps provide the technology and wealth required to sustain the environment. But, trade can exist only if the environment is protected to ensure that the natural resource base is sustained.

What then is the priority? Much was said at the Rio de Janeiro conference about the need for increased development assistance. That point has also been made at this conference. My Minister wants me to strongly make the point that more probably also needs to be said about the fundamental need for access to markets and a more liberalized trading system that will allow market forces to reflect efficiency rather than the outcome of subsidy laws. This is where the real challenge lies if the goal of environmentally sound and sustainable development is to be attained by pressing the market access case. The Minister does not want to downplay the need for international cooperation and assistance to the developing countries. He makes the very real point that in the developed world, six times as much money is spent on subsidizing agriculture as is spent on assisting the developing countries.

Once the Uruguay Round is completed, do we need a "Green Round?" In our view, until the present negotiations are satisfactorily resolved, the way ahead will remain uncertain. Without a successful conclusion, we will have no foundation on which to construct an international system which satisfies both environmental and trading needs. The vision at Rio of a new framework for relations between developing and developed countries, of a multilateral system which would integrate environmental concerns into economic and social policies, will otherwise remain an elusive goal. Mr. Storey and his government, therefore, feel very strongly that the first priority is to finish the job in hand. At stake in the Uruguay Round is not only the credibility and indeed the viability of GATT but also the effectiveness of multilateral action in dealing with global problems of development and of the environment.

Conclusion

In summary, in reference to the question of whether or not we need a Green Round, we think it is probably too early to know the answer. What we must do is complete the job in hand. As we do that, we are confident that GATT can and will act in an environmentally friendly way. In addition, all environmentalists must be very careful that their very valuable movement is not infiltrated by protectionists who are operating for protectionists' means and desires and not for the betterment of the environment.

Section VI: Practical and Policy Implications of a Sustainable Agriculture, an Environmentally Sound Agro-Industry, and a Greener Trading System

Chapter 25

Reflection on the Conference Agenda

John Block

(Transcribed from conference tapes.)

Farm Programs and the Environment

As a United States farmer and citizen, I am happy to see the set-aside program instituted in Europe. However, it is a bad policy. You take good land, your best land in some cases, out of production. Taking land out of production by buying it out would be a program more like our conservation reserve program where we take the fragile land out. I understand why you are doing it and why you must do it to cut production because it is not as politically painful as the way it was done in New Zealand.

Cross Compliance

The cross compliance between farm payments and environmental obligations will become more pervasive. As Mr. Gummer said, and I believe he is right, there is no justification for a farmer to be paid just because he is a farmer. I am a farmer but I agree with that point.

New Zealand

I think Brian Chamberlin is right when he says world prices discourage the use of chemicals and fertilizers because world prices are not artificially high. Artificially high prices encourage excessive use of chemicals and fertilizers and excessively intensive farming. It is just an economic reality but I think in the end we need to approach the problem by getting prices in line with the world market place.

Agribusiness

It is my judgement the attacks on chemical companies and the use of chemicals in farming and biotechnology definitely can and may force the cost of new technology to unacceptable levels. The poor, who can hardly afford to do so, pay the most. The cost of bringing a new chemical on line today is $100 million in some cases. How many new chemicals are we going to get at that rate? It is bad for the people of the world to be subjected to this. It is not just the farmers that are paying a price. It is not just the chemical companies. It is the consumers of the world.

Trade and the Environment

The examples have been given more than once of tuna and dolphins and hormones and beef, where countries, the United States in one instance and Europe in the other, used their own unilateral standards as a tariff barrier. I do not believe it is the way to do it and I think in the long run it undermines the GATT process and global trade. I think we need to have some international standards. I realize they have to be somewhat flexible because different countries are different in different ways, but we have to be very careful to guard against the possibility of country after country creating a whole set of new non-tariff barriers.

I do not believe that we need to green the GATT anymore than it is. The GATT is a trade organization. I realize that we need to look towards dealing with our environmental problems. There are some serious abuses that have been imposed on the environment by farmers and businesses, but they need to be dealt with on a case-by-case basis. Many countries have different problems and you cannot just have a world standard and lay it across the globe.

I regret to say that many of our critics in agriculture, farming, and agribusiness are irresponsible. I have not heard from irresponsible ones at this conference, but I hear from them back home. I think they are irresponsible when they distort scientific facts and promote unjustified hysteria and when they oppose new technology such as irradiation, biotechnology, and new chemicals. They suggest natural fertilizer is better than commercial fertilizer, which I do not think the Dutch would agree with necessarily, as much manure as they have here. They argue that organically grown food is safer than other food even though there is no scientific reason to prove its truth. They put species and critters ahead of people. If the spotted owl was in a poor country, they would eat the devil. If they had their way, the rich countries would do just fine because we are rich and we can afford this pickiness and these luxuries. The poor countries are the ones that will suffer as the price of food goes up and as the cost of production rises, as they are denied the right to make a rightful living with the available resources.

Chapter 26

Reforming and Shifting Agricultural Policies

Michael Franklin

(Transcribed from conference tapes.)

There are two things during this conference about which there was a general consensus: 1) that agricultural policies are moving in the right direction and 2) that, even though too slowly for our Australian and other friends, we are taking support out of the market, even in the European Community. That again is a step in the right direction and, indeed, is probably the single most important contribution agricultural policies can make to improving the environment. Environmentally favorable measures are also being gradually introduced into agricultural policies. Over the last few years it is important to register that there has been a greater raproachment between governments, the farming community, and the environmental lobby.

Summary of Section II

I want to discuss three issues which came up during my panel discussion. First, how far should one go in introducing environmental policies into agricultural policies? My impression is that there are still some countries where environmental policies are no more than add-ons. I think we have used the phrase "integrated agricultural and environmental policies," which seems to me to be a good phrase. However, I do wonder whether in fact we might not think of going even further. Farmers have driven agricultural policy for the last thirty or forty years. Maybe the driving force needs to be reversed.

Secondly, we debated without resolving the difficult question of whether you want to go as far in all countries or whether there is a differential that can be built in, particularly between developed and developing countries. This turned around the argument of whether environmental policies are a luxury or not, which all of them are manifestly not.

I want to suggest here that perhaps it is the nature of the environmental issue which may be determining to what extent some differentiation is desirable or justified. You could certainly argue that some forms of environmental policies, such as maintaining the landscape just like it was when grandmother was alive, is a luxury. As far as I am concerned, that is something you can take or leave. If, however, there is an acute pollution problem, which is actually doing damage to the rest of the economy, then a different line should be taken. That type of differentiation perhaps did not come out at the conference as much as it should.

Third is the question of how to adjust policies. There is no question of choosing between the carrot and the stick. We have to have both. Indeed, we do have both. Not forgetting the role that voluntary changes can play in this particular area, it is perfectly understandable that farmers should prefer the carrot to the stick. But, the argument that high farm incomes will automatically guarantee acceptable environmental practices will not wash. Indeed, I suspect the opposite is the case. There is, of course, room for the carrot.

When I was in charge of the British Ministry of Agriculture, the best thing I ever did was put in hand the work which led to the concept of the environmentally sensitive areas that is now extended throughout the European Community, where you take a certain view of how you would like a particular area of land to be managed from an environmental point of view and you pay the farmer to manage in that particular way. That seems to me to be a perfectly acceptable concept, but clearly there has to be room for regulation as well. There are areas where there is no particular reason why the farmer should not be subjected to the same kind of controls as have been found to be necessary in other parts of the economy.

On this question of the choice of instruments, I do not have a lot to say, except that it seems to me again that it depends a bit on the nature of the problem and who it is who is suffering. For example, control over nitrates seems to be a case where regulation has already been accepted in a number of countries and will be accepted more widely. As for the question of the preservation of the landscape, since we want in Europe to have animals on the hillside, it would be actually better to have cardboard animals than to have real animals. I could not, however, in the time left to me think of how to preserve the terrace landscape in Japan without having the rice, but perhaps somebody could think about that.

Cost of Compliance

Where the cost of compliance should fall will, of course, effect the competitive position of agriculture, though I think the debate has somewhat exaggerated this problem. It ought not to decided on the basis of who has the deepest purse. As it is, it is always going to be exaggerated by those who insist that they cannot play the game unless the playing field is wholly level. That is a dangerous argument in agriculture.

CAP reform might have produced money to spend on environmental policies, but the so-called MacSharry reforms do not bring with them any peace dividend. The cut in the cereal price, which will clearly benefit the environment, has been possible politically only in exchange for an expensive system of income aids. The benefit to the consumer has been matched by a higher burden to taxpayers. While we may take the view that this particular compensation was excessive, it is clear that politically it was felt to be necessary. I think the argument that for example Ministers Bukman and Gummer were putting forward, which I certainly prescribe to, is that if you are making these payments, increasingly society will not support them or be prepared to defend them unless they produce some material benefit, whether it is in the environment or some other desirable social objective. Those income payments are vulnerable unless they have conditions attached to them.

In conclusion, yes, we can go along with the idea of the BBB but we must not loose sight of the PPP either. Furthermore, it is quite clear that while, we may be moving in the right direction, we have a very considerable way still to go in transforming agricultural policies in a way which accurately reflects these other and very important policy objectives.

Chapter 27

Concerns of Less Developed Countries

Liberty Mhlanga

(Transcribed from conference tapes.)

If we voted here today, we would find relatively no conflict or contradiction about the question of agriculture, the environment, and trade: is there conflict or cooperation? I think the majority, myself included, would go for cooperation.

From an agricultural standpoint, the point has particularly been made about lessening the use of chemicals, fertilizer, insecticides, fungicides, and herbicides. Those elements are very expensive for our agriculture. From what some of our learned friends were saying here, we could use biotechnology to reduce the use of these chemicals or eliminate them all together (e.g. by doing a few tricks to the plants so that they repel these insects and fungus and by treating the weeds so that if these weeds grow next to some of these plants, they are going to die). It is really the transfer of these technologies that maybe at some point a gathering like this should look at, especially transferring the process of some of this technology inexpensively.

In my own country, the main foreign currency earner is tobacco. I hope that within the context of tobacco, the PPP rule does not apply. My room in this hotel was assigned to me because it was a non-smoking room. I hope we do not get to a point where you get to a hotel like this and they tell you it is a non-smoking hotel. That would spell doom to countries like Zimbabwe that are tobacco growers. I suppose that this would effect the United States

264

also because I am told the United States is a big producer of tobacco.

What is frightening about this question of "greening," especially within the context of the United States and EC countries, is that a lot of commodities are going to be accepted within that context. Given the other commodities that are not going to be accepted and the many starving people particularly in the developing world, it is obvious that what does not turn green is going to land in the ports of the developing countries. I think this is an element that really needs to be taken quite seriously.

In my own country we normally consume meal white maize. Whenever we receive yellow maize, we eat it after all of the white maize has been exhausted. This year we have imported yellow maize from the United States and Argentina because there is very little to eat and have found ourselves really enjoying the yellow meal that we do not normally favor. One can see that element of enjoying the not-so-green being a market place for those people who cannot afford to green their own products.

Chapter 28

Agricultural Policy
and Its Environmental Impacts

Robert L. Thompson

(Transcribed from conference tapes.)

Section II concerned the effect of agricultural policies and production practices on the environment. Because of the time constraints, the three authors tended to focus relatively less on the impact of production practices on the environment than they did on the impact of agricultural policies. Agriculture is a very heterogeneous industry, both within and among countries, and it is extremely difficult to generalize the relationship between agricultural production practices followed and the alleged environmental negatives associated with them.

The two key points here are that agricultural production practices do vary greatly within and among countries and that the empirical evidence of causality between practices and the environment is not always clear cut. For example, in my own state, in places where there are elevated levels of nitrates in ground water, the most important culprits are 1) septic tanks and 2) intensive animal agriculture. Probably the best place to have a well is in the middle of a corn field because there it is away from both the septic tank and the hog house. Yet, if you listen to much of the environmental rhetoric, they would forcibly require farmers to reduce the level of nitrate applications on their corn production. The point is that the causal relationships between production practices and the quality of the environment need to be well-documented.

266

Most of the time in the session was spent discussing the effects of agricultural policies on the environment. All three speakers made the observation that higher levels of assistance to agriculture tend to be positively correlated with higher applications of inputs per hectare of land. In other words, more intensive agricultural production is achieved as a result of higher levels of agricultural assistance that are linked to the volume of production. This statement is true because you raise the optimum application rates as a result of raising product prices relative to input prices. But, it is also true because where you have set-aside programs, you often create artificial scarcity of land, which causes more land-saving inputs to be used and induces the country's research establishment to focus its attention on land-saving technological changes which lead to further intensification of future production.

The United States

Relating to the United States, general observations were made that the 1985 and 1990 farm bills had significantly reduced income transfers to American farmers and decoupled payments from current and future production. Also, positive observations were made related to the creation of the Conservation Reserve program as well as the Swampbuster, Sodbuster, and Conservation Compliance provisions, which had positive impacts on soil erosion and water quality.

But, at the same time, it was observed that as farm program benefits have been reduced, principally as a result of tight budget constraints, there has been less for farmers to receive from government programs. Therefore, the incentive to participate in some of these programs is reduced because the cost of compliance may be perceived by some farmers to exceed the dollar value of the benefits that might be derived from government payments. It was also pointed out that there is evidence that at least in the first few years of these programs, enforcement tended to be both slow and lax.

The European Community

On the EC, it was observed that the new CAP reform, which is moving internal crop support prices in the direction of world market prices, will indeed reduce the incentive for as heavy input use per hectare as has been the case in the past. It was observed that the CAP reform pays lip service to the PPP but has very little content in support of that. In fact, the intent seems more to pay farmers to follow good environmental practices than to force them, when they are polluters, to pay themselves.

Also, in the attempt to put more teeth into the CAP's new fifteen percent acreage reduction program than the US has had in its programs, the new EC policy will require that there be a rotational set aside (i.e. that you cannot set aside the same 15 percent of your land every year). I think a very interesting perspective in the Dubgaard paper is that this may actually increase nitrate pollution. He suggested in fact that "there could be a nitrate time bomb associated with this policy because the cover crop that is planted may indeed not adequately use the nitrates in the soil and that you'll end up with the nitrates moving down towards groundwater." He suggests as an alternative to the present policy what he calls his "second-best policy" of controlling supply in the Community, one of high eco-taxes on agricultural chemical use combined with some price support.

Recommendations

We need to design policies that induce researchers, both public and private, to develop new technologies that save scarce environmental resources. This suggestion is in opposition to the land-saving technological changes which have tended to be the products of our research establishments in the past.

Countries need to continue to decouple income assistance to farmers from current and future production, especially when it is associated with production per hectare.

Animal manure is more often an environmental problem than chemical fertilizer is. Therefore, farmers need incentives to make better use of animal manure for plant and nutrition. Also, there needs to be more appropriate incentives for making sure that the animal manure gets applied at the most beneficial time of the year. One example was pointed out in Dubgaard's paper that in Denmark they require farmers to have a large tank to hold manure for nine to ten months out of the year. The manure tends to not be applied in the spring, because that is the time when labor is scarcest. So, even though you are storing a nine to ten month supply, the manure still tends to be applied during the fall just before the time when there is the maximum likelihood of runoff into surface water.

The bottom line is that where real environmental problems caused by agriculture exist, the appropriate government policy is to provide suitable policy signals to reflect the true cost of environmental assets that are not priced in the market place. We have to recognize that the first best solution from an economist's perspective is not always politically attainable. The optimum mix will be a balance between regulation and price incentives. Since farmers respond rationally to economic incentives, the consensus in our group was to use price incentives to the greatest extent possible, supplementing with regulations only when necessary.

Chapter 29

Lessons to Learn from History

Dale Hathaway

(Transcribed from conference tapes.)

A consensus ran through this whole conference that: 1) agriculture can and does contribute to environmental problems; 2) changes in agricultural practices will be required on a broad scale in most of our countries; 3) payments to producers, with the possible exception of Germany, will be made conditional upon following certain production practices; and 4) environmental issues will enter trade relations. It is interesting to me that there was a very substantial consensus that agriculture should get special treatment in environmental matters. Although lip service was paid to the Polluter Pays Principle, the Ministers of Agriculture said something else. After all, Ministers of Agriculture have a constituency who have for years gotten huge amounts of public funds for doing, in many cases, the wrong things. Indeed, if we mean polluters pay, we should not pay polluters to stop polluting.

Repeating Earlier Efforts

We did not, however, view the Food and Fiber Sector as broadly as I believe it should have been viewed. It strikes me that it is very unlikely that in the Food and Fiber Sector outside of the regular agricultural farm production we are going to adopt the principal of bribing people to do what has to be done. Yet, this is what we are saying for agriculture. There was an amazing consensus that we will in fact use bribery. I am not surprised but amazed that once again we are sitting here with a new set of issues that are about to enter the GATT negotiations and we are going to establish that agriculture is a special industry that should indeed have special rules.

About 46 years ago a group of people gathered in Havana to talk about trade rules. For reasons that were also very good, they decided that there should be special rules for agriculture. Forty-some years later we are desperately trying to get the special rules for certain agricultural activities removed from the GATT. Meanwhile, we want to hurry up and get that done so we can put some special rules into the GATT regarding agriculture and the environment. We ought to think about whether we are in fact laying down a set of rules that over the long run we will regret and have to undo.

Future Outlook

I hope that your optimism about the wonderful impacts CAP reform will have on the environment turn out to be true. We, in the United States, have had the system that the EC is now adopting for a long time and I do not believe that we are without environmental problems in agriculture. Therefore, it seems to me that we should not expect too much from changes that are made for their own good reasons and concentrate on looking at the changes we have to make regarding the environment.

Chapter 30

The Need for Multilateralism

Aart de Zeeuw

(Transcribed from conference tapes.)

I have experienced in the GATT that you need to have international agreements to limit the possibilities of governments doing what they sometimes politically are forced to do by their farmers or other sectors of the economy. When I look at the change already in domestic policies during the negotiations in the Uruguay Round, it is very clear that this was the reason.

According to Brian Chamberlin, New Zealand has already changed its policy by getting rid of farm subsidies. This is a very good example but is not only prevalent in New Zealand. Australia and Japan have made progress in their own domestic policies. Also, the Community is changing its domestic policy in the direction of more market orientation.

Furthermore, almost everybody is convinced now that reducing subsidies has to be done to encourage the farming population to have incentives to use and to produce more efficiently. It is also very clear that we may expect that moving towards a more market-oriented and efficient agricultural policy, it will also be good for the environment because farmers are aware that they cannot spoil the number of inputs.

This relates not only to what we have in the GATT now but also to other international agreements concerning the environment. We heard that also this afternoon from the UNCED and the Montreal and the Basel Protocols.

There was a consensus at this conference that you may not go the unilateral way and you must not go the multilateral way. But, we must not hide the fact that we are going to see conflicts, because we do not exactly know what are standards for the environment. We all know that it is not possible to harmonize standards easily because the local situations in many countries are so different at looking from the environment that we must do a lot from this prospect. We must not have internationally harmonized standards but at least to work on standards on a rational basis that get away from emotions.

Chapter 31

Conference Summary

Lord Plumb of Coleshill

(Transcribed from conference tapes.)

I would first of all like to thank you all for the contribution you have made in what obviously is the first major conference since the Rio Summit. Let us just remind ourselves that we had eleven Ministers who are responsible for agricultural and environmental affairs here over the course of the last two days, as well as officials from 34 countries and representatives of virtually the world, including the World Bank and the United Nations, and many other institutions and organizations.

There has been, I believe, a general endorsement here for the key messages which emerged from Rio:

1) that the health of the environment and the economy are interlocked and, indeed, almost indivisible;

2) that environmental and economic issues are global and not national in character and that the world has moved to environmental and economic interdependence; and

3) that in proposing new policy initiatives, we have to strike a balance between environmental and economic interests and in the case of this conference, between environmental, agricultural, and trade issues.

The game is not about choosing one over the others or, to use John Gummer's own words, "extolling one issue beyond its proper place." Certainly, in terms of the environment and trade, it is clear that we need to weigh the needs of the environment with the interests of world trade.

Areas for Discussion

There are still though many questions to pose. Among this group of experts here as moderators you can tell that it would be impossible to reach a final conclusion or agreement and answer all those questions that have been posed over the last couple of days. Will, for example, higher environmental requirements or standards for agriculture force the cost of farmers' products to rise? Will consumers pay higher prices in the shops? Mr. Eglin, in what I thought was an excellent paper, reminded us that the policy challenge is to get environmental prices right while interfering as little as possible with the efficiency of the market.

Do we enforce environmental standards through subsidies or through taxes? Both Ministers Gummer and Bukman supported one method of rewarding farmers for good environmental conduct and penalizing them for bad behavior. This obviously requires an appropriate mix of carrots and sticks, which will include payment provisions and tax incentives and penalties. Sir Michael Franklin has said it is a question of using both and mixing the two.

Trade

If we are going to move towards establishing international standards, then surely we have to set proper domestic standards first. Of course, this may upset the conditions of fair trade. It may distort competition between producers. It may mean they are playing to different rules or, in other words, creating somewhat of an acute disadvantage, particularly in the developing countries. If so, we quite obviously need to find ways of helping the LDCs.

As far as trade is concerned, do we need a separate "Green Round?" Or would it not been more sensible and more effective to further green the GATT? I sensed the mood of the meeting when Aart de Zeeuw was moderating in Section V that greening has to be incorporated in the present discussions. We have not got six or ten years to wait for yet a further "Green Round."

275

Obviously, agriculture has occupied a crucial role in the current Uruguay Round because of the distorting influence of present government policies on world trade. Whatever the outcome of that round, we ask how can we create a truly level playing field in terms of subsidies and market access? Should we not accept that there will always be differences between us and try to work within them? We know that agriculture is not yet green enough in many parts of the world. We know more has to be done. We know governments will do more, especially in the context of the post Rio agenda.

Yet, we have to remind ourselves, and I do not think this came out perhaps forcefully enough in the debates that we have had, that a five to ten fold increase in growth over the next 50 years is needed to maintain the global standard of living for ten billion people. Food production will have to increase four times to feed that many mouths and will consequently place a heavy demand on the environment. That is why I think the Earth Summit recognized that the goal should be sustainable development, a lasting balance between economic growth and the environment.

The Three Great Satisfactions

John Gummer reminded us of three great satisfactions. I took them to heart as a farmer: tilling the land, trading the goods, which he said one did with excitement, and passing on to the next generation something better than we ourselves inherited. Well, of course, he is right.

But, we cannot ignore that those satisfactions become less sufficient if you are a Russian earning 2,000 rubles (the equivalent of $10 a month) as a milk producer or an African seeing everything you produce shrivel in drought stricken land. Their perspective on stricter environmental rules or the conditions of trade is inevitably somewhat different when their priorities are to be able to produce enough and to earn enough to eat and when perhaps their water is heavily polluted or they face massive soil erosion. Yet, it will be in their interests and I believe it will be in all of our interests if we try to get the balance right.

That is why, for example, I believe the conference itself strongly endorses Rio's contention that correcting the imbalances among economic trading interests should not be the only game in town for trade negotiators. That is why we in the International Policy Council serve notice on the GATT negotiators that policies must be designed to sustain the planet and provide for fair trade and development around the world. We cannot, as I say, wait ten years or more for a "Green Round." We need to green the results of the present round.

Goals Require Commitment and Leadership

None of us who are involved in this International Policy Council underestimates that this will require sustained political commitment, strong political leadership, and clear thinking among Ministers who have spoken of the importance of cooperation.

Yet, we know in trying to answer that question which we posed at the beginning (Cooperation or Conflict?) that there are many instances of conflict. Many have been highlighted over the last two days. We have to urge all of us politicians not to rush the job or hurry through ill-considered changes and above all to consider policy reforms in the right context, not in isolation. They must recognize the urgency of changing public attitudes which we so often hear.

If I may use a little story of an actual case of going to a conference with 300 young members of Friends Of The Earth, a strong movement we have in the United Kingdom. I was booed and jeered as I walked in the room. I was the enemy who had arrived among them. As I got on the platform, I realized that I was not a very welcome guest. I said I was born and bred a farmer. My father was born and bred a farmer. My grandfather was born and bred a farmer. The motto of my family is you will leave this Earth in better shape than you found it. So, I think I have been a friend of the Earth longer than you lot.

Now, I thought I was pretty good but they did not. I had an hour and a half of purgatory. A group of them came up to me afterwards and one of them pointed at me and said, "You're a liar." I said, "I'm sorry. What have I done to offend you?" And he said, "You said you've been a Friend of the Earth longer than us." I said, "That's true. I gave you my family history." He said, "You couldn't have been a friend of the Earth. It hasn't been going that long."

Thus, as John Gummer reminded us the other night, it is those, of course, who have little knowledge of what is actually happening on the ground who seem to have so much influence over what in fact we are doing. So, if we can harmonize the different interests, that is good. But, we should also do what is in our best environmental interests.

Conclusion

Therefore, I offer as a summary the three little conclusions to which I have come.

Trade policy imperatives

Environmental problems are the result of domestic distortions in both rich and poor countries. In the case of rich countries, they have largely been involved with price supports and in poor countries with taxation of agriculture. Finding solutions, therefore, requires multilateral negotiation and cooperation. Trade barriers are not the most efficient way of achieving environmental or, for that matter, farm income objectives. This does not necessarily imply that we should rush into a "Green Round" but rather that green considerations should prevail in the GATT negotiations. Thus, the fortunately titled "green box" of the current Uruguay Round discussions can form the starting point for reviewing the environmental dimensions of trade agreements.

Domestic policy imperatives

Efforts both multilaterally and domestically to shift farm support away from price support to direct payments should be encouraged and built upon since they will benefit the environment. It is fair to immediately begin defining the environmental requirements that these payments should be conditional on, so that farmers will be paid to enhance and protect the environment and the landscape. So, while pressures on farmers' cost structures from the new lower prices created by the switch to direct payments will force some environmental benefits, they are insufficient on their own to bring about the changes that consumers and taxpayers will demand. The progress made so far by developed countries on this should only be considered a beginning. For example, the CAP reform should move onto the next phase without delay. Policy reforms therefore must be a combination of the carrot and the stick. The Polluter Pays Principle is fully endorsed but must be complemented by incentive programs as well.

Agribusiness imperatives

Agribusiness can and does contribute to improving agricultural practices for the benefit of the environment. While it is recognized that agribusiness could also have negative environmental impacts, it is vital to create an economic environment that maximizes the potential for new technologies emerging from agribusiness to contribute positively to conservation and environmental protection. Agribusiness should not be stifled by regulation from making positive contributions. So, while some regulation of business activity is necessary for environmental reasons, governments must resist demands to hold back by regulation emerging technologies for emotional or non-scientific reasons that fail to recognize the linkage between the economy and the environment.

Summary and Conclusions

Robert E. Wise

Conflict or Cooperation?

The answer to the seemingly simple question "Conflict or Cooperation?" was given in the first moments of Minister Bukman's opening address. Thus, it might appear that the conference organizers gave themselves an easy question to answer when designing the format of this conference.

However, as the interventions of more than two dozen speakers amply demonstrated, the complexities of the issues involved in trying to understand and analyze the interrelationships between agriculture, the environment, and trade are multi-faceted and multi-layered.

A sense emerged from this conference that policymakers around the world share a considerable consensus on the direction in which agricultural, environmental, and trade policies must move but that the details of new policies and the mechanisms by which they are to be achieved are far from clear or straightforward. There is an imperative for cooperation, but it cannot be taken for granted that this goal will always be achieved.

Understanding the Issues

Agriculture, the Environment, and Trade

Agricultural production and trade affect the state of the environment universally around the globe. However, the precise nature of these effects varies based on a number of factors.

The most obvious is the divide between rich and poor countries. Environmental degradation in OECD countries can occur because of overly intensive production stretching the capacity of the natural resource base. Positive environmental benefits can also result from the adoption of high tech production methods coming from both private and publicly funded research. In less developed countries, population growth is perhaps the single largest factor leading to environmental degradation, while the mere lack of economic access to purchased inputs prevents the situation from being worse.

Environmental goods and bads fall into many categories. When discussing production agriculture, there is a tendency to focus immediately on such issues as soil erosion and water quality. Bringing trade into the frame of reference suggests consideration of comparing resource endowments between countries and how they are exploited. Increasingly, especially in the developed world, concern for the environment is also expressed in terms of amenity and landscape values.

Economic Activity and Environmental Quality

However many different aspects of environmental quality we wish to define, they all share a direct and important relationship with economic activity. The results of man's economic actions have inextricable impacts on the environment; and, vice versa, as soon as we lay down environmental objectives for society to meet, we circumscribe the forms of economic activity we can undertake.

This interdependence between economic activities and the environment led the speakers to conclude in general terms that, on balance, a market orientation in economic policies will result in the greatest possible environmental benefits. For agriculture, this has immense implications, given the extent to which, especially recently, governments have intervened to affect agricultural markets.

Irrespective of environmental considerations, other pressures have come to bear in recent years to start moving agricultural policies around the world towards greater market orientation. Much of what has already happened has occurred through national domestic pressures, such as budgetary constraints, influencing the decisions of governments. Multilateral efforts to bring further changes have reached new heights in the ongoing Uruguay Round of GATT negotiations. It must be remembered though that these multilateral efforts also have their origins in issues of economic rather than environmental policy.

The Role of the Nation State

While every individual has a role to play in affecting the environment around us, the most obvious unitary player on which to focus attention is the nation state. This conference highlighted speakers from around the world, and their presentations largely emphasized differences in physical circumstances or policy approaches at national levels. The nature of the interaction between agriculture, the environment, and trade is primarily determined by the actions of national governments, either in terms of what occurs domestically or internationally.

So, while it is important to appreciate the roles of farmers, taxpayers, consumers, politicians, traders, and others individually, it is also important from a policy perspective to consider each grouping in national terms. At the individual level, it is possible to comprehend the meaning of the Polluter Pays Principle. Taking this concept to national and international levels is somewhat more complex but, in essence, will help form a basis for multilateral cooperation for achieving mutually beneficial environmental goods. It is perhaps partly because of this complexity that international trade negotiations have so far not seen environmental concerns as major driving forces.

Implications for Institutions

The Earth Summit at Rio and other multilateral efforts such as the Brundtland Commission and work in the OECD are, however, turning the tide in a new direction. Taken together with national and regional actions (such as within the EC, ASEAN, or NAFTA), it is possible to discern the emergence of a willingness on the part of individual countries to let multilateral cooperation on environmental issues circumscribe national policymaking.

In contrast to this, it is also clear from the general reaction to the GATT tuna/dolphin ruling that national governments are preparing to accept that individual countries should not be allowed to impose their own environmental imperatives on others through the exercise of trade policy interventions. Finding the best forum in which to argue the case multilaterally is one of the major issues that this conference debated.

As currently constituted, however, the GATT does not have any direct mandate or mechanism for considering environmental policies, *per se*. While the GATT has established a Group on Environmental Measures and Trade and the UN, through UNCED, has raised environmental issues onto the multilateral agenda, no mechanisms or modalities have yet been developed for negotiating international agreements.

The Role of Agribusiness

Agribusiness has the potential to be both a protector and polluter of the environment. If we define agribusiness to mean that part of industry which is developing and marketing products to aid farmers in the production of goods from the land, then it is clear that the potential purposes, and therefore the potential environmental consequences, of its products are within agribusiness' direct control. In addition, they are also externally influenced by the rest of the agricultural economy and agricultural policy.

The output-increasing technologies that have come from agribusiness were generated from an economic and policy environment driven by food shortages. At the time of their genesis, there is little doubt that these technologies made positive contributions not only to world food security but also to world environmental conditions. Yet as agricultural policies around the world became more focused on income goals that were mechanistically production related, these same technologies have sometimes become viewed as detrimental to environmental goals.

While the politicians and their bureaucrats take the work of reforming these policies forward, economic actors in the marketplace, including agribusiness, will continue to influence agriculture, trade, and the environment. Speakers at the conference indicated that agribusiness has played a significant role both in agricultural production and its consequent effect on the environment.

The New Policy Environment

The consumer-driven, invisible hand of the marketplace has also been paralleled by the more visible hand of government regulation. Surplus production and environmental degradation, often spurred on by past (and continuing) agricultural policies in many developed countries, have led in turn to the imposition of regulatory constraints on the use of certain technologies in particular situations or locations.

The pendulum has also swung fully the other way in that government interventions to promote sound environmental practices are either competing with or have replaced production-intensifying policies. The consensus of the speakers was that developing the appropriate balance for agricultural, environmental, and trade policies for the future will require the use of both "carrot" and "stick" approaches. The single most central concept that will help policy makers achieve this balance is the pursuit of "sustainable development."

The new policy environment has had the effect of redirecting the research and development work of agribusiness. The increasing importance in society at large of environmental concerns has meant that there has been a major shift in investment towards technologies that reduce the use of inputs that have potentially damaging environmental effects.

Policy Conclusions

This conference identified that the goal of achieving sustainable development in both rich and poor countries for the mutual benefit of agriculture, the environment, and trade creates imperatives for both the public and private sectors. In the public sector, this will involve both multilateral and national level policy imperatives. Imperatives are apparent for the private sector as well, but these will be to a large extent circumscribed by public policy.

Multilateral Policy Imperatives

Many environmental problems are the result of domestic distortions in both rich and poor countries that have resulted in the erection of trade barriers. More often than not, these policies fail to meet the farm income and other objectives for which they were established. Eliminating these barriers will require multilateral negotiation and cooperation.

The fundamental principles that should underline such negotiations should include:

- commitment to an open and competitive trading system;
- appropriate values attached to environmental goods;
- recognition that environmental standards must vary amongst countries;
- and the desire to develop multilateral dispute settlement procedures.

These principles, as suggested by GATT officials and others, imply that the GATT's mandate could be expanded to encompass specifically an environmental brief. This does not necessarily imply that the Uruguay Round be followed by a new exclusively "Green Round." Rather "green" considerations should inform all GATT negotiations. Since it now appears likely the Uruguay Round will not be finished soon and that a fairly lengthy period of continuing negotiation may ensue, it may be possible to begin this process now.

National Policy Imperatives

Multilateral efforts to bring greater market orientation to agriculture are only going to go so far. Already in the Uruguay Round we have seen an acknowledgement on the part of negotiators that national governments will be allowed to continue to provide subsidies for income objectives. Many governments already want to link these payments to the provision of environmental benefits: farmers will be paid to enhance and protect the environment and landscape. Such national initiatives should be encouraged and built on.

It is possible to view such cross compliance as either a carrot or a stick, and indeed both sorts of policy need to be developed. Basic benefits of income support should be conditional on environmental performance, while incentive programs should be made available to further encourage the adoption of appropriate production techniques where taxpayers have expressed a willingness to pay for such programs because of perceived environmental or amenity benefits.

Private Sector Imperatives

It is vital to create an economic environment that maximizes the potential for new technologies emerging from agribusiness to contribute positively to conservation and environmental protection. This means above all that agribusiness should be given the freedom to develop new technologies without the imposition of luddite regulation: governments must resist demands to hold back, by regulation, emerging technologies for emotional or non-scientific reasons that fail to recognize the linkage between the economy and the environment.

The private sector also has a responsibility to prioritize its research and development programs to produce technologies that are environmentally beneficial. While a freely operating market economy, where the value society places on environmental goods is adequately enumerated, will be the best circumstance for achieving this objective, it is also recognized that some degree of regulation is inevitable.